AF643016

Supply Chains in Action

Supply Chains in Action

A case study collection in supply chain, logistics, procurement and operations management

Richard Wilding

KoganPage

Publisher's note
Every possible effort has been made to ensure that the information contained in this book is accurate at the time of going to press, and the publishers and authors cannot accept responsibility for any errors or omissions, however caused. No responsibility for loss or damage occasioned to any person acting, or refraining from action, as a result of the material in this publication can be accepted by the editor, the publisher or the author.

First published in Great Britain and the United States in 2020 by Kogan Page Limited

Apart from any fair dealing for the purposes of research or private study, or criticism or review, as permitted under the Copyright, Designs and Patents Act 1988, this publication may only be reproduced, stored or transmitted, in any form or by any means, with the prior permission in writing of the publishers, or in the case of reprographic reproduction in accordance with the terms and licences issued by the CLA. Enquiries concerning reproduction outside these terms should be sent to the publishers at the undermentioned addresses:

2nd Floor, 45 Gee Street
London
EC1V 3RS
United Kingdom

122 W 27th St, 10th Floor
New York, NY 10001
USA

4737/23 Ansari Road
Daryaganj
New Delhi 110002
India

www.koganpage.com

© Richard Wilding 2020

The right of Richard Wilding to be identified as the author of this work has been asserted by him in accordance with the Copyright, Designs and Patents Act 1988.

ISBNs

Hardback 9780749483708
Ebook 9780749483715

British Library Cataloguing-in-Publication Data

A CIP record for this book is available from the British Library.

Library of Congress Cataloging-in-Publication Data

A CIP record for this book is available from the Library of Congress.

Typeset by Integra Software Services, Pondicherry
Print production managed by Jellyfish
Printed and bound by CPI group (UK) Ltd, Croydon CR0 4YY

CONTENTS

CONTRIBUTORS

Professor Richard Wilding OBE is recognised globally for his thought leadership in Logistics and Supply Chain Management. Richard is a highly acclaimed presenter and regularly speaks at Industrial Conferences and has undertaken lecture tours of Europe and Asia at the invitation of local Universities; Confederations of Industry. As Chair (Full Professor) in Supply Chain Strategy at the Centre for Logistics and Supply Chain Management, Cranfield School of Management UK, Richard works with European and International companies on Logistics and Supply Chain projects in all sectors including pharmaceutical, retail, automotive, high technology, food, drink and professional services to name a few. He has published widely in the area of Supply Chain Management and is Editorial Advisor to a number of top journals in this area. He is currently Chair of CILT.

Erica Ballantyne, Sheffield University Management School, has expertise in the areas of urban and city logistics, freight transport operations, reverse logistics and local authority freight transport planning and policy decision making. She has been employed in various operational and management roles within the logistics and transport industry, working mainly in the FMCG and grocery markets.

Anastasia Christodoulou is a postdoctoral researcher at the School of Business, Economics and Law at the University of Gothenburg, Sweden. Her research interests focus on sustainable shipping, maritime energy management, intermodal transport systems and short sea shipping. She has published several scientific articles in peer-reviewed journals and presented her research work in various international scientific conferences.

Graeme Heron, Sheffield University Management School, has research interests that include the emerging roles of data enabled food value chains, quality management in the transport sector, and adapted management science tools for equal participatory and inclusive learning. He has over 28 years' experience in manufacturing industries, and working in the food sector.

Peter Hilton is a director at Hilton Productivity Services Ltd., providing consultancy services in the management of productivity and performance in operational sectors, including retail, logistics and manufacturing. He has over 20 years' experience in the development of effective operational workforce planning processes.

Ingrid Hunt is a Lecturer in Supply Chain Management at the School of Engineering at the University of Limerick, Ireland.

Gendao Li, Associate Professor in Operations Management, Department of Marketing, Operations and Systems, Newcastle Business School, Northumbria University.

Jie Ma is Senior Lecturer in Operations Management, Department of Marketing, Operations and Systems, Newcastle Business School, Northumbria University.

Mark Manning is the Founder and CEO of iTRACE Technologies, a Silicon Valley company specializing in supply chain security. Mark is a serial entrepreneur and has been involved with brand protection and product security for over 15 years, delivering technology solutions to some of supply chains biggest problems. iTRACE 2DMI helps companies stop Production Overrun, Diversion and provides secure product authentication to global fashion accessory brands. iTRACE has deployed blockchain and traditional track and trace solutions through a suite of desktop, on-product and cloud-based security applications. Mark studied Engineering and Telecommunications in London England and currently resides in the San Francisco Bay Area.

Steve O'Sullivan has held SCM positions in complex business-critical environments for global firms, and within diverse industries, including aviation and consumer electronics, where he has consistently created and implemented superior process improvement solutions across the entire supply chain process, while supporting international management teams in meeting and exceeding established targets. Great mentors in companies, such as, SIFCO Turbine Components, instilled a deep-rooted appreciation for customer support, and Logitech (Ireland Services) provided a powerful full-spectrum foundation in the art of SCM.

Henrik Pålsson is Associate Professor at Lund University. He has conducted research and taught master's students within packaging logistics since 2004. Lund University specializes in this topic and is world renowned for its research in this area.

Noreen Spillane is the Chief Operations Officer at UL Hospitals Group.

Alireza Shokri, PhD, Senior Lecturer in Operations and Supply Chain Management, Department of Marketing, Operations and Systems, Newcastle Business School, Northumbria University.

Todd Snelgrove, Consultancy Experts In Value, has over twenty years of business to business procurement and sales experience, most recently as Global Vice President of Value for a global industrial company. Todd's focus has been on creating and implementing programs, systems, and processes with tools, so companies can measure, sell and buy based on best quantified value. Todd now runs his own consultancy and shares his experiences and best practices globally at executive meetings, conference keynotes, and supporting academic courses at LBS, Kellogg, IMD and others. Todd can be reached at todd@expertsinvalue.com

Daniel Stanton is a global supply chain executive and Co-Founder of SecureMarking. He has worked with Caterpillar, U.S. Navy, APICS, and MHI. He's also been a professor at Bradley University, Jack Welch Management Institute, and National American University. Daniel is the author of the bestselling *Supply Chain Management For Dummies* and online courses from LinkedIn Learning. SecureMarking is a powerful new tool for manufacturers, distributors, and their customers to combat the growing threat of counterfeit, black market, and grey market products in global supply chains. It securely ties physical products to the digital supply chain using high security inks.

Allen Woods is a chartered member of the British Computer Society who, on leaving the British Army after 24 years' service in 1995, worked in defence logistics information management for the following 23 years as an independent consultant and software developer. His credits include building a distributed financial management platform for the Army Catering Branch, building and maintaining the MoD Health and Safety Information System (HSIS) and the construction of a number of policy and governance distribution portals for major Defence Support Chain management organizations. He now works on developing an information management strategy to support EU General Data Protection Regulation (GDPR) compliance.

ACKNOWLEDGEMENTS

The editor wishes to acknowledge all those who have helped in the production of this book. In particular, I am especially grateful to all the contributing authors, from diverse backgrounds and specialisms, who have dedicated time and expertise in writing the case studies included.

I am also grateful to my colleagues in the Centre for Logistics, Procurement and Supply Chain Management at Cranfield University for their support and encouragement.

A special thank you to all at Kogan Page for their patience and support of all those involved in this project and for supporting our innovative royalties model, ensuring that all those involved in this project receive some reward.

I also thank those who have helped with this project but not specifically named above. In particular, I acknowledge the patience and support given by my wife, Janice, for bearing with me while I was distracted by this project.

> My son, there is something else to watch out for. There is no end to the writing of books, and to much study will wear you out.
>
> After all this, there is only one thing to say: Have reverence to God, and obey his commands, because this is all that man was created for.

Ecclesiastes 12:12–13

Introduction

This book is purposely designed to be accessible to both the practitioner and the academic. The purpose of the content is to educate, inform and give real-life examples of supply chains, logistics, operations management and procurement in action. Its goal is to enable innovation by both individuals and organizations to ultimately create sustainable value for the stakeholders served and reduced costs for those serving those stakeholders.

Innovation through sharing ideas

I define innovation as taking ideas that are new to the individual and creating economic, social or environmental value. To innovate, it is important to be exposed to new ideas and insights and for individuals and organizations to proactively seek opportunities for 'idea exposure'. This can occur through engagement in, for example, professional organizations, universities, factory visits, face-to-face networking and, increasingly, virtual networking through social media platforms. Importantly, ideas are shared through the stories and experiences of others. This is how knowledge and wisdom have been passed down over the millennia. Within the context of the supply chain, logistics, procurement and operations management, the same principles apply. Stories and experiences need to be shared, enabling ideas and knowledge to be shared and thus cultivating innovation. Many important innovations within the supply chain have occurred through taking ideas from one environment and applying them to another. It is reported, for example, that the founder of the fashion manufacturer and retailer Zara visited Toyota, the automotive manufacturer, witnessed their systems and innovated by taking ideas from the automotive supply chain and applying them to the fashion supply chain, creating a revolution in fast fashion. Case studies are effectively stories – stories that illustrate key concepts and approaches, thus enabling innovation.

Taking knowledge and creating action in the supply chain

My passion is taking knowledge and creating real-world action. My objective is to take and develop knowledge so that it creates impact in the real world. Enabling learners to bridge the gap between the 'classroom' and business has been a theme throughout my career. This has been a goal since starting my career in industry and then 'accidentally' falling into academia.

The 'learners' I work with range from those currently based in full-time education to those managers and directors who recognize the need for continual professional development and are challenging themselves to gain and apply new knowledge to benefit their company, society or the environment.

The majority of learners with whom I interact demand that learning should be embedded rapidly. I therefore develop learning and assessment that are integrated effectively to ensure the individual and organization benefit (ie a 'return on investment') at each stage of the learning and assessment journey. The learning environments I have been responsible for creating have had significant impact on business performance (profits, society and culture, environment and planet) through encouraging, enabling and inspiring practitioners to apply and adapt learning within their context.

A foundational element of facilitating learning is the use of case studies. Case studies demonstrate theoretical concepts in an applied setting, giving insight into the context of a problem while demonstrating a key principle. The use of case studies has been found to be significantly more effective than many other methods at encouraging active learning, increasing enjoyment and hence the desire to learn and apply the insights gained. Case studies can take many forms, from short 'case vignettes' providing a short description or account to provoke discussion and reflection to lengthy 'book case studies' that tell the whole story of a company or situation. Whatever the length of the case study, learners and practitioners need to critically reflect on the knowledge gained and what can be applied. It may be a great story, but how will the story impact on personal and individual action?

During the delivery of teaching and learning interventions, whatever form they take, I always end by allowing learners time to consider three questions:

1. What knowledge did I gain?
2. What action should my organization take?
3. What action am I going to take?

It seemed appropriate that during the production of this book, the authors preparing case studies for this collection should consider these questions. This ensures that the case study is not seen as a 'story' but as a practical tool to share knowledge and encourage action for both the individual and the organization. My hope is that by studying and reflecting on the case studies contained in this book, both individuals and organizations will innovate, thus creating a positive impact on profits, people and planet.

The building blocks of supply chain strategy

In structuring and editing this book, my perspective on supply chain strategy has influenced its organization.

The supply chain and its management are fundamental to the success of any organization, both profit-making and not for profit. Put simply, within all environments an organization will have some form of corporate strategy defining its mission, direction and objectives. This in turn will define the competitive strategy of how an organization will compete and thus gain competitive advantage. The competitive strategy, it can be argued, is focused on 'creating demand' for the organization's products and/or services; that is, it is focused on how value is created for the customer or stakeholder the organization serves.

The supply chain strategy in turn defines how 'demand is fulfilled', that is, how value is delivered to the customer or stakeholder the organization serves. It is focused on the operational execution of the business mission. For effective strategic alignment to occur, it is imperative that those involved in the design, development and execution of the competitive and supply chain strategies collaborate effectively.

In simple terms, there are four key elements to any supply chain strategy: process design; network, infrastructure and equipment design; information system design; and organizational/people design. Importantly, these are all interrelated; for example, if the supply chain network is changed, it will potentially have implications for the processes, information system and the organization. If, for example, a new additive manufacturing (3D printer) is utilized within a warehouse so that components can be manufactured on demand, processes will need modifying, the network will have to be adjusted, there may be different information system requirements and, importantly, the skills of the people within the supply chain may have to change, along with other organizational implications. The increasing complexity of these interactions is a constant challenge for any professional working within supply chains.

It therefore seemed appropriate to categorize the case studies within this book under the themes of Process, Network and Infrastructure, Information Systems, and Organization and People. However, many cases span a number of themes, so readers should not see this as definitive. I wanted to move away from a traditional classification of, for example, sector (eg public or private), industry type and so on, because as already mentioned, it is important that ideas from different environments are shared to create innovation and action.

The four themes of the book are as follows. Each has a symbol, and each chapter is marked with its appropriate symbols.

SUPPLY CHAIN PROCESS DESIGN

(1)

The process design of any supply chain requires serious attention; poor process results in poor performance. In recent decades, many process analysis approaches have been utilized within supply chain improvement. The majority of approaches are utilized to gain transparency of the process in order to provide a foundation for further analysis, for example cost-based analysis through activity-based costing and cost-to-serve approaches. Process re-engineering, with its foundations in the Toyota Production System, including just-in-time (JIT) methodology, lean and six sigma analysis, also has an important part to play in enabling the redesign of the supply chain, thus taking techniques from a macro, individual-facility focus and applying the approaches at a more holistic supply-chain-centric level.

SUPPLY CHAIN NETWORK AND INFRASTRUCTURE DESIGN

(2)

Supply chain network and infrastructure design occurs at multiple levels, from the global network of facilities and flows down to the configuration of individual facilities, for example warehouses and factories and the associated equipment utilized within them. Network design is often a complex decision requiring multiple trade-offs, and multiple variables may need to be balanced, including cost, time, environment and social considerations. One may be balancing location decisions to minimize flows of materials to, for example, manufacturing operations but also flows of goods to the customer. The trade-off is increasingly time related in some environments, for example if you need to deliver to customers within 2 hours you need a different network compared to delivering to customers in 48 hours. For the short lead-time, depots and inventory may have to be located close to the customers, whereas on longer lead-times an individual regional or even global warehouse may suffice. Accessibility to key resources may also impact on the network and infrastructure, people being one such example; some locations may seem attractive for minimizing materials and finished goods flows, but if there is not adequate population or infrastructure to support a facility, a compromise needs to be found.

Within individual facilities, the nature of the product and market characteristics will define the equipment utilized for handling and management. Product characteristics such as size, fragility, temperature requirements and so on will define the required equipment, but also market characteristics such as volatility of demand and required lead-time for delivery, for example, will define the level of automation required.

SUPPLY CHAIN INFORMATION SYSTEM DESIGN

3

The information system design is an important element of the supply chain. It is required to create transparency and visibility of the utilization and flows of key resources. Data on resources create information, which leads to knowledge and ultimately understanding (and wisdom). The supply chain needs systems to monitor multiple variables and can include demand, inventory, lead-time, even vehicle positions. Information systems to support the management of the financial resource, which is the life blood of any supply chain, are also fundamental (if one stakeholder runs out of money, supply chains rapidly collapse!), and methods to enable transparency of the cost-to-serve specific markets with individual products against a particular services level require robust and timely information. In today's world, the abundance of data requires appropriate processing, technologies and approaches, including Big Data analytics, artificial intelligence and cloud computing. The blockchain concept is currently being piloted to ensure provenance and an auditable unhackable record of supply chain transactions, enabling greater levels of trust and requiring further adjustments to information systems design.

SUPPLY CHAIN ORGANIZATION DESIGN

4

The supply chain organisation encompasses the people dimension of the supply chain. This can be planned at a global, regional and local level. The organisation design can include decisions on, which suppliers to work with, the organisation structure of the supply chain network and specific skill and training requirements for individuals working within a particular facility.

For supply chains to operate effectively there is what can be described as human chain. Whether a new product is being launched, sales and operations planning undertaken or new logistics services provided they all involve people, in relationships, influencing each other. The organisation structures implemented will influence relationships as will culture and human resource management. One definition of for Supply Chain Management states, "Supply Chain Management can be defined as the management of relationships with all key stakeholders to achieve greater customer value at less cost to the supply chain as a whole". It could be argued from this definition that every process, system, infrastructure decision should strive to improve a relationship with a particular stakeholder. Relationship management is therefore receiving increased emphasis within supply chain networks and in recent years ISO44001: Collaborative business relationship standard has been developed to support and emphasis relationship management.

The organisation design will also consider the skills, both soft (Emotional Intelligence) and hard skills (Technical Intelligence) required to operate the supply chain function effectively. This can include the leadership skills for different supply chain environments and information technology skills, for example. Critically "values" of the organisations and individuals is an area of increased focus, for example, ethical procurement and corporate responsibility requires an alignment of values within the supply chain with appropriate decisions on process, network being supported by transparency and information within the extended supply chain network.

Conclusion

This book provides a number of case studies that demonstrate supply chains in action. It provides an insight into the decisions and approaches that impact the supply chain, logistics, operations and procurement professionals. It has been structured around a simple strategic framework with an emphasis on Process, Network and Infrastructure, Information system and Organization design. As editor, I accept this is simplistic and that more comprehensive frameworks are available, but my intention was to make the structure accessible to both specialists and those just taking a glance at this critical area of business. It is recognized that, with the limited number of cases presented, not every topic can be addressed, but it is hoped that by considering the individual cases and perhaps the book in its entirety the reader will be motivated to create action and innovate. Case studies can be reviewed individually but often it is more powerful to share with colleagues to provoke discussion, as the different perspectives and insights of others further enhance the impact and learning gained. It is hoped that perhaps individuals may also be motivated to tell their own story, to share by writing a case that can be included in future case study collections in order to enable academics and practitioners to learn and innovate.

Case Studies

01

Efficient integration of shipping into intra-regional supply chains

ANASTASIA CHRISTODOULOU, ZEESHAN RAZA AND JOHAN WOXENIUS

(2) (4)

Knowledge

You will be able to identify crucial operational and managerial parameters that influence the employment of maritime transport chains for certain routes and recognize the different types of potential cooperation under these transport systems.

Action

You will be able to identify the potential benefits from the cooperation and shared planning with other agents in these maritime transport chains and adopt appropriate innovative strategies for these joint operations. By adopting innovative logistics and management strategies for the integration of shipping into their supply chains, companies can acquire a significant competitive advantage in the market, thus reducing the per-unit transport cost of their products and enhancing the overall system efficiency and sustainability.

Introduction

Container shipping is the backbone of intercontinental trade in manufactured and semi-manufactured goods. The integration of shipping into intra-regional supply chains has been a challenge, although it has been widely stated as a transport policy aim during recent decades owing to the supreme sustainability performance of maritime transport compared to road and, in some respects, rail transport. Despite a wide range of initiatives taken by different stakeholders, the level of integration of intra-regional shipping transport chains has been quite slow, and the desired environmental results have not been achieved. The identification of crucial operational and managerial parameters to enable the development of maritime transport routes is quite important for shippers and supply chain managers.

The cooperation between a major forest company in Sweden and Finland and a shipping company is analysed in this case study, providing a real-life example of successfully integrating shipping into supply chains and giving some insight into the factors that contribute to the effective operations of these maritime supply chains. The case will describe the unique intermodal logistics system developed by the forest company for the transport of its products using an innovative cargo unit, which can be transported by Roll-on/Roll-off (RoRo) ships and trains in countries with a generous rail loading gauge, such as Sweden. Apart from the SECU (Stora Enso Cargo Unit) innovation, the case illustrates the operations of these RoRo shipping services chartered by the company, whose demand has a great impact on service design, potentially affecting the frequency of departures and even stipulating the use of specific vessels.

The two companies cooperate in two ways. The first concerns ship management, that is, the operations management of vessels, while the second is related to selling the excess freight capacity available on board the vessels and in SECUs to third-party shippers. The case study will shed light on these different types of cooperation – operational and commercial – and highlight the benefits for both firms.

This real-life example of maritime supply chains may enable the supply chain actors to discover and understand the real-life phenomenon of successfully integrating shipping into intra-regional supply chains on mid-distance routes and recognize the potential benefits from developing these logistics systems.

The forest company

This is a world-leading Swedish-Finnish forest company that produces paper and packaging products, biomaterials and wooden construction materials and exports them all over the world. The Swedish component started as a copper mine in the 7th century, and a share certificate dated 1288 makes it the world's oldest limited company still in business. It merged with the Finnish forest industry in 1998. The company employs around 26,000 people in more than 35 countries and had a turnover of €10 billion in 2017. Sea transport is the main traffic mode employed by the company, accounting for approximately 89 per cent of the transport work, followed by road (9 per cent) and rail (2 per cent) transport. They have developed a unique intermodal transport system, using SECUs moved in a combination of ships and trains on Swedish tracks. SECUs are large intermodal containers, with dimensions of 13.8 m × 3.6 m × 3.6 m and a cargo capacity of 80 tonnes, compared to the ISO container's 26.5 tonnes. Although SECUs are innovative cargo units for multimodal transport, their employment is quite restricted owing to the special equipment that is required for their transhipment (eg special translifters), and their use is mainly located in Finnish, Swedish, Belgian, British and German ports, where the main production and consumption centres are located.

Cooperation scheme

The company has developed a short sea shipping (SSS) network of services for the transport of its products to consumers that includes three main routes: the Gothenburg–Zeebrügge route, the North Finland routes from Kemi/Oulo and the South Finland routes from Kotka. Compared to container vessels, the high frequency of departures of RoRo vessels, in addition to the fast cargo-handling (the cargo is horizontally loaded onto the vessel, towed into the vessel or brought in on wheeled vehicles), enhances their competitive advantage and facilitates their integration in intermodal transport chains.

Since 2009, the company has outsourced the operations of the eight RoRo vessels that were employed in its SSS network, as ship ownership and ship operations management are not the company's main activities and could be better performed by a shipping company. The company assigned ship management of its SSS system to the shipping company Transatlantic, but a carrier has gradually taken over the traffic since 2014. To manage the company engagement, the carrier founded a single-purpose company (SNES) that acts exclusively on behalf of the shipper, being the long-term charterer of the vessels. Some of SNES's operations on behalf of the company include the operation and maintenance of the vessels, the instruction of master mariners on board, and the scheduling and booking of the cargo to their contracted shippers.

Apart from this type of cooperation, in 2015 the carrier was selected by the shipper as the 'sales agent' for the excess freight capacity, either the empty space on board or the empty space inside the northbound SECUs, for external customers on the Gothenburg–Zeebrügge route. The same year, the company restructured its SSS transport network by replacing the Port of Gothenburg with the Port of Zeebrügge in Belgium as the hub of its logistics system. About 1.5 million tonnes of cargo per year were shifted from Gothenburg, significantly increasing the logistics system's efficiency, as the cargo from the paper mills in Kemi and Oulu in Northern Finland was directly transferred to Zeebrügge. Despite this shift, the role of the Port of Gothenburg is still crucial for the flows from the company's four mills in Sweden, all located rather far from the coast.

In Sweden, the forest company employs the SECU rail system for the transport of its products from the inland mills to the Port of Gothenburg, where the cargo is transhipped to RoRo vessels. Although this rail system is owned and operated by the state-owned rail operator Green Cargo, they have certain control of the 190 wagons deployed in the SECU rail system and they are responsible for the rail operations to the port. Every day, three trains carrying their cargo reach the Port of Gothenburg. The efficient transhipment of cargo flows from trains to RoRo vessels at the port is achieved in close cooperation between the carrier and the shipper and with the continuous exchange of information about the cargo flows. While enhanced transhipment efficiency from rail to RoRo vessels at the port has been accomplished, the cost of port operations is extremely high, accounting for 60 per cent of the company's total shipment cost.

The Gothenburg–Zeebrügge connection is the backbone of the company's SSS network, offering frequent RoRo services vital for the transport of the company's products to continental Europe and major consumer countries. Two chartered RoRo vessels, which were purpose built for their cargo, operate between Gothenburg and Zeebrügge and execute two round trips per week. These vessels have two levels of loading ramp, a technical feature that enables reduced time of vessels at ports and allows them to run at 15 knots, compared to some 18 knots by other RoRo vessels on the route.

The vessel speed reduction offers both financial and environmental benefits, as it implies a dramatic decrease in fuel consumption and reduced harmful emissions from vessel operations. The size of the vessels is 2,600 lane metres, and ISO containers on cassettes can be double stacked. There has been a significant expansion of the Gothenburg–Zeebrügge line over the years, owing to a modal shift from land-based modes of transport to sea and the adjustments in the production patterns of many companies that transferred their operations around Gothenburg and increased their shipments in this line.

Under the cooperation scheme between the carrier and the forest company on the Gothenburg–Zeebrügge route, the carrier is responsible for third-party sales and receives a commission, but the full commercial risk of utilizing the vessels is borne by the forest company. Freight forwarders and road haulage firms are the main external customers on the Gothenburg–Zeebrügge route, as they occupy the third-party freight capacity on board, load semi-trailers or fill the empty space inside the SECUs. The allocation of both the case company and third parties' cargo depends on the agreed capacity and the current demand. The case company, for example, has reserved an agreed freight capacity of 260 SECUs per week on vessels operating on the Gothenburg–Zeebrügge route, and the carrier is not obliged to transfer any excess cargo volumes, especially when demand from external customers is high. Third-party forwarders are usually given priority over the case company, as the carrier does not want to risk losing these external customers. In these cases of capacity shortage, despite the additional transport cost, the case company either stores SECUs in Gothenburg to fill up empty capacity in a stand-by consignment scheme or moves or reroutes a vessel from North Finland to satisfy its customers' urgent needs.

This commercial cooperation between the case company and SOL developed quickly, resulting in the carrier selling the RoRo capacity for nearly 100,000 third-party cargo units on the Gothenburg–Zeebrügge route in 2017. Another interesting feature of these RoRo operations is that their utilization rate reaches about 95 per cent in both directions, which is rare for the RoRo industry, although many SECUs are empty on the northbound leg. This high utilization rate can be reached owing to the high flexibility of vessels' operations, with the final load plan made half an hour before the vessels' departure. Apart from these successful third-party sales, this commercial cooperation resulted in another beneficial outcome. The case company's SSS network was expanded with other partners – P&O operations in the North and Mediterranean seas and the carrier in Scandinavian regions – with a significant increase in the cargo volumes of their chartered vessels.

The short stay of SECUs at the port – a few days, maximum – before their shipment is achieved owing to the flexible allocation system with external customers that enables the utilization of the excess capacity by third parties. To arrive on time to the right customer and at the right place, SECUs are given a date based on the cargo unit that has the earliest arrival time in the destination port, and then they are put in lanes with dates. Apart from their function as loading units, SECUs sometimes act as warehouses when the case company needs to produce earlier to satisfy the client's required delivery time; in this case, the cargo is produced, directly loaded on SECUs and shipped. However, SECUs never reach the customer, as the cargo is always reloaded to semi-trailers and the last leg of the 'trip' includes road transport.

At this point, it is important to again highlight the fact that the case company and the carrier share two different cooperation types, operational and commercial. The operational cooperation concerns the operation management of vessels by SNES on behalf of the case company acting as the long-time charterer of the vessels, while the commercial cooperation is related to SOL acting as the 'sales agent' for the excess freight capacity to third-party shippers. These different types of cooperation are quite distinct, and the benefits they offer for both companies present great differentiations.

Learning outcomes

This case study provides a real-life example of effective maritime supply chains and brings new insights for the shippers and supply chain managers, highlighting the importance of cooperation and shared planning with other transport modes for the establishment of efficient maritime supply chains. The development of a management 'culture' that promotes the complementarity of inland and maritime carrier operations and relies on carrier–shipper relationships can have a significant impact on the further employment of RoRo shipping services, as these services usually do not offer door-to-door transport but are the core parts of an intermodal transport chain.

Successful integration of shipping into supply chains implies efficient port operations with low cargo-handling costs and short times in ports. As shown in this case study, the efficient transhipment of cargo flows from trains to RoRo vessels at the port is achieved by the continuous exchange of information about the cargo flows and close cooperation between the carrier and the shipper.

The potential benefits from the development of maritime supply chains are apparent in this case study. Apart from the successful management operations of the vessels, the commercial cooperation between the shipper and the carrier resulted in increased sales of shipping services for third-party units and the utilization rate of these services reaching about 95 per cent. Another beneficial outcome from this cooperation is the expansion of the shipper's SSS network with other partners in different regions, significantly increasing the cargo volumes of their chartered vessels.

The adoption of a different management approach that relies on a carrier–shipper relationship and the consideration of the transport chain as a 'whole', giving particular emphasis to the ports – the 'nodes' of the maritime supply chains – could enable the integration of shipping into intermodal transport chains, enhance the whole system's efficiency and sustainability and lead to reduced lead-times, emissions and costs for all the collaborating parties. Sailing at reduced speed, thus decreasing bunker consumption and emissions, is a major benefit of the short turnaround time in port.

QUESTIONS

Based on this case, with a focus on the development of efficient maritime supply chains and the further integration of shipping into intra-regional supply chains, a number of discussion points should help you identify crucial operational and managerial parameters that influence the employment of maritime transport chains as well as the potential benefits from their operations:

1. In what way is the efficient integration of shipping into intermodal supply chains important for its further employment in intra-regional trade?
2. What is the role of efficient port operations for the enhancement of maritime supply chains?
3. How do managerial and cultural parameters affect the establishment of efficient maritime supply chains?
4. What are the potential benefits from the development of maritime transport chains for the supply chain actors?
5. Based on this case, what can be done to facilitate the integration of shipping into intra-regional supply chains?

Answers on page 220.

02

Overcrowding in a hospital emergency department

A supply chain management referral pathway to reduce overcrowding

INGRID HUNT AND NOREEN SPILLANE

(1) (2) (4)

Knowledge

You will be able to identify the need to implement a new supply chain process to provide GPs with an alternative referral pathway for their patients. Ultimately, this leads to a more positive experience and outcome for their patients and fewer bottlenecks at the ED.

Action

You will be able to recognize the impact of a supply chain decision on a hospital's ED by understanding the link between the GP and the patient and the effect the communication process has on the patient experience and outcome. The case study also demonstrates that by streamlining the patient pathway process through a single point of contact, previously underutilized resources were maximized, while also ensuring that patients received the care they required and avoided the ED altogether. With the introduction of a Bed Bureau pathway, an ED has a more focused process to improve patient experience and avoid overcrowding in the ED. There is a standardized referral pathway which allows for effective and efficient use of available resources and a more positive patient experience.

Introduction

The nature of emergency medicine has changed dramatically in recent years with the introduction of new treatment options and the availability of modern medical technology. Nevertheless, patients presenting to the ED with conditions today are considered time critical. The ED is often seen as the 'safety net' for patients, and many experts have noted that the ED is really the 'gateway to the rest of the hospital'. If, at this early stage of the supply chain, problems arise in the ED, they have the potential to affect the rest of the hospital's supply chain processes.

The healthcare supply chain is characteristically complex. One is not just dealing with products and services, but also dealing with real people and their health and wellbeing. Additional complexities include the involvement of GPs, government, insurance companies and regulatory agencies. Each part of the supply chain often works independently, which prevents it from working as an interrelated and interconnected system. Patient flow through the ED is a multifaceted supply chain, starting with the patient who may arrive at the ED on the recommendation of their GP.

The purpose of this case study is to review the introduction of a single point of contact, known as 'the Bed Bureau', and how it offers options for the GP and for patients to avoid poor outcomes, poor patient experience times and spending extended periods of time on a trolley awaiting an inpatient bed.

Patient pathway

Currently, if a patient is unwell, they can attend the ED either by self-presenting or by calling the ambulance service. Alternatively, several patients attend their GP who in turn refers them to the ED, and it is this cohort of patients that are referred to in the case study. Overcrowding is often blamed on patients attending for 'minor illness', but most patients with minor illness prefer not to be in the ED at all. Nevertheless, overcrowding in the ED is a regular phenomenon and causes negative reputational damage to the organization. The hospital group under review for this case study makes regular media headlines in terms of the number of patients awaiting treatment in the ED and patients spending time on trolleys.

The hospital group comprises six clinical sites functioning collectively as a single hospital system. This group, known as the UL Hospital Group (ULHG), provides a range of acute inpatient and day-care services to a relatively largely populated area in the mid-west region of Ireland. University Hospital Limerick (UHL) is the only hospital in the group that provides major surgery, cancer treatment and care, and a range of other medical, diagnostic and therapy services, and has the busiest ED in Ireland, providing the only 24/7 emergency services in the group. The rest of the group is made up of specialty hospitals providing, for example, obstetric, neonatal, medical assessment units, local injuries units and day surgeries.

The GPs in the region, through their GP Forum, have advised that they are unable to access services in the local hospitals and therefore often use the ED as a default option. The patient pathway through the ED at the hospital is viewed as a very complex and challenging supply chain path. There are regular issues over patients waiting for a bed and therefore patients spend excessive time on trolleys. This then results in a very poor experience for the patient and often leads to a breakdown in trust with the patients who are the 'customers'. Prior to the introduction of the Bed Bureau at the hospital, there were several steps taken by the GP to get their patient treated appropriately. Medical assessment units (MAUs) are located across the area within the six clinical sites and they serve the main hospital. Each MAU functions as an independent unit, requiring separate phone calls to book appointments. The GPs have stated that they must wait too long for outpatient appointments to the units and viewed the steps noted below as too complex:

1. Patient is seen by the GP and a hospital assessment is determined.
2. The GP establishes what hospital assessment unit is suitable for the patient's needs.
3. A call is made to the appropriate MAU.
4. If there is a medical assessment appointment available, the patient can attend on the day and time appointed.
5. If there is no appointment available for the patient, the patient is sent directly to the ED.

What is a Bed Bureau?

The Bed Bureau facilitates a highly efficient and more structured supply chain process to deal with patients accessing the ED. The Bed Bureau introduces a single point of contact for the GPs, offering options for the patients for applicable care other than the ED. This single point of contact required the establishment of a centralized Bed Bureau at UHL. This was staged by competent staff using a carefully designed computer system for receiving and processing referrals based on a single criterion for the patient to access a relevant MAU as opposed to going to the ED directly. Communication with all the players/stakeholders in the pathway was critical and their buy-in to the process was imperative. The partakers of interest included the chief executive officer (CEO) and the chief operations officer (COO) of the hospital group, the executive management team and clinicians, as well as the communication manager, GP Forum, clinical directors, bed managers, patient flow staff, ED staff and the staff at the MAUs at the clinical sites.

With a newfound focus on the patient pathway, this supply chain improvement process gave rise to an increasing championing of the Bed Bureau. While approaches may differ from hospital to hospital nationally and indeed globally, the common drive for this Bed Bureau from the stakeholders was a need for the patient to have a better experience and reduce the number of patients attending the ED. This common goal has led to all agreeing that the healthcare supply chain for patient pathways needed to be more efficient and provide a better service for all.

Implementing the Bed Bureau

The setting up of the Bed Bureau for the hospital group was a new and innovative way to improve access for the GPs and in turn improve the patience experience. Unscheduled care and the flow of patients through the hospital system is the brief of the COO. It is the responsibility of this post holder to manage and mitigate the associated risks of poor patient experiences and poor patient outcomes. Keeping these metrics in mind, there was clear support to introduce a Bed Bureau. With the support and operations of key stakeholders, noted previously, software was developed by a lead clinician and an external information technology (IT) company to produce a database system that would now be known as the 'Bed Bureau'. In summary for this case study, several activities took place:

- A room to host the Bed Bureau was identified and desks, computers and headphones were installed.
- Staff were recruited through the nursing and Human Resource (HR) department.
- A paramedic coordinated the transfer of patients from UHL to other hospitals or returned the patient home.
- An administrator redeployed to work with the team became the superuser of the IT system and provided training to the Bed Bureau staff and to the staff on all the other sites.
- The governance of the Bed Bureau was provided by the Bed Manager and her office was near the staff answering the phones.

Initially 30 GPs were contacted to test the concept. Communication to the MAUs was also imperative as their work lists would now be generated by the Bed Bureau staff. The staff at the clinical sites would no longer take calls from their local GPs and book the patients in. There would now be a group-wide approach and the sites would no longer work in isolation. Each site agreed a number of slots every day that the staff in the Bed Bureau could populate. The staff in the Bed Bureau travelled to each of the sites, met the local staff and discussed the criteria and number of slots allocated. Each site had visibility of the other sites and agreed to use the criteria set up on the software system.

In addition, when the Bed Bureau commenced, the ED was very busy and it was decided that patients attending the ED with a GP letter and who met the criteria for MAUs at UHL would be transferred there once booked in through the Bed Bureau booking system. The ED staff in this instance rang the Bed Bureau and booked the patient in. This alleviated the pressure in the ED and ensured the other MAUs were populated first with appropriate patients.

The Bed Bureau was set up on a phased basis initially, with the key aim to formalize the interaction between the referring doctor in primary care and the acute hospital and to ensure patients are streamed to the most appropriate clinical site within the hospital group that has the appropriate environment to deal with the patient's problem in an effective and timely manner. The steps now taken by the GP are identified as follows:

1. Patient is seen by the GP and a hospital assessment is determined.
2. The GP telephones a dedicated phone line for the Bed Bureau.
3. The GP is offered an appointment for one of the relevant assessment units or referred to the ED as appropriate.

Data measured

Over the period of design and implementation of the Bed Bureau, a collection of data using both quantitative and qualitative methods was obtained, reviewed and analysed. Surveys were carried out and interviews undertaken with relevant staff, and the Planning, Performance and Business Intelligence Unit at the hospital and the Bed Bureau software program extrapolated certain data criteria for review. This also coincided with pre and post the implementation of the Bed Bureau. Data measured included:

- The number of attendances to the ED in the four months preceding the introduction of the Bed Bureau and the same information for the four months after the introduction of the Bed Bureau.
  - These data were also used to establish the age profile of the patients attending, the total number of hours spent in the ED, the number of patients on trolleys and the total number of admissions to the hospital group.
- Attendances at the MAUs on all sites were measured pre and post implementation of the Bed Bureau.
- In addition, data from the Bed Bureau IT system were obtained to establish the number of calls made by the GPs and the number of slots filled in each MAU as well as the numbers of patients who attended their appointments and those who did not attend.
- Furthermore, the numbers of admissions and the number of patients discharged from the MAUs were identified.
- Additional information available included:
  - Identifying the number of times GPs used the Bed Bureau to access the system and alternatively identify the number of GPs who don't use the Bed Bureau and continue to refer their patients to the ED.

During this period the satisfaction rate of the GPs was continuously monitored.

Analysis of Bed Bureau data

The data generated by the Bed Bureau for the period January to April 2017 were analysed post implementation and noted as follows:

- The total number of GP referrals processed by the Bed Bureau for a four-month period = 6,042 referrals.

- The average number of GP referrals per month processed by the Bed Bureau for this period = 1,510 referrals.
- The highest number of referrals by a single GP per month for this period = 15 referrals.
- The average number of referrals by a single GP per month for this period = 5 referrals.
- The lowest number of referrals by a single GP per month for this period = 0 referrals.
- The total number of referrals to one of the MAU sites per month for this period is 184 GP referrals.

Patient experience times and outcomes

Patient flow through the ED is a complex supply chain, and overcrowding results in poor outcomes and poor patient experience. The introduction of the Bed Bureau simplified the supply chain for patients who attended their GP and required further medical assessment. Prior to the Bed Bureau, these patients were often referred to the ED because accessing an appointment in the MAUs was so complex, with each MAU having a different criterion and a different contact number. The Bed Bureau introduced a single point of contact for GPs across the whole region, offering options other than the ED for patients. This reduced the number of GP-referred patients going to the ED, as these patients avoided the ED altogether and were more appropriately assessed, diagnosed and treated in the MAUs, which previously were resourced but underutilized.

In setting up the Bed Bureau, the GPs were considered to be key players in managing the major queues that occur in the ED, and their feedback, although mainly informal and through a short survey, was given due consideration. The setting up of the Bed Bureau in UL hospitals was a new and innovative idea to improve access for GPs and to improve the patient experience. Communication on the sites was also very important, as their work lists would now be generated by the Bed Bureau staff and the staff on the sites would no longer take calls from their local GPs and book patients in.

The Bed Bureau facilitates a group-wide approach and the sites no longer work in isolation. Each site agrees on a number of slots every day that the staff in the Bed Bureau can populate and each site has visibility of the other sites. This ensures that all available slots on all sites are utilized. When the Bed Bureau commenced, the ED was very busy, and it was decided that patients attending the ED with a GP letter who met the criteria for the acute MAU in the UHL would be transferred there. Once they were booked in through the Bed Bureau booking system, they avoided the bottlenecks in ED. The ED staff in this instance ring the Bed Bureau and book the patient in. This alleviates the pressure in the ED and ensures the other MAUs are populated first with appropriate patients, as the available slots on the UHL site are prioritized for ED. Eventually, it is anticipated that these patients will be referred directly to the Bed Bureau by their GPs. The Bed Bureau is now available 24/7, so that out-of-hours GPs can also use this resource.

Benefits of the Bed Bureau

The Bed Bureau was set up and introduced on a phased basis and its impact to date has resulted in a number of benefits for GPs and in turn patients. The benefits include:

- GP referrals are triaged at a central point: the Bed Bureau.
- GP referrals admitted via the MAU remove that cohort of patients out of the ED, which in turn reduces the number of patients that contribute to the overcrowding.
- The Bed Bureau generates data to evaluate referral patterns for GPs over time.
- The Bed Bureau creates a database for oversight of bed availability across the hospital.
- The Bed Bureau process standardizes referral/admission criteria against which to audit for compliance.
- The Bed Bureau addresses the inefficiencies of the previous process, reducing the patient pathway to three key steps as opposed to five complex steps. This is now a lean process that addresses the risk of variation in the system.
- The Bed Bureau facilitates a more efficient bed utilization of bed capacity in the hospital.

Conclusions

The Bed Bureau has facilitated a single point of contact for GPs and has improved the experience of suitable patients who can be referred directly for a medical assessment in the MAUs across all the hospitals in the group. These patients avoid the ED altogether and the resources available are utilized in a much more efficient way. The process for referring the patient has been refined to reduce the many steps that were previously used by the GP to refer patients to the MAUs. This leaner process has reduced the variation that existed by standardizing the process for all MAUs in the region.

Managing patient flow and pathways in healthcare is a complex supply chain and the introduction of the Bed Bureau has addressed the requirements for one group of patients, namely those referred by GPs.

The approach of managing GP referrals to reduce overcrowding in the ED at ULHG is pioneering work; nevertheless, we do appreciate that the Bed Bureau may not or cannot address the overall overcrowding issues that arise in EDs nationally or indeed globally. It is widely recognized that there are many other issues contributing to overcrowding. Examples include a lack of acute bed capacity, difficulty in attracting consultants to work (specifically in this case) in the Irish health system and a lack of development and expansion of services in the community, to name but a few. These are major challenges facing hospital supply chains. For those patients who are referred via the Bed Bureau directly, the patient experience time and the patient's outcome are much improved. Access to the MAUs is much less cumbersome for GPs and the revised pathway through the Bed Bureau is efficient. This allows GPs to give the patient their appointment date and time before they leave their GP surgery. The entire process can take less than a three-minute conversation on the telephone now.

QUESTIONS

1. Why is the healthcare supply chain complex?
2. Explain why the ED is critical to the supply chain process in a hospital.
3. What is the function of a Bed Bureau?
4. What benefits can be drawn from the introduction of a Bed Bureau to the healthcare supply chain?
5. What suggestions can you make for improving the patient pathway in a hospital's ED?

Answers on page 221.

03

Company X's OTD (on-time delivery) performance improvement

The application of Lean Six Sigma methodology

GENDAO LI, ALIREZA SHOKRI AND KYRILL NUSSBAUM

(1)

Knowledge

You will be able to understand the impact factors of OTD and will also have seen the Lean Six Sigma methodology in use in different settings.

Action

You will be able to use Lean Six Sigma to continuously improve the operations of their organization.

Introduction

Manufacturers are facing great challenges in fulfilling demand, owing to the speed of change in demand and ever-increasing product varieties. However, OTD not only has an effect on customers' satisfaction, but also has a great impact on company's financial performance through better service, enhanced profitability and greater market share. Lean Six Sigma (LSS) is a systematic methodology to continuously improve business performance. It is of vital importance that practitioners are able to use the LSS tools to improve OTD.

This case study investigates the OTD problem in a cable gland and cleat manufacturer and illustrates how LSS could improve OTD performance.

X company introduction

Case-company X is a leading technical solution provider that designs, manufactures and sells industrial cable management products worldwide. Its products target the oil and gas, mining, construction and infrastructure, energy and power, food and agriculture, pharmaceutical, chemical and petrochemical, and rail industries. Continuous improvement and innovation ensure that its products lead the way in quality, safety and performance. Company X is based in the UK and has offices across the world, including the United States, Asia, Australia and South Africa, employing over 500 employees. Owing to its superior engineering and technical capabilities, the company grew from a family-sized business to a multinational enterprise (MNE) and has doubled its sales turnover in the past decade.

Their product range varies from high-volume standard goods to make-to-order goods. Here, the 80/20 rule can be applied. Eighty per cent of their sales volume comes from fast-moving, high-volume products, and the remaining 20 per cent from 'make-to-order' goods. However, the 20 per cent in volume products account for 80 per cent of their product range and only 20 per cent of the range covers all high-volume goods. Therefore, the uniformity or distinction of processes at the company considers the high-volume aspect of production, with a high amount of customized 'make-to-order' products. The challenge for Company X is to find the right balance between economies and diseconomies of scale in order to stay competitive within the market. A well-known and long-time weakness of Company X is its delivery performance. OTD is almost non-existent, which frustrates the company's customers. One of the authors has been employed to investigate the problem using Lean Six Sigma methodology. An LSS project was initiated and carried out using the DMAIC (Define, Measure, Analyse, Improve, Control) cycle, which will be described in detail in the following sections.

The Define phase

Before the LSS project began, Company X was suffering from late deliveries to customers. Measures for OTD were very weak and customers were dissatisfied. Also, the company's bottom line was directly affected.

The labour cost involved in producing non-conformance reports (NCRs) for processes or products that don't meet quality standards is a so-called 'hard cost'. Soft costs, such as lack of efficiency within the process and the potential loss of customers, are among the current costs to the business that are related to the weak OTD performance. This weakness came to the attention of the company directors and was the main reason for this LSS project.

'Voice of customer' (VoC) analysis

To prepare for the VoC analysis, customer opinions were collected by the customer service department via phone calls and e-mails. The analysis was used to develop measurable critical-to-quality (CTQ) factors, which help he company to understand which activities, functions or tools they should focus on. The project team developed a VoC to CTQ diagram as shown in Table 3.1.

SIPOC analysis

SIPOC (Supplier, Input, Process, Outcome and Customer) analysis is a tool for identifying the suppliers and their inputs to the process under study, as well as the outputs (CTQs) of the process under study and the customer segments for its outputs. The project team conducted the SIPOC analysis linked to OTD performance, which is listed in Table 3.2.

TABLE 3.1 VoC to CTQ tree

Voice of customer	Focus point	Critical to quality
		Quantity checks
	Defect-free processes	Quality checks
		Stable process flow
	Accurate lead-times	Accurate lead-time measures
On-Time/in-full orders		Stable process flow
	Feasible due date	Feasible delivery dates
		Accurate planning
	Accurate inventory	Accurate stock levels
		Stock counts

TABLE 3.2 SIPOC analysis

Supplier	Input	Process	Output	Customer
Customer services Manufacturing Assembly Warehouse Packing/dispatch	Shop order Customers' requirements ERP (IFS) BoMs Routing Finished goods	Order placement (IFS*) Manufacturing Warehouse processes Assembly Quality check Quantity check Packing Dispatch	Shipped goods Shipping documents ERP(IFS)	External customers Customer services Carriers Finance department

* NOTE *IFS is the ERP system used in X company.*

Final project objectives

Designed for the identified CTQs, OTD is the key performance indicator for all products in this project. To measure OTD, the following formula is used

OTD (%) = Number of deliveries on time/Total number of deliveries

The estimated goal of this project was to increase OTD to 50 per cent at the end of December 2017.

The project team also developed a Gantt chart for planning the project.

The Measure phase

The Measure phase enables a company to understand current processes in order to create a current baseline which can then be compared with future changes in the process. While the impact factors in the CTQ and SIPOC analyses are complicated, the measurement of OTD is very simple. At the beginning of the project, the OTD in Company X varied from 30 to 35 per cent.

To further measure the OTD, a process map was developed illustrating how different activities are linked to delivery. The map is depicted in Figure 3.1.

The process starts with the incoming order from the customer. The customer service department negotiates the delivery terms with the customer. Usually, the lead-time for make-to-order products is 2–4 weeks, while stocked items range around one week. Next is operations planning, which schedules the order using material resource planning (MRP). After planning has been completed, the order will be on hold until the scheduled production

FIGURE 3.1 OTD process map

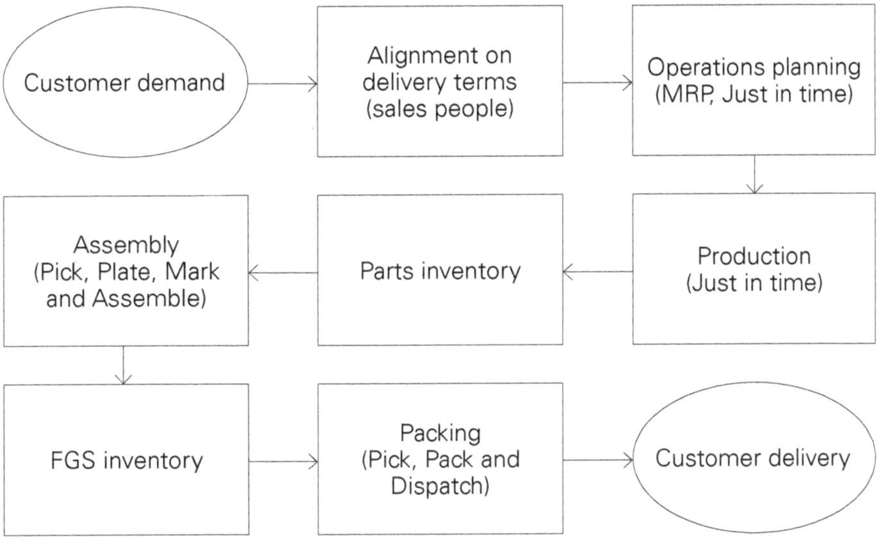

date, which is backwards scheduled by deducting the lead-time from the shipment date. That is, production is scheduled just in time to be completed before the order is scheduled to be dispatched. Following the production of parts, the newly produced semi-finished products are stored in inventory. When it is time for the products to be produced, employees in the inventory store pick the appropriate parts to be sent to the assembly department, where the semi-finished parts are assembled into finished products. These go to the warehouse for packing and dispatching. At this point, the production schedule is expected to have been met so that all orders are dispatched on time.

Based on the CTQ and the process map, the project team developed an OTD value chain, derived from Porter's value chain, by classifying the activities into primary activities and supporting activities. The OTD value chain is presented in Figure 3.2 with the corresponding relationship with the process map presented in Table 3.3.

The factors in the OTD value chain demonstrate areas with potential for improvement in Company X. The bottom row indicates the primary activities and the other rows show the support activities. 'Quarantine' stock means stock that is reserved for orders that are on hold because of defective or missing parts.

These activities then became sub-projects in the Improve phase.

FIGURE 3.2 OTD value chain

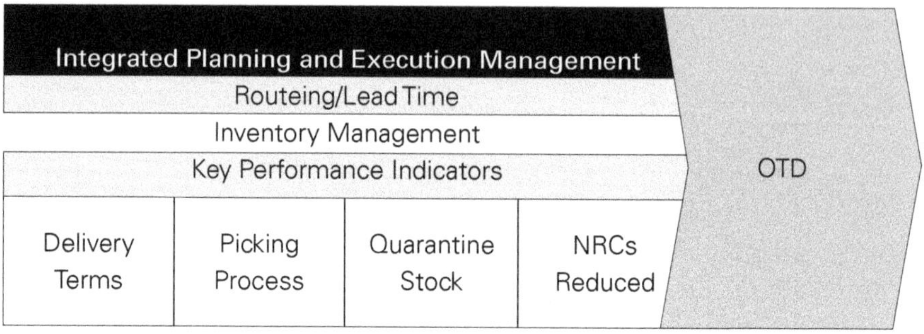

TABLE 3.3 Relationship between the OTD value chain and the process map

OTD value chain activity	Process
Integrated planning and execution management	Operations planning
Routings/lead-time	
Inventory management	Parts inventory control FGS inventory control
Key performance indicators	
Delivery terms	Agreement on delivery terms
Picking process	Assembly
Quarantine stock	Assembly
NCRs reduction	Packing Production

The Analyse phase

This stage is about investigating the current baseline to identify the root causes of the business problem.

As stated in the Measure phase, the current performance of OTD was only about 30 to 35 per cent. The team analysed each area identified in the OTD value chain using various data sources.

They collected primary data on NCRs using brainstorming, participative observation and semi-structured interviews. After analysing the data, they identified the most significant cause of that problem as human error, which is related to a lack of training and leadership.

The quarantine stock was analysed using historical data across a five-month period. It was found that 15 work orders per day on average were affected and moved to quarantine. In addition, 70 per cent of all these work orders involved 200 different part-numbers, representing only 20 per cent of the total part-numbers affected.

The quarantine stock analysis showed that 50 per cent of all work orders in quarantine were due to errors in the quantities received. Reducing the picking errors would reduce the on-hold work orders and improve OTD performance.

The inventory analysis mainly focused on stock level and accuracy. It revealed many out-of-stock situations in which orders could not be dispatched because of missing products.

The lead-time analysis was conducted by analysing the actual lead-time from the ERP system. Table 3.4 presents the comparison between the expected lead-time in the agreed delivery terms and the actual lead-time. It is clear that the actual lead-time is significantly greater than the expected lead-time.

For planning, delivery terms and KPIs, which were of a qualitative nature, the project team conducted a root-cause analysis, which also included the above areas.

A cause-and-effect diagram, also known as a fishbone or Ishikawa diagram, was used to structure a brainstorming session with the employees. The discussion focused on the six Ms: Man, Machine, Management, Measurement, Material and Method. Figure 3.3 presents the diagram.

Putting the above analyses together, the project team developed a root-cause matrix relating to each area (Table 3.5).

Table 3.5 was used to develop the scope of the sub-projects in the Improve phase.

TABLE 3.4 Lead-time analysis (unit: day)

	N	Mean	Mode	Median	StDev
Actual	1633	7.838	4	5	9.203
Expected	1633	2.5419	2	2	1.1244

FIGURE 3.3 Cause-and-effect diagram

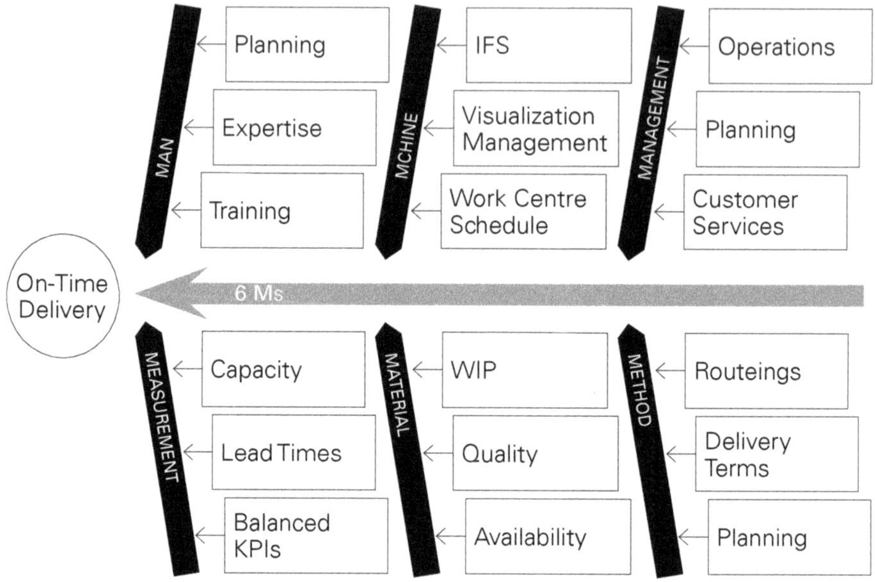

The Improve phase

Based on the above analysis, eight sub-projects were designed to improve the root causes.

Sub-project 1: NCR reduction (packing department)

This sub-project focused on standardizing the packing process. Scanning technology was implemented, HR adjustments made, quality inspections initiated and additional work-instructions developed.

Sub-project 2: Quarantine stock (WIP)

This sub-project identified 200 parts that were stored next to quarantine stock and replenished on a regular basis. This enabled 70 per cent of parts affected by failure to be replaced immediately, which reduced reaction time for work orders in quarantine.

Sub-project 3: Picking process

The picking process was improved through improving communication and performance measures and streamlining the process.

TABLE 3.5 Root-cause matrix

		NCR reduction (packing)	Picking process (Unit 3)	Quarantine stock	Inventory management	Lead-time review	Integrated planning and management	Delivery terms	KPI development
Man	Planning	X			X	X	X	X	X
	Expertise					X	X	X	
	Training	X	X				X	X	
Machine	IFS	X		X	X	X	X	X	
	Visual management	X	X	X	X	X	X		X
	Schedule	X			X	X	X	X	X
Management	Operations	X	X	X	X	X	X		X
	Planning	X			X	X	X	X	X
	Customer service	X			X	X	X	X	X

(continued)

TABLE 3.5 Continued

		NCR reduction (packing)	Picking process (Unit 3)	Quarantine stock	Inventory management	Lead-time review	Integrated planning and management	Delivery terms	KPI development
Measures	Capacity				X	X	X	X	X
	Lead-times	X	X	X	X	X	X	X	X
	KPIs	X	X	X	X	X	X	X	X
Material	WIP	X	X	X	X	X		X	X
	Quality	X		X				X	X
	Quantity	X	X	X	X			X	X
Method	Routings	X				X	X	X	
	Delivery terms	X			X	X	X	X	X
	Planning	X			X	X	X	X	X

Sub-project 4: Inventory management

Several actions were taken in this sub-project. Process changes, technology, daily cycle-counts and fast-moving inventory levels were developed to improve product availability and inventory efficiency.

Sub-project 5: Lead-time review

Owing to the large discrepancy between the expected lead-time and the actual lead-time, lead-time was constantly monitored and reviewed in this sub-project.

Sub-project 6: Integrated planning and execution management

Owing to the lack of coordination between different departments, operations planning was unfeasible. This sub-project proposed to change the current one-way process to an integrated planning system as illustrated in Figure 3.4.

Sub-project 7: Delivery terms (promised delivery dates)

This sub-project brought the sales team and the operations planning team together to come up with reasonable delivery terms when negotiating with customers, based on the company's capacity.

FIGURE 3.4 Integrated planning

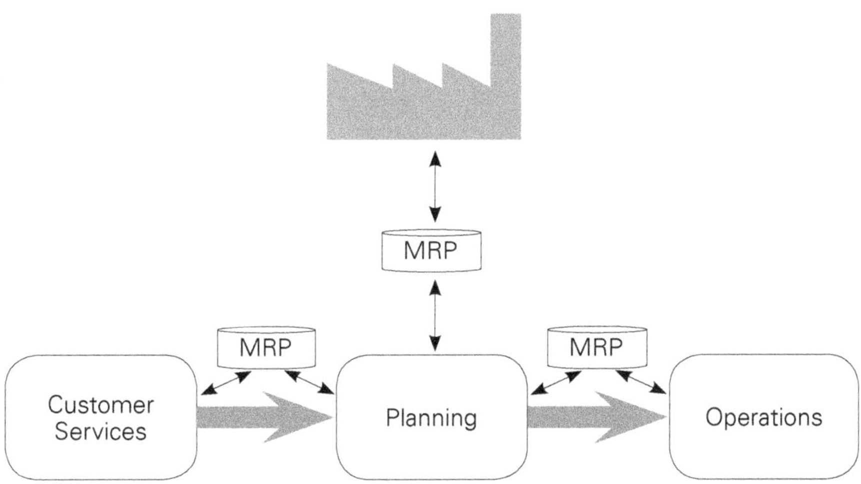

Sub-project 8: Key performance indicators (KPIs)

Lack of good balanced KPIs was the major issue for the company. This sub-project aimed to develop a system of KPIs. However, because of the scope of KPIs, this sub-project was implemented as an independent project beyond the LSS project.

During the implementation of the sub-projects, improvement started to emerge. By November 2016, the OTD was already 49.90 per cent.

The Control phase

The achievements of this project were disseminated across the company. The revised processes were stabilized. Cross-department communication/collaboration mechanisms were designed. KPI development became an independent project. To improve the results over time, a continuous improvement philosophy was introduced, and the above steps will be repeated in the future.

Conclusion

Company X was experiencing problems in their OTD performance but had no solution. Weak OTD performance not only caused customers to be dissatisfied, but also incurred huge costs. The project team applied LSS methodology to tackle this problem and achieved significant improvement.

QUESTIONS

1. Critically analyse what could be the soft and hard enablers of, and barriers to, implementing LSS for this particular project and explain why. Critically evaluate this for SMEs and MNEs.
2. What could be the major strategic and operational benefits and drawbacks of implementing an LSS project in the manufacturing sector and why?
3. Calculate the defects per million opportunities (DPMO) and Sigma value of the baseline measurement and final output of this particular project and critically analyse the difference in terms of waste reduction, quality enhancement and customer satisfaction.

Answers on page 223.

04

Developing best practice in operational workforce planning

PETER HILTON

1 2 3 4

Knowledge

- **Workforce planning** is a continual process used to align the needs and priorities of the organization with those of its workforce to ensure it can meet its legislative, regulatory, service and production requirements and organizational objectives.
- **Operational workforce planning** is on a person-to-person level and streamlines daily employee-related operations. This approach can help managers develop work schedules and employee hours to maintain business productivity and continuity.
- **Industrial engineering** is an engineering profession concerned with the optimization of complex operational processes. Industrial engineers are concerned with developing, improving and implementing integrated systems of people, money, knowledge, information, equipment, energy and materials.
- **Standard Minutes** are used to measure the amount of work content for a defined method at a defined performance level that any task requires. That defined level is Standard Performance (BS100). Producing 60 Standard Minutes per hour, having taken appropriate rest, is Standard

Performance. The Standard Minute or Standard Hour is the same unit of measurement used to identify the time value of tasks in every business sector – admin, retail, finance, manufacturing, distribution, service, construction, transport etc.

- **Key performance indicator**. A performance indicator or key performance indicator (KPI) is a type of performance measurement. KPIs evaluate the success of an organization or of a particular activity (such as projects, programmes, products and other initiatives) in which it engages.
- **Operational workforce planning** requires the development of a representative operating model, usually in the form of a spreadsheet, to analyse the variances between the forecast for workload demand and the availability of labour resources. The operating model is organized across a hierarchy incorporating the activity within teams, departments and sites so that it is possible to match resources for any forecast level of demand and to resolve any gaps and variances that are identified.

Actions

The project sponsor creates a project team that develops a work plan with clear objectives and timescales. In this case the aim was to integrate an industrial engineering department into the operations management structure.

The project consisted of a number of work streams. Progress against particular activities and milestones was tracked by the work-stream leaders and fed back to the project team for review.

Expertise and specialist skills were brought into the project team in order to fill gaps in knowledge and to add resources to shorten the timescales for delivering the project.

Collaboration across departments was required in order to deliver the change programme and to manage the risks associated with the impact of change on people and processes.

The project incorporated a number of initiatives that contributed to the overall plan. In addition to providing coaching for the industrial engineer employed by the business and the development of six-month and one-year industrial engineering work plans, practical exercises in work measurement, process improvement and training in operational workforce planning techniques all contributed to the overall success of the project.

Introduction: What is operational workforce planning?

Within an organization that manages a production system, the operational areas where production processes are executed require a number of planning systems to support the management of inputs and outputs, inventory, machinery, equipment and transport. Often, these production planning processes are integrated into enterprise resource planning (ERP) systems and are managed by operations management teams. Operational workforce planning is the aspect of planning that is focused on mapping the existing skills and capabilities of labour resources against current and future operational business requirements. An effective plan will be able to identify the variances between the resources required and the resources available across time periods.

The responsibility for operational workforce planning straddles the operations and HR areas. Operations managers are usually tasked with identifying the number of people required and the HR department is then responsible for delivering those requirements, both in terms of numbers and in skills, as part of its remit for workforce planning across the organization. Larger organizations may set up a central planning team to provide a link between the two areas and to relieve the operations management team of what can be a technically challenging process to maintain.

The case for operational workforce planning

Workforce planning is a core function of human resource management, and an established business process. However, operational workforce planning is far less likely to be integrated into business processes. In my experience it is very unlikely to be supported or subject to the same quality management systems that are required in, for example, business processes covered by ISO accreditation or by internal audit teams.

Recent research (Aberdeen Group, 2014) in the operational aspects of workforce planning shows that the capability in organizations to create effective and accurate resource plans is highly variable and that this can have a significant impact on operational performance. Fifty-two per cent of 'best in class' organizations have the ability to integrate data from ERP, financial and human capital management systems. The figure for the 'industry average' is 35 per cent, and for 'laggards' it is just 29 per cent.

A poor operational workforce planning process has two main consequences. It will result in inaccurate estimates of the resources required at any point in time. This can lead to shortages that can impact quality and service or excesses that result in higher costs and lower profit. It will also result in poor decision-making generally, across the business, because the operating budget will be distorted by the inaccuracies in the plan.

This case study focuses on a real example of the steps that a business, in its national distribution centre, has taken to develop a basic and underperforming operational workforce planning process into one approaching 'best in class'. The project took 10 months from start to finish and resulted in a new planning process that reduced the weekly forecast for resources by 15 per cent.

The case study

The framework for process improvement provided by industrial engineering

The project started with a request from the business to support a newly appointed industrial engineer in the development of a new department to focus on process improvement. I undertook an initial review over a four-week period to get to know the business and the industrial engineer, and developed a strategy looking a year ahead and an action plan for the first half of the year. I presented my plans to the business, which were agreed, and I was engaged to deliver them soon after.

There are a number of steps that are required to build up a solid platform for organizing effective process improvement activity and to incorporate productivity information into an effective operational workforce planning process. These follow a standard approach that is transferable across most, if not all, production systems. There are some similarities to the lean management approach. In fact, almost all the process improvement techniques in the toolkits are interchangeable, but with the important exception of work measurement. In this case, the business was very clear that work measurement was to be an important aspect of the work, and so it was clearly identified as an industrial engineering programme. This aspect is vital to be able to establish a platform for developing best-practice operational workforce planning processes.

The business had recently moved into new premises and had undergone a period of expansion enabled by new technology and automation. It had a well-established and effective management team able to deliver large-scale and complex projects, increasing the capacity of the site and also its capability to improve service to customers. The industrial engineering department was required to provide an objective and measured approach to evaluating new methods of working and the effectiveness of the new processes that had been implemented.

To provide a framework I segregated the project into five work streams:

- project planning;
- labour standards (work measurement);
- process improvement;
- productivity metrics and KPIs;
- operational workforce planning.

This approach enables a business to properly evaluate benchmarks for productivity and performance, identify process improvement opportunities and prioritize them by looking at the associated costs and benefits. The last piece of the jigsaw is the planning process that provides the business with accurate forecasting of resource requirements and labour costs, and a planning process that guarantees that cost savings will be delivered, as metrics are updated in the planning model.

Turning data into information

A theme running through each work stream was a requirement to establish, validate and organize data sources to provide an integrated information management system that would support productivity and performance management and the operational workforce planning process.

Operations in the business were fully supported by various automated systems and an overarching warehouse management system. However, much of the information being used to manage labour resources day-to-day was created and organized independently across departments and shifts. Spreadsheets were the main data tool but there was little coordination of effort or standardization and most data were input manually rather than being fed directly from systems. From an initial review of the main spreadsheets being used, I felt that there were too many inconsistencies and gaps in the data to be able to have much confidence in the management reporting process.

Evaluating the existing operational workforce planning processes

In this case, there was a central operations planning team who designed and maintained the existing operational workforce planning process. The main source of operational data was a master spreadsheet for departments to record daily volumes processed and hours used. This was a manual process, with the data then being linked into summary tables to create operational metrics. These were then referenced in the main planning model. This team also received data on contracted hours and attendance from HR that were also integrated into the planning model, and into the volume forecasts that were prepared by the finance team.

HOW AN OPERATIONAL WORKFORCE PLANNING MODEL WORKS

Part 1

Workload demand calculation

Starting with the site volume forecast:

1. Organize the hierarchy of the model by department and task.
2. Apply volume drivers to calculate volumes at task level.
3. Build up standard task times and metrics for unmeasured work.

The outcome is the forecast for workload hours for any given volume forecast.

Part 2

Calculation of available hours:

1. Site contracted hours.
2. Available temporary hours.
3. Account for unproductive time (absence and allowances).
4. Account for performance factors (where department performance varies to the standard).

The outcome is the total available productive hours.

Part 3

Establish a process to balance workload demand and available hours to eliminate variances.

In this case the planning model was in spreadsheet format and was used to create the annual forecast as well as supplying weekly updated forecasts so that the amount of agency labour required in the next period could be agreed. This process culminated in a weekly meeting with the agency representatives and the operations managers to finalize agency requirements.

The business operations employed approximately 80 per cent of its 'own' staff on permanent contracts, with the remainder supplied by agencies. This requirement was based on the output of the planning process and outwardly appeared to follow the correct steps.

My concerns were that the information being provided by the manual data-gathering processes, across the operational departments, was subject to too many risks:

- relying too heavily on manual processes;
- not enough data validation elements in the master spreadsheet (so errors were not prevented or identified);
- metrics that were determined at department level that could be more accurately determined at task level;
- parts of the operating model that were still based on estimates, where metrics had not been validated;
- the potential for errors to be created in the data processing steps from the master spreadsheet to the operating model spreadsheet, for example by the misuse of cell references, since validation and audit steps were absent.

In summary, in the early stages of the project I had major doubts over the information being used as the primary source for both tactical and strategic planning, and being used by the business in the operations budget and for setting high-level performance targets.

Work stream 1: project planning

Once the initial phases to get the activities started had been established, the business organized a stakeholder meeting, scheduled for every two weeks, where the project plan was reviewed and issues arising were discussed.

Work stream 2: work measurement of warehouse operations

The priority in this case was to start to take observations of processes on the shop floor so that we could start to get a realistic and objective view of process efficiencies in all departments. This would also allow the newly qualified industrial engineer to hone his work measurement technique and so the first period of the plan was heavily weighted towards work measurement activity. The target was to establish labour standards for all operations processes, based on relatively small but meaningful samples.

All direct tasks associated with processing activity were to be measured, and so these were broken down into element lists in readiness for work measurement. We also recorded the indirect tasks, for example waste removal, quality checking and stock checks, so that we had a full picture of all the activity that had to be resourced and that could be included in the process improvement review.

As we gathered information, we noted any potential process improvement opportunities and any questions we felt needed further discussion about the methods being used. By looking at the same processes on different shifts, we were able to identify variations in methods and the way that flows and work volumes were managed. As a result we generated an extensive issue log. This was to form the basis of process improvement plans that would be developed for each department.

The work measurement programme, covering around 100 separate tasks, took 400 hours of measurement activity (10 weeks). The whole process, including setting up and analysis, waiting for the right work to be available at the right time and writing up the process improvement action plans, was spread over a period of about four months, as we also progressed with the other work streams.

Work stream 3: process improvement

As the work measurement progressed, the business was continuing in the development of operational processes. During our observation phase we had already identified a potential solution to some process issues in the goods-in department. An upcoming capital project was going to temporarily restrict space in the department, and this gave us the opportunity to design and implement a new layout that improved the organization and flow of products, as well as addressing the space restrictions. This was a successful exercise and introduced the operations team to the benefits of a collaborative approach using the new information being gathered and evaluated by the industrial engineering department.

The approach to process improvement was to engage more with the operations teams, and as we put together our issue log the business agreed to invite members of the departmental management teams and supervisors to be nominated as process improvement champions. They would be our main point of contact and take responsibility for the actions that were to be agreed, and would also receive some informal problem-solving coaching. A group of champions were soon in place. There was no formal recognition of the role; it was seen as cementing the general responsibilities for process improvement already set out in the job description in a more structured way.

Work stream 4: productivity reporting

Soon we had started to compile the first set of Standard Minute values for direct tasks. We followed a plan to focus on one department at a time, moving on to the next when we had only the remnants to pick up. As the list grew, we could start to compare them with the production targets being used informally to manage individual performances, and to fill in the gaps where targets were not being used.

We also set about extracting and evaluating activity reports from the warehouse management system. There had been no proper evaluation of the systematic data that were available in the form of standard productivity reports. We began the task of identifying the key reports and validating them. As we highlighted various problems with the standard reports, we were able to work with an IT analyst to reconfigure reports so that the data produced in them reflected exactly the information we wanted to see and to report on.

The new reports enabled us to validate the labour standards against actual performances across the whole population working at any time of the day or night. This was important, as some of the new information showed up significant issues with the accuracy of the production targets in use, and confirmed that our standards were accurate, reasonable and achievable. Using the correct systematic data to demonstrate performance levels was a key step in building confidence in our techniques across the operations management team.

Work stream 5: operational workforce planning

It was an obvious step to use the new production targets to update the operational workforce planning model. Unfortunately, the scope of the existing model couldn't be adjusted to reflect the increased level of detail required from moving from a department-level hierarchy to being activity based.

Having built and used models that met similar requirements, I recommended that we should start again, and with the cooperation of the planning team I started the process of creating a new model using a pre-existing spreadsheet format. I agreed to create a version that would allow the output from the new model to be compared directly to the output of the existing model, so that the business would have the final decision on whether to adopt the new model based on a period of parallel running.

I had to ensure that the model had enough functionality to optimize the data-processing elements and be simple enough for the planners to use and maintain, with supporting materials available to ensure a smooth handover process.

In the first phase I used all the information available to account for direct and indirect tasks in each department and assembled the components of the model. In the second phase we hosted separate meetings with all the departments to validate all the tasks and agree ways to quantify the time spent on indirect tasks. Finally, in the third phase we had follow-up meetings to walk through the first output from the new model and to do a final validation of the numbers. By this stage, we had identified the variations between the two models, and I could quantify the key differences and create a waterfall chart for each department.

A SELECTION OF KEY FINDINGS

- In one department, an estimated production target generated 15% more hours in the existing model compared to the measured standard in the new model.
- In another department, volume drivers that had not been updated resulted in 35% more hours in that part of the existing model compared to the re-validated version in the new model.
- One department had not been modelled at all and the workload was calculated using estimates that proved to be inaccurate compared to the newly validated information. In this department 22% more hours were estimated by the existing model compared to the new model.
- The percentage allowance added on for 'job training' in the existing model was much higher than required. This allowance was reduced by 2% in the new model after re-validation by the training department.

Although there were many issues with the workload calculation process that had to be resolved, the process that had been developed to extract contract hours and availability from HR systems was working well and did not have to be changed. We did, however, make some process improvements to ensure that the information contained in the HR databases was more effectively aligned with the information used by the training department to maintain the skills matrix and individual training plans.

I was able to demonstrate and evaluate all the key differences between the new model and the existing model and to explain why the new approach had created a more accurate reflection of the operating model. In the validation stages, all the key changes had been discussed in depth with the operations management teams and the planning team, and relayed in summary to the general manager. The planning team started to use the new model as soon as the final version was handed over, and used a parallel-running period to familiarize themselves with the model before switching over completely.

The total impact of the output from the new model compared to the old model was a reduction in agency resource requirements, on average, of 15 per cent. This was to be phased in over a period of time.

Summary

A key finding of research (Aberdeen Group, 2010) on warehouse management excellence was that over 70 per cent of the companies in the study reported that they tracked events at the employee level. However, only about half of these were taking this process to the full operational workforce management step of correlating these data to a standard or a plan.

In this case study, the business was, in the main, tracking productivity rates at employee level, or in the absence of that information, at department level. It was also using that information to drive a planning process. However, it recognized that it didn't have the level of skills within its management team to fully interpret the data and organize them in a way that would provide accurate and meaningful information.

Recognizing that the managing of productivity management and operational workforce planning processes is a specialist area is a key step in establishing operational workforce planning within a structure of well-defined business processes that will support the organization as a whole.

As shown in this case study, it enables the organization to improve its overall performance by providing accurate information for creating operating budgets that improve the distribution of resources. It also supports the development of strategies to optimize operational performance and reduce labour costs.

QUESTIONS

1. Describe how operational workforce planning fits into the overall business process of workforce management.
2. From this case study, identify the five project workstreams and one key deliverable for each.
3. Describe the risks associated with the original operational workforce planning model in this case study and the benefits that were identified when the output from the new model was compared directly to the original model.
4. Identify three ways how Industrial Engineering techniques can be used to support an organisation to improve its overall performance.

Answers on page 224.

References

Aberdeen Group (2010) *Warehouse Management Excellence: Maximizing resources and efficiency*, Aberdeen Group, Boston, MA

Aberdeen Group (2014) *Bottom Line Reasons for a Total Workforce Management Strategy*, Aberdeen Group, Boston, MA

05

Why procurement should want to pay for performance

A case study of how buyer and sellers aligned to create the most profit for both

TODD C SNELGROVE

(1) (2) (3) (4)

Knowledge and action

Evolving procurement is a strategic asset of a company: moving from being a 'buy something that meets the minimum criteria at lowest price' company to 'buy the best value for the company that realizes the most sustained profit'.

A procurement team from a large industrial company (that shall remain unnamed) evolved from being a 'necessary evil, back office function' to a strategic resource. How did this evolution occur and why? It started when we realized that we needed to move away from buying products and services that met the minimum requirement at the lowest price, towards buying and delivering true value to our stakeholders. I will share my experience, which I have helped to replicate in numerous other companies as they evolve procurement to being a strategic asset for their companies.

During the evolution of procurement departments, in any organization, there comes the time when the list of suppliers and how they will be chosen, based on the company's priorities and the processes, scoring system and ranking to be used, will be defined. Procurement departments that evolve and become seen as strategic start by changing the methods and systems they use to choose suppliers.

In numerous companies the user and the body funding a purchase, whether they are concerned with capital expenditure (CAPEX) or operating expense (OPEX) costs, is a hindrance to the buying community by preventing them from getting what they want. To paraphrase, 'once procurement gets involved they take over the process, and when we say that's the offering we want and need, we are pushed back into a corner and told that they will buy based on the best "value for the company"' – for which *read lowest price*.

It seems that the procurement department forced the process, weighting and scoring system handed down from the corporate level onto each stakeholder, failing to ask them to specify weightings based on their needs but making generic allocations, as if all purchases had to be based x per cent on price, x per cent on meeting quality requirements, x per cent on lowest TCO (total cost of ownership; we will come back to TCO later), x per cent on delivery requirements and so on. The feeling was that the buyer was not getting what they wanted (needed) and they were being ignored (despite the fact that they might value different things). In these scenarios the actions of the business units across numerous companies seemed similar. To minimize procurement's impact:

- Bring procurement teams into the buying process as late as possible, so you force their hand.
- Work with 'pre-chosen suppliers' to help them win the bid (the exercise of bidding was just that – an exercise).
- Tell procurement that they must contract with a certain supplier for specific reasons and that no substitutes will be countenanced.
- Make the specification request for proposal/request for quotation (RFP/RFQ) so technical that when the user says that only one supplier can deliver, you get less pushback.
- Use non-quantifiable reasoning, such as 'we have a great relationship with XXX' – not 'we have four projects we're working on and we think they will deliver x profit dollars, and if we switch suppliers, we lose that...'.

Introduction

ORGANIZATION

Strategy should be set from corporate, by a chief procurement officer or the like who reports to the CEO, not just finance. Procurement is much more than a cost, but to be seen as strategic it needs its rightful seat at the boardroom table. Second, if you have a matrix structure, embed procurement in the geographic and corporate business functions. This does two things: first of all it brings the resource closer (and yes, proximity matters) to the customer. Sitting in on meetings concerned with marketing, production, HR and so on gives a procurement person a better flavour of what is going on 'early'. Also, the comradery of being one of them vs someone from head office makes a difference. Finally, you might get a better perspective on what value is, living, breathing, and watching it happen. If you have a new product development process, I would want a procurement person involved 'as support' from the first meeting. They then can ask questions, change thinking and provide much more value vs being brought in once the product has been designed and is ready to build (it's too late).

UNDERSTANDING VALUE

Spend some discovery time, with a structured process, walking a day in the life of the user of the product or service you will be buying, identifying all the different pain/value points based on how the product or service will be used. This will open your mind as to what should be measured and how it should be weighted when making a buying decision. The visual I like to use for this is the 'priceberg' (Figure 5.1). Yes, we can all see the price of the offering (and maybe the associated shipping, receiving and process costs), but are we really looking at all the different profit drivers?

We need to look at everything. What I find is that price might be the most visible measurement, but often it has the lowest impact. To be clear, we should challenge our suppliers on what value drivers they can affect and how they think they can do it. They are the experts, that is what they do daily, so work with them and gain their knowledge.

FIGURE 5.1 The priceberg

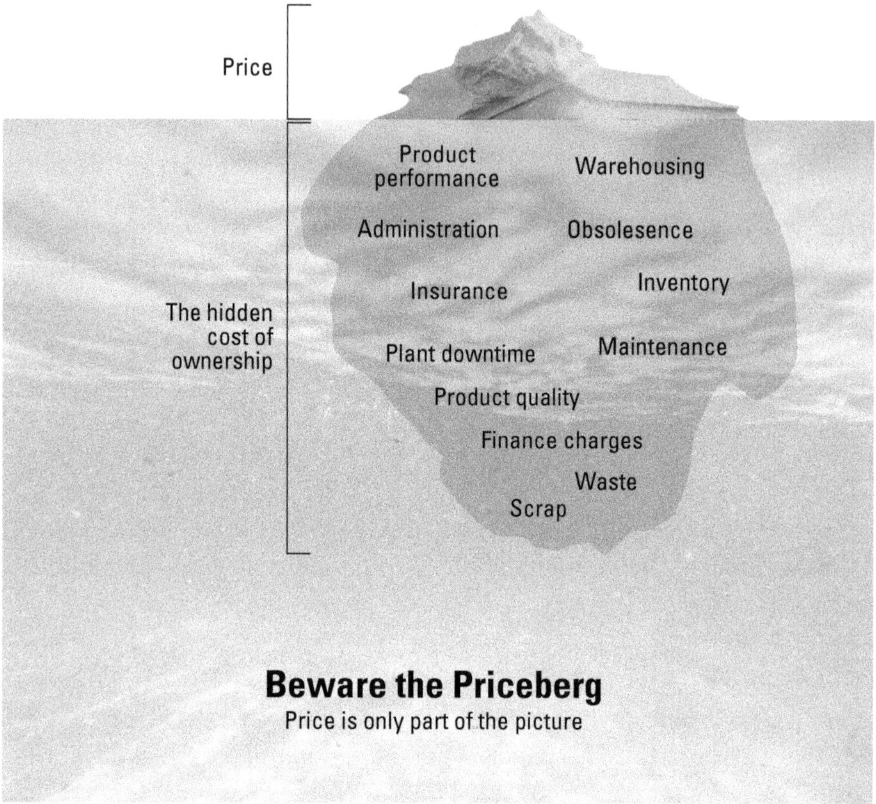

SOURCE Todd C Snelgrove

Here is a personal example of not understanding all the costs and potential value. Years ago, I used to spend a fair amount of time in London. Sometimes, leaving after my work sessions and heading to Paris, I got into a habit of taking the Heathrow Express (a fast train from London Paddington station to Heathrow). It ran every 15 minutes and the journey took 15 minutes, so I was sure of when I needed to be at the station. Then I would fly to Paris, and over the years I learnt that it was faster (and cheaper) to take a train that ran beneath Charles de Gaulle airport into the city than take a taxi to my hotel. I wasn't doing this to save money but rather time and the uncertainty of Paris traffic. So, all was well, until one of my colleagues suggested that I take one of the low-priced carriers and save some money. I thought why not, it's only an hour's flight and they must be safe, or they wouldn't be allowed to fly. I was doing some good and saving the company £100. As I left the session we were running at London Business School, my co-presenter Rob Maguire asked what time my flight was. I pulled up the itinerary and said it leaves in 2.5 hours from LGW. It turned out that LGW is a 'London Airport' but it was Gatwick, not Heathrow. I regrouped and asked Rob (a UK resident) the best way to get to LGW (this was before they had a direct train). He laughed... the only way was a black cab (or I could take the Underground, walk, get a train, walk, take a bus or taxi, or run). In those days, black cabs wouldn't take credit cards or debit cards. So, I made it to Gatwick, ran to the desk of the low-priced carrier and was then charged £25 for my large checked bag (free on BA) and £20 to select a seat. Finally, I got on board, stressed, but I had made it. I must have shut my eyes because as I woke up, we were landing and the pilot was welcoming us to Paris. I looked outside and knew I was in the wrong place: this was not Charles de Gaulle airport, it was Paris Airport at Orly – the Tourist, Cargo, Other airport. No big deal, *but* no direct train into Paris, so the choice was to rent a car (by the way: the low-priced airline companies make money from the car rental companies) – not a chance I am driving into Paris during rush-hour traffic, let alone parking a car downtown for two nights. So black cab it was – say €40 (and 90 minutes wasted in congestion). I spent more time than needed and a considerable amount of money. So, all flights between London and Paris are not the same. Had I walked the options, I would have been able to see all the potential value and cost drivers.

MEASURING VALUE

As a company we first looked at the generally accepted methodology of measuring total cost of ownership or TCO (Figure 5.2). What I realized was that even though my chief purchasing officer (CPO) was using the same term as I was, we both meant something different. I looked at all the costs associated with acquiring, installing, operating and maintaining an asset, and even the disposal cost at the end of the useful life of that asset.

My CPO, on the other hand, was referring to landed costs. For example, his measurement was solely focused on price, delivery, quality, shipping costs, currency, lead-time, minimum order quantity, terms and conditions, return policy and so on, which are very CAPEX focused. These are important,

FIGURE 5.2 Cost and time graph

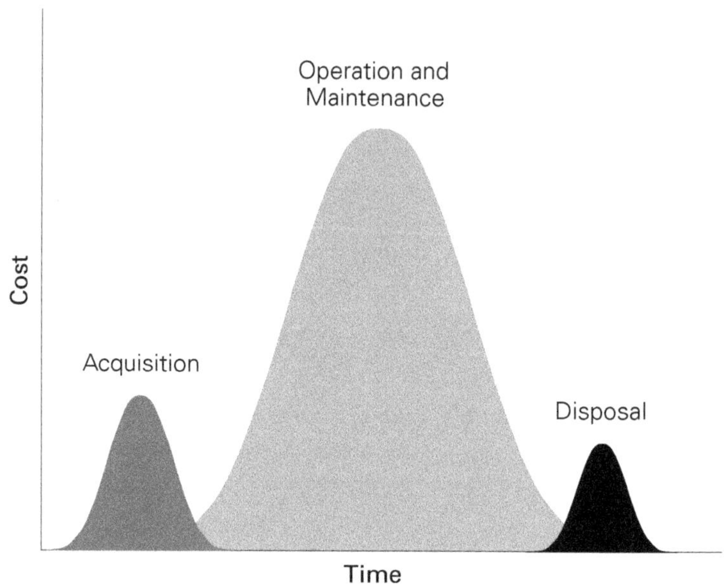

SOURCE Todd C Snelgrove

but my experience said that value is created during the usage (or operational phase) of an asset, and that phase is where the big expenses occur. I liked to remind people that the machine we were buying had *potential value* such as 'manufacturing a part', but that value was realized only when the machine ran in the operation phase. So, we started to look at all the costs that would be incurred during the installation and usage phase, such as energy, water, ink, lubrication, installation costs, repairing parts and/or services costs, speed of machine or output of machine, number of operators to run it (is it easy or specialized?), setup time, expected life of the machine and so on. I think we had 380 of these drivers. So at least we started looking past the acquisition phase and into the usage phase. As we started to build out the value drivers, how would we quantify it? A lot of value that was created was not a cost per se, and didn't fit a true TCO model; the offering was not a cost reduction, but it did affect our profit.

Where is the focus vs where is the value?

CAPEX or OPEX: where is the biggest impact and where should you focus to realize the greatest profit impact? Research shows that it's during the installation, maintenance, operating and disposal phases of a piece of equipment by a wide margin. In the early 2000s, Accenture did a study appropriately called *Equipment Today – Service Tomorrow: The Total Cost of Ownership Vision*. The purpose of the study was to demonstrate to original equipment manufacturers (OEMs) that the potential in service revenue is a multiple of the OEM market (nine times larger). So, looking at commercial aircraft, Class 8 trucks (large 18-wheelers) and industrial equipment (fans, gearboxes, pumps, and light duty pickup trucks (for work)), they found that only 8–12 per cent of the total expense for the buyer occurred when they bought the asset. As you can see, the fuel (energy), uptime, labour, production, repair costs, parts, water and so on represented 90 per cent or so of costs, that is, costs were nine times greater than the cost of buying the original equipment.

Sometimes, buyers focus narrowly on the initial purchase price of the product. Many companies I know look very hard at the initial purchase price and use numerous negotiating techniques to try to get, say, 10 per cent off the price. However, they *assume* that the OPEX costs are either smaller or the same, no matter which piece of equipment they buy. This could be because we (or the sales team) have done a poor job (intentionally or not) of enumerating the bottom part of the 'priceberg'. However, maybe customers should buy a piece of equipment that has an initial purchase price that is 10 per cent more expensive, but either it is a better piece of equipment, or they install and start up the machine and then find they get a 2 per cent saving on the OPEX cost. Numerous times I have heard people say, well, 10 per cent is bigger than 2 per cent, so that's where we will focus. To make the number useful, it needs a denominator. A 10 per cent saving, or a higher price on an asset that represents only 12 per cent of its lifetime costs and value, is only 1.2 per cent, whereas a 2 per cent improvement of the 88 per cent is 1.76 per cent or 47 per cent more impactful; you need to do this work so you can understand the real impact of decisions. So, let's research, let's challenge suppliers on the OPEX costs we can expect, and maybe even sign a contract based on the performance or outcome of the asset.

During a session in Oxford for the Centre for Advanced Procurement Studies, I was explaining our evolution on understanding and buying value, and saying that we needed to measure the impact of more than just cost, but all the value that procurement can create. However, I knew that the term value had been overused so many times that it didn't resonate, and that to some people the word value meant lower price. So, I looked at Professor Choi and said: 'What I want to do is buy from suppliers that drive up my profit, so it should be called Total Profit Added™' (Figure 5.3). A new, more accurate term was created.

Moving from TCO, which focuses on costs, to something much more holistic, looking at all costs and upside value, I term this Total Profit Added™ (TPA™). The concept of TPA™ not only looks at all the costs but also measures all the benefits that are created, thereby aligning the focus of selling companies and buying companies on what option creates the most profit. Let's remember, profit is generated by fewer costs but also by more value. Using a TCO methodology, value was only calculated if it led to a cost reduction, omitting other tangible measurable benefits that drive profit,

FIGURE 5.3 Total profit added

Design	Acquisition	Operation	Disposal
Robustness	Inventory amounts	Energy and lubrication	Dismantle
Ease of manufacture	Payment terms	Product life	Shipping
Tolerances	Contract management	Auxiliary repair costs	Disposal costs
Design costs	Supplier consolidation	**Production amounts**	Recycling costs
Margin	Finance charges	**Production quality**	Treatment costs
Sales	Obsolescence	Machine reliability	Government fees
(*Customer TPA™*)	Receiving	Cost to install	Sustainability
	(*Unit price*)	Taxation	
		Warranty costs	

SOURCE Todd C Snelgrove, 2019

specifically not on the reduced side of the balance sheet but on the increased side (sales side). Here are few examples, which are not perfect, but should help illustrate how added value can increase profits over and above just cost reductions:

- Choosing a higher-priced offering in the pharmaceutical or technology industry that helps you launch a new product sooner than your competition (earlier months × revenue × margin). Some lifecycles are only 12–16 months, so even one week earlier to market is huge.
- A remote monitoring system that allows you to speed up a machine, increase hours of production and increase the yield of saleable product.
- Create an offering that has a higher residual value, maybe build it better so it has a longer service life, meaning that after 10 years of use you could sell it in a secondary market where the cheaper version was at the end of its life. Think of a car that might have a higher initial acquisition cost but has a better resale value in the future or has a longer useful life.
- Risk reduction, relationships, access to best and first resources: State of Flux, in its annual 2015 Global Procurement Survey, found that suppliers that practise value co-creation and supplier relationship management realize 4–6% more value than contracted levels. Specifically: 'SRM is a discipline of working collaboratively with those suppliers/customers that are vital to the success of both organizations, to maximize the mutual value of those relationships.'
- You co-design with a supplier a better new product for you to market. The inclusion of a higher-priced solution allows you to charge a higher price (vs the increased cost of your offer) that your customers are willing to pay for (yes, we will spend an additional $1,000 on that offering, but it will save our customer $5,000 in energy costs, so we can sell our machine for $1,800 more, or choosing this offering increases our profit by $800 per machine (higher profit generated per unit sold × number of units). This might be an assumed impact prior to launch; however, payment models that allow for bonuses based on actual improvements would make the buyer's and seller's benefits aligned, based on generating more profit.
- Service field management software that allows you to increase your field's utilization, increase your service revenue, reduce your contract leakage etc. Maybe it has a higher price per month but it helps you sell more (www.servicemax.com).

For companies today, software exists out of the box that has the calculations of value; you just need to determine what numbers you want your suppliers to use in the formulae and then you can compare all offers. The one I am most knowledgeable about is from Tim Underhill of Underhill and Associates: http://www.sbs4me.com/total-cost-sourcing.html

TCO 'evolved' in other industries

Technology companies have been discussing TCO for over four decades. Getting companies to buy into the benefits of the investment requires a believable and reasonable business case.

Medical, pharmaceutical, hospitals and governments have started to evolve the TCO concept into something more usable for the health industry. Total Cost of Care is a look at the costs and value of utilizing different medical treatments, for example effectiveness, number of days in hospital for invasive surgery, number of follow-up tests required and so on. Some companies are even based on their ability to reduce a hospital's or government's healthcare cost in an area – not by substituting a lower-priced offering but taking out the overall costs and increasing the value (quality of life) for the patients.

The *renewable energy industry* is starting to work on a framework called Levelized Cost of Energy or LCOE: what is the total expected investment – new build, power generation, maintenance costs, expected life of the asset (so all the costs) – compared to the number of kilowatt hours (KWh) produced? This then generates a better look at the best payback. For example, maybe nuclear produces lots of KWh for the cost to build, but once you start looking into the disposal costs (shutdown), the calculation for wind or solar energy might look like a much better investment.

Best practices for buying best value (TPA™) determine:

- Calculations you will use to quantify value. These calculations are the same everywhere in the world. Energy savings is KWh saved × Number of days × Price per KWh. If they affect your business, the numbers to put into the calculation might be different. Again, I suggest using a pre-existing tool, instead of creating calculations, and focus on implementation.
- Corporate benchmarks to be used at the beginning of the year. These are defaults, unless a country has better numbers: Downtime for this range of products is $10,000 an hour, Energy is 10 cents a KW, Cost of capital is 15% etc.

- What you value. Sometimes these can be broken down into hard and soft savings. People debate the terms; however, hard savings go right to the bottom line (energy, water, ink, quality/scrap), whereas with soft savings you know a benefit exists, but the direct correlation is not always immediate. The soft savings can turn out to be the biggest over the longest period (employee satisfaction, brand value etc). I have seen companies say 25% of the annual target in value can be soft savings, and that they are valuable and will have a huge impact vs looking only at this year.
- Assumptions are okay. Do not get stuck spending months or years looking for an exact number. As all options you are reviewing are using the same input, it's the relative difference that matters. If 13 cents vs 12 cents a KWh is going to make the difference on which machine you should buy, call it a tie. We're looking for magnitudes of difference.
- Sign-off process. The supplier makes an offer using expected benefits, your company buys/implements the solution, then annually or at whatever interval is appropriate it is tracked to see actual value created to the best of your ability.
- Calculate over the life of the new solution but allocate. Say a supplier is able to reduce energy savings by $10,000 a year for a new application that has an expected life of 10 years; booking the $10,000 savings per year is best vs it all being taken in year one. This is why TPA targets are always incremental (last year we targeted $1 million, this year $1.75 million, an additional $750K). This also stops the price switching suppliers every other order.
- Communicate with suppliers. Do you ask on your RFPs etc that the proposal have an estimated value breakdown? Do you say that this number will be the primary driver of who wins the award? Do you have annual supplier days where you explain that you want all supplier best ideas to come to you first, that you don't mind paying more if you get more, that you have a structured tool and process to quantify different value proposals? Salespeople tell me that they sometimes stop creating and bringing the best ideas to help a company as they assume that all they care about is the lowest price that meets the minimum criteria.
- Motivate the business units to look at best value. It's not just procurement's responsibility to find and buy best value. However, in some companies I have seen that if procurement finds a more valuable offer, the savings are pulled 100% out of a business unit's budget: 'If we help you buy a

machine that costs less to operate, then we will reduce your total budget equal to this amount.' What I see is that this does not incentivize the business unit to save money or create value – as it is all getting stripped away. A best practice is that, say, 50% of the savings is deducted from the budget *but* 50% goes back into the project budget for them to buy another solution they need. So, you get the mentality that says if I help save money over here then I can buy those new tools our team needs vs the improvement being swallowed up by head office in another country.

- Engage all employees. Companies should have a simple way for employees at all levels to submit improvement ideas. They should be rewarded for those that are implemented with some of the improvement profit that was generated. Sometimes, the shipper or receiver, the janitor or someone who is closest to the actual situation might see improvement ideas that management would never recognize. These suggestions could be sorted by biggest impact, then reviewed and classified into easy or hard to implement and cost to implement, then the top five submitted to a committee every quarter. I once had a president mention to me 'what do we do if we get too many ideas?' – that's a problem I think I would like to have.
- No 'similar' substitutions. A very large Fortune 100 CPO decided he was 'sick and tired of paying all these bonuses to Procurement when they created these substitution savings... but somehow Total Costs never went down'. The similar offering might seem like a direct substitute, but there is a good chance that it does not perform as well, or other costs go up. With that in mind, the company did not allow for price/substitution savings.

Finally, look at what is good for the company. Your company reports earnings per share as a company, not as a function. So, drive a corporate culture focused on what's good for the whole business, not just a department at the cost of another function. Be willing to move money between departments for the good of the whole if needed. Maybe one team needs new software that allows its service and asset management teams to be more productive and reduce the costs of maintaining the facility or increase production, but the money to pay for that software needs to come from the IT budget. Make it happen.

Contracting/rewarding based on value

Penalty-clause service level agreements have been introduced. Over the years, I have been involved, on both the buy and sell side of numerous negotiations, in situations where the buyer wants to put in some service level agreements.

This makes sense; we need to know what 'good' looks like. If the supplier is not meeting these expectations and it is their fault, penalties should be applied. However, with all the penalty clauses, why are so many agreements not fulfilling the desired targets? The carrot and stick analogy makes sense.

One thing to do is to put yourself in the position of the supplier. For example, let's say that a supplier guarantees 4 hours to respond and fix a fault, machine availability of 95 per cent and so on. Let's assume that the supplier is delivering at, say, 90 per cent, not the 95 per cent agreed in the service level agreement (and ignore customer happiness and suchlike, just looking at this from the viewpoint of rationale economic theory). As a supplier I would do a calculation that says what will the penalty be, and what will it cost me to get to the threshold. If the penalty is $100,000 and I think I would need to spend $200,000 to hit the target (adding more inventory, adding a full-time service person or whatever), it doesn't make sense to spend more than I get back. By the way, just so buyers know, the higher the target and penalty, the more *all* suppliers will add to the cost of the bid to 'insure' themselves against the risk.

Let's take a different scenario: the supplier is delivering and the machine is running at 95 per cent, but the field engineer sees an opportunity to improve that number (upgrading a part on the machine, for example); this would get the machine to 97 per cent availability (less downtime). As a rational business professional, would you spend your money (the part and service) on something that helps the customer do better and get *no* return? Probably not. You will manage to hit the threshold and the lowest cost to your company to increase your profitability. However, as the buyer I want the best value for my company, so I should want to reward the supplier with a bonus of, say, 50 per cent of the first-year improvement ($50K for $100K improvement). If it is something new and provides a hard value that affects profit, I get this benefit each year for the rest of that machine's life. Reward in conjunction with penalties will lead to the desired actions you really want.

Conclusion

It is the most advanced supply chain that will enable your company to be a leading differentiator and disruptor in your market. No longer can companies hope and bet that all innovation will come from within their own four walls. You must engage your supply partners, so that they bring their best ideas and newest innovations to you first. To do so, you need to treat your supply base as an asset, not a cost of doing business that needs to be reduced. You must entice them; you want to be their customer of choice. If you want innovation, the newest ideas, the A-team from the supplier, do you think treating them with threats, punishments and commoditization strategies (three bids and the lowest price wins every time) will entice them to help you the most? In most industries, the odds are that your competitors have access to the same suppliers, similar information and expertise, and therefore the one differentiator you have is to get your suppliers to partner with you so that you get that leading edge. That might be the newest ways to reduce costs or the best ways to increase your revenue. I love the evolution of procurement chart (Figure 5.4) that my good friend and retired Chief Procurement Officer Bo-Inge Stensson put together (bo-inge.stensson@saphire.biz).

FIGURE 5.4 Past and future practices of B2B buying

	Past best practice		Future best practice
Main purchase criteria	Cost, quality	→	Total cost and total value of ownership
Consideration of soft factors	Generally not	→	Yes: sustainability, agility and innovation are key differentiators for suppliers
Relationships with suppliers	Adversarial BTI/BU (bring them in, beat them up)	→	Colaborative: objective is joint value creation
Time horizon	Short term	→	Long term
Inter-company collaboration	Limited – purchasing department operates largely autonomously	→	High-cross functional collaboration with marketing, finance and operations
Contribution	Tactical, low impact	→	Strategic, high impact
Main explicit assumption	Products are commodities	→	Suppliers are a source of innovation
Main implicit assumption	Companies compete against each other	→	Ecosystems compete against each other

SOURCE Hinterhuber, A, Snelgrove, T and Stensson, B (in press) *Value First, Then Price: The new paradigm buying and selling in B2B*, Routledge, Abingdon

Moving from service level agreements and performance penalties to rewards for exceeding targets allows procurement and suppliers to work together for a sustainable competitive advantage and more profit. Companies that buy based on best value, and measure all costs and benefits, are 35 per cent more profitable than companies that do not.

It is time for most businesses to rethink their procurement strategy and evolve from costs down and efficiency focused towards value added and strategic. It is not easy, but the benefits for the business are phenomenal. Each journey starts with a step or an action, and within this book you have many practical ideas to use to help your company to the next level. I wish you well on your successful and profitable journey of co-creating value with suppliers, with the focus on driving the greatest Total Profit Added™ for your company.

QUESTIONS

1 How do you start to align?

2 How should you measure your success?

3 What categories are easiest to start with?

Answers on page 226.

Reference

CAPS Research (2019) [accessed 7 June 2019] Home Page, *CAPS Research* [Online] https://www.capsresearch.org/ (archived at https://perma.cc/L6LJ-K9NT)

06

Closing the cycle from tree to product

Company X's sustainability journey

GENDAO LI, ALIREZA SHOKRI AND JIE MA

(1) (2)

Knowledge

You will learn the sustainable supply chain management principles and practices used in the case company.

Action

You will be able to use sustainable supply chain management principles in their own organizations.

Introduction

Sustainability is one of a modern company's major concerns owing to limited natural resources, climate change and increasing consumer demand. This is particularly true for wood product manufacturers, because forests are decreasing rapidly. Sustainable supply chain management is becoming more and more important. Closing the supply chain loop by reusing and recycling is one approach to achieving sustainability.

Company X, founded in 1961, is a leading multinational enterprise in the production of wood materials, with 17 plants and 24 sales offices worldwide. As a market leader, Company X produces an extensive product range of wood-based materials (chipboard, OSB and MDF[1] board) as well as sawn timber. It has localized its supply chain in different countries by sourcing locally and serving local markets. Its UK branch is called Company X UK Limited, and has been operating since 1984. There are two manufacturing plants, headquartered in the North of England and Scotland. Currently, the company directly employs about 783 people in the UK across a range of different disciplines, including production, engineering, sales and marketing, customer services and forestry. As a wood-based material manufacturer, the company consumes a large quantity of wood as its major raw material. In this case study, we will analyse how Company X closes the supply chain loop to achieve sustainability.

Company X's main supply chain

The company's main supply chain is not very complex. It purchases timber, its main raw material, from local suppliers and produces solid wood in the sawmill, followed by the production of wood-based materials for furniture manufacturers.

Although forests are renewable, demand for wood as a construction material, as raw material for paper, bioplastic and textiles, as well as a renewable energy source, is growing steadily. Studies show that there will be a deficit of around 70 million cubic metres of wood in Europe by 2020 if management of the resource continues as it is today. Considering both cost and environment, Company X follows the concept of cascading use: high-quality logs are used to produce sawn timber, while sawmill co-products, roundwood from the forest and recycled wood are turned into wood-based materials.

Closed-loop production cycle

Company X emphasizes the sustainable use of raw materials in its core values. Besides the first use of raw materials, from timber production in the sawmill to the production of wood-based materials, the company proactively collects used wood products from customers, either end consumers or business customers.

In 2000, a wholly owned subsidiary was first established in Leeds as a wood waste recycling centre. Since then, four recycling centres have been developed across the UK. The subsidiary works with large furniture groups, civic amenity sites, industrial users and waste management companies to collect acceptable used wood products or wood waste.

The materials are classified into different categories as follows:

- Grade A: All packaging wood – items used to contain, support, carry, enclose, wrap or protect. It comes from construction, manufacturing, distribution, warehousing and engineering.
- Grade AC: All wood destined to be sold to consumers and also wood items from the manufacturing process (no MDF).
- Grade B: All solid untreated natural timber products from construction sites, demolition companies, skip firms or transfer stations.
- Grade C: All mixed wood sources, either natural and manufactured (no MDF).
- Grade CA: All waste wood from civic amenity sites.

A collection service is offered by a fleet of specialist vehicles along the M62 corridor, across the North East and from the central belt of Scotland. Within a 25-mile radius of each recycling site, all waste wood is collected. For palletized bulky waste wood nationwide, the collection service is provided by third-party hauliers. In this way, the recycling subsidiary provides continuity and reliability for the production of wood materials. The recycling process is as follows:

1 Inspection. Material is inspected on arrival from the recycling site to remove MDF.

2 Sorting. The material is then reduced in size using an electrical shredder which also releases trapped metal.

3 Cleaning. The materials pass though specialist cleaning equipment to remove contaminants, including plastics, glass, stones and textiles.

After this process, recycled materials suitable for the production of wood materials are identified. Those that cannot be used for producing wood materials will be used for energy generation.

Company X also collaborates with large furniture groups to reclaim waste wood products. Since March 2017, an outstanding partnership between the company and a large furniture group has developed. As the International Head of Safety and Sustainability at the group said: 'We use Company X board in the manufacturing of our desks and work systems. The waste that is generated is sent to Company X's subsidiary for initial reprocessing and then to Company X for further reprocessing. The clean recycled wood is then used as part of the mix to make new particle board, which we then use to make more furniture.' The recycling process is similar to that described above:

1 Offcuts and wood waste generated at the group's production facility are collected and delivered to Company X's recycling subsidiary site, utilizing empty vehicle space and back-loading.
2 Wood is sorted into chipboard or MDF before being broken down to a suitable size.
3 Graded material is transferred to Company X's production site for sophisticated cleaning and then broken into chipped wood.
4 Finer wood dust, which cannot be used in board production, goes into Company X's heat plant, generating heat for its chipboard production processes.
5 Clean recycled material goes into the production of new particle board, used to construct the group's products, such as the Ratio desk.

The recycling of waste wood into new products has environmental benefits as well as business efficiencies for both the furniture group and Company X. The benefit to the furniture group is significant. The closed-loop process enables the group to ethically dispose of more than 1,000 tonnes of wood waste each year, which was previously sent for heat recovery. The benefit to Company X is of course the raw materials for wood material production. In addition, empty backhaul is also reduced, which improves transportation efficiency.

The materials closed loop means that Company X is saving the environment 1.56 million tonnes of CO_2 per year.

However, from the above discussion, there is a proportion of unrecycled waste. If not disposed of properly, it will go into landfill, which is not environment friendly. Company X puts unrecyclable wastes into the energy circle, which makes the system a real closed-loop ecosystem.

Energy closed loop

Besides the materials closed loop, Company X also closes the energy loop.

> WHOLE CLOSED-LOOP ECOSYSTEM
>
> Those wastes that cannot be used as recycled wood are neither sent to landfill nor discarded, but rather go into the energy circle.

In 2007, a wood power plant was built to generate electricity for use in the chipboard manufacturing processes at the site. This biomass energy facility runs on waste wood from chipboard production and a proportion of recycled wood fibre that has gone through the recycling plant and been cleaned but cannot be used as raw material. Waste wood first turns into gas, which then is turned into electricity. During the gas generation process, heat is produced, which, if not used properly, will go to waste. Company X reuses this heat to power a drier that can be used to dry wet woodchips, which are then used in biomass boilers. In 2013, the plant had a heat capacity of 50 MW and in September of that year an expansion plan was agreed. Energy generation capacity has been greatly increased. Now, the biomass plant not only supplies energy to the production plant, but also supplies clean energy to local residents.

Conclusion

By closing the supply chain loop, Company X has reduced its consumption of raw materials significantly and it has also become completely independent in terms of its primary energy supply. It is estimated that the use of recycled wood can avoid the escape of 1.73 million tonnes of CO_2 per year. In addition, the use of renewable energy on its own site can avoid approximately 1,487,001 tonnes of CO_2 emissions from fossil energy sources escaping into the environment per year.

QUESTIONS

1. What are the challenges faced by Company X in its business?
2. Why does Company X want to close the supply chain loop? What are the advantages and challenges in closing the supply chain loop?
3. What are the key success factors in Company X's closed-loop ecosystem?

Answers on page 226.

Note

1 MDF: Medium-density fibreboard.

07

Environmentally responsible packaging in global supply chains

HENRIK PÅLSSON

1 2 3 4

Knowledge

After completing the case, you will be able to:

- analyse the total environmental impacts of packaging (from the packaging material and from the impacts of packaging on transport and logistics efficiency as well as on product waste);
- recognize how various supply chain decisions affect packaging, which, in turn, affects supply chain sustainability;
- determine possible analyses to reduce the environmental impacts of packaging;
- recognize the major potential of packaging to improve supply chain sustainability and the circular economy.

Action

The knowledge gained from this case can be put into action by developing management principles for environmentally responsible packaging. In this process, the differences and similarities between a circular economy and a sustainability perspective on packaging should be considered. The management principles should be developed by applying a framework. In particular, the ways to tackle each factor that determines the environmental impact of packaging should be applied. This will enable you to understand how packaging practices and decisions influence logistics operations, transport efficiency, product waste and the effectiveness of the packaging material. To support holistic decision-making where both specific operations and overall supply chain performance are taken into account, a key issue is to apply a system perspective. To facilitate the development of management principles for environmentally responsible packaging, you can get inspiration from the case of packed table grapes in a global supply chain.

Introduction

This case presents a structured approach towards developing and selecting environmentally responsible packaging. The approach identifies and categorizes the environmental impacts of packaging in supply chains to determine its potential to reduce them. A study of the environmental performance of packaging in a global food supply chain of grapes from South Africa to Sweden illustrates the approach. The study analyses the environmental impacts of the material in the packaging system and the environmental impacts of packaging on logistics, on transport efficiency and on product waste.

The way supply chain practitioners manage packaging has a direct impact on the financial and environmental performance of their organizations, their suppliers and their customers. The decisions taken by packaging decision-makers affect the cost and environmental performance of operations in the company, as well as the performance of the suppliers and customers in terms of efficiency of transportation, replenishment, material handling and other logistics operations. It is important that practitioners can understand the impact of their decisions on both specific operations and overall supply chain performance. This supports holistic decision-making and a competitive supply chain. This chapter discusses how a circular economy can be used as an instrument for decision-makers to move a business or a supply chain towards sustainable packaging.

The chapter highlights the potential of packaging logistics for effective and efficient supply chains and categorizes the environmental impact areas of packaging. It uses the case of a global supply chain of table grapes to illustrate the challenges and dilemmas of environmentally sustainable packaging. The aim of this case is to describe and illustrate a structured approach towards identifying the environmental impacts of packaging on supply chains.

Sustainable packaging

Sustainable packaging should fulfil economic, environmental and social dimensions. Sustainability can be defined as 'the balanced integration of economic performance, social inclusiveness, and environmental resilience, to the benefit of current and future generations' (Geissdoerfer *et al*, 2017: 766). From an economic perspective, this means that packaging should save more than it costs in terms of enabling supply chain efficiency and supply chain effectiveness. Efficiency can be obtained by facilitating efficient replenishment, transportation and material handling. Packaging affects the costs of purchasing material as well as the costs of converting, material handling, processing, picking, printing and transport. Effectiveness can mean that the packaging increases sales, through attractiveness or by making products available, and that it enhances the consumer value of the packed product. Packaging can help to extend shelf life and increase sales through communication and marketing as well as by providing convenience for consumers.

From an environmental perspective, sustainable packaging should minimize the packed product's environmental impact in terms of the use and reuse of resources for material, product waste, and logistics and transport operations. For instance, the selection of packaging material affects the environment, and packaging affects energy consumption and emissions from various activities, such as converting packaging, material handling, processing, picking, printing and transport. The protection that packaging provides can reduce the amount of waste and damaged products, for example food waste.

Finally, the social perspective of packaging is about helping consumers and users modify their behaviour in the direction of sustainability. For instance, packaging can foster unsustainable consumption habits by making it easy for consumers to adopt a 'throw-away mentality' or to disregard the value of materials (Lewis, 2005). However, by understanding consumer perceptions of sustainable packaging and factors that determine purchasing decisions, it is possible to influence their behaviour by developing packaging in a sustainable direction that consumers appreciate (Nordin and Selke, 2010). This can potentially induce proper disposal and facilitate sustainable behaviour for different lifestyles, for example single-household portions and large packs for families. The social dimension of packaging also covers the fact that packaging provides employment and can enable food availability in both disaster areas and developing regions.

Circular economy and sustainability

A circular economy is an approach, or an instrument, for moving a business or a supply chain towards economic and environmental sustainability. Geissdoerfer *et al* (2017: 766) define a circular economy as: 'a regenerative system in which resource input and waste, emission, and energy leakage are minimized by slowing, closing, and narrowing material and energy loops. This can be achieved through long-lasting design, maintenance, repair, reuse, remanufacturing, refurbishing, and recycling.' Thus, sustainability can be seen as the objective, while the circular economy can be an instrument for achieving this objective.

The characteristics of sustainability and a circular economy have many similarities, and some differences. According to Geissdoerfer *et al* (2017), some typical similarities include integrating non-economic aspects into business development, using a systems approach and innovation as a core idea, the need for collaboration between different stakeholders, and the key role of private businesses' resources and capabilities. A vital difference is that in sustainability, responsibilities are shared but not clearly defined, whereas in a circular economy the responsibility by definition lies with the private businesses as well as with regulators and policymakers. Another noted difference is the ultimate goal. A circular economy aims for a closed loop that eliminates resources going into and leaking out of the system, whereas sustainability focuses on an open-ended system with multiple goals for various stakeholders and interest groups. A third difference is who has an interest in applying sustainability or a circular economy. With sustainability, the view is that the stakeholders' interests align; for example, less waste is good for the environment, organizational profits and consumer prices. In the circular economy, the view is that there are financial advantages for businesses on the one hand, and less resource consumption and pollution for the environment on the other.

In the context of packaging, the circular economy is based on the idea of an ecocycle society where product and packaging values are maintained for as long as possible, while waste is minimized and used as a resource for recycling or energy recovery. In supply chains, consisting of a number of companies from packaging filling at a producer to the point of consumption, packaging makes a circular economy possible through packaging waste, product protection that can minimize product waste, volume and weight efficiency, and stackable and unitized packaging that facilitates logistics and transport efficiency.

The role of packaging in environmentally sustainable supply chains

The previous section described three pillars of sustainable packaging and their links to a circular economy. To analyse the environmental pillar and the roles of packaging in a circular economy, we can group the environmental impact of the packed product into three factors (Pålsson, 2018):

- packaging material;
- logistics and transport efficiency;
- product waste.

Packaging material affects the environment in terms of energy consumption and emissions from the packaging manufacturing process. This depends on the raw material and its processing. This factor also affects the environment when it is disposed of, including aspects such as energy consumption and emissions from recycling, landfill, incineration and reuse. The latter includes the washing and handling of empty packages. The *logistics and transport efficiency* factor refers to how well the packaging enables high fill rates in logistics processes and transport. For instance, if one packaging system enables a vehicle to carry 20 per cent more products than another packaging system, then 20 per cent fewer vehicles are needed. Similarly, the packaging system also affects the number of products that logistics equipment can handle simultaneously. Finally, the *product waste* factor refers to how well the packaging avoids product waste, which can occur due to product damage, obsolescence and difficult-to-empty packaging. The product waste factor is what determines the accumulated energy and emissions of a packed product. Thus, the further down in the supply chain a packed product becomes waste without being used, the greater its environmental impact. Apart from packaging filling, the environmental impact of the packed product in food supply chains originates from food supply and packaging. Food supply includes the growing, processing, production and refinement of food, which generally accounts for a substantial proportion of the total energy consumed for packed products in food supply chains.

To manage the environmental impact of packaging in food supply chains, we must first analyse the impact of each of the three factors. Figure 7.1 shows a structured analysis approach highlighting four complementary ways to tackle each factor.

FIGURE 7.1 Three factors that determine the environmental impact of packaging, and four ways to tackle each factor

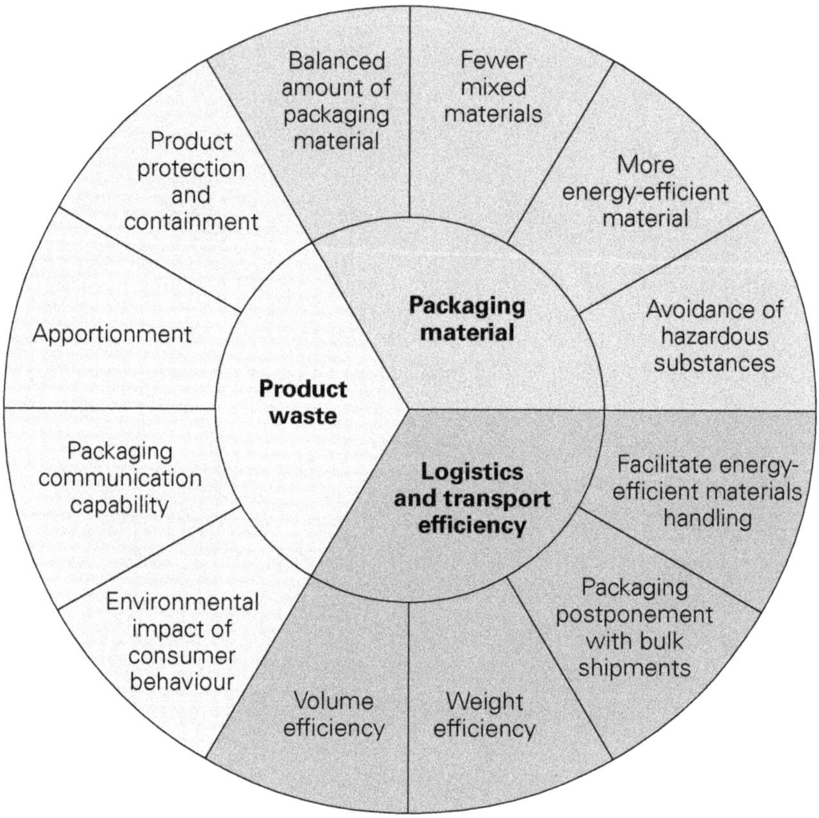

The packaging material factor needs to balance the amount of packaging material against the amount of product waste. A product can be overpacked, using more packaging than necessary to protect the product. A product is overpacked if the environmental impact of the excess packaging material exceeds the reduced environmental impact of less product waste. Similarly, a product is underpacked if the environmental impact of added packaging material can reduce the total environmental impact of product waste plus the packaging material. In the process of finding a balance between the amount of packaging material and product waste, companies need to consider protection from mechanical shock and vibrations, chemical and microbiological reactions, and temperature variations. For some food, more packaging can prolong shelf life. For instance, with a thin plastic bag around a head of iceberg lettuce, it takes a few days more before the outer layer must be disposed of.

The next way to tackle the packaging material factor is to use as few mixed materials as necessary, which improves recycling efficiency. Mixed materials can consist of laminated layers of plastic, cardboard and aluminium foil. These materials often have excellent properties for food and beverages. They can extend the shelf life of food, provide weight-efficient packaging (as an alternative to metal or glass) and eliminate the need for refrigeration for some products, but they are challenging to recycle. Thus, mixed materials should be used to the extent that the reduced environmental impact from their beneficial properties is greater than the environmental impact of reduced recycling. For a large company, the recycling capability of their materials can vary between different markets, which also should be taken into consideration.

The third way to tackle the packaging material factor is to use energy-efficient materials. This means scrutinizing the packaging material market carefully to find materials that minimize the environmental impact of the packaging production process and the energy sources used in that process. Finally, the packaging material factor should minimize the hazardous substances in the packaging material, as these can affect both the users of the packed product and the environment.

As shown in Figure 7.1, the logistics and transport efficiency factor also need to be tackled in four ways. The volume efficiency of packaging affects the use of transport vehicles and logistics equipment. The more products that can be packed in the same volume, the more volume efficient the packaging system becomes. The same logic applies to the weight efficiency of packaging.

The next way to tackle this factor is the concept of packaging postponement, which is related to volume and weight efficiency. By postponing the final packaging system, products can be shipped in bulk to regional packing centres, warehouses or assembly sites. For instance, instead of bottling a beverage in a central production site, large barrels can be shipped to regional bottling centres. This minimizes the need for transport.

Finally, packaging should facilitate energy-efficient materials handling. This can be achieved by designing packaging systems with stacking capability, which optimizes space utilization in storage areas in the production stage, in warehouses, transports, and in logistics equipment, such as on forklifts. It can also be achieved through the modularization of packaging systems. Designing packages in modules enables co-loading and co-handling.

A related concept is unitization, which means designing each level of the packaging system as units of the next level, so that a number of primary packages fit exactly in the secondary package and so on. Unitization affects the number of packages or unit loads that are handled simultaneously, which in turn affects the environmental impact of materials handling.

The final way to tackle this factor is to use packaging as an insulating barrier to sustain the correct temperature of the products. This could eliminate the need for certain logistics equipment for maintaining the cold chain, which reduces energy demand for cooling.

To address the product waste factor, food waste should be avoided in the entire supply chain. One way to tackle this is by making sure that the packaging system has sufficient protection and containment capabilities. From an environmental perspective, it is important to minimize food waste, but it is also essential to balance this against the type and amount of packaging, as the packaging material for several food categories has significant environmental impact. Figure 7.1 shows that the average energy consumption from the packaging system in a food supply chain in the UK is 23 per cent. Another way to tackle the product waste factor is to analyse apportionment. This is because the amount and size of each packaging level affects the level of obsolescence and product waste in different stages of the supply chain. For instance, having excessively large secondary packaging can lead to food waste in stores, and with excessively large primary packaging consumers may not consume all of it before the expiry date. A third way to tackle this factor is to address the communication capability of packaging. This includes track-and-trace information, which should be used to minimize takebacks, avoid unnecessary product waste and reduce obsolescence. The final way to tackle this factor is to design packaging so that it facilitates environmentally responsible consumer behaviour. Thereby, packaging can be designed to avoid product waste through easy-to-empty packaging and packaging that can be resealed, which extends shelf life.

A case: table grapes from South Africa to Sweden

A global supply chain of table grapes from South Africa to Sweden illustrates the three factors that determine the environmental impact of packaging. Table grapes are sweet berries that are sold throughout the year. They are a low-margin product, quite delicate and sensitive to heat. This case focuses on packed table grapes from farmers in the Western Cape in

South Africa. The grapes are harvested from November to April. At the beginning and end of the period, an individual farmer ships 5 containers of grapes per week, and in the peak season the farmer ships 12 containers per week. The farmer grows, harvests and packs table grapes for both the domestic and European markets. This case focuses on the table grapes that are sold on the Swedish market, where the main customers are three major retailers. The total cost to the farmer of finalizing a 500g box of table grapes is less than €0.70, which includes the product (70%), labour (15%), and packaging (15%). In addition, there are shipping and handling costs. Figure 7.2 illustrates the supply chain.

After harvesting, the grapes are transported in a plastic crate to a packhouse on the farm where they are precooled to 20–22°C. In the packhouse, the grapes are quality checked regarding size, freshness and sugar content. The quality control is conducted both by an independent South African quality organization and by the exporter. The exporter has higher quality requirements than the South African quality organization, but it is compulsory to use the quality organization to ensure that fruit from South Africa maintains a certain quality. After quality control, the grapes are packed and stored. From the packhouse, the farmer sends the grapes by truck 5km to a cooling facility where the grapes are precooled for 48 hours, and then cooled down to –0.5°C for 3 days. From the cold storage room, the pallets of grapes are moved with forklifts to a non-refrigerated waiting area for

FIGURE 7.2 The supply chain for table grapes from South Africa to Sweden

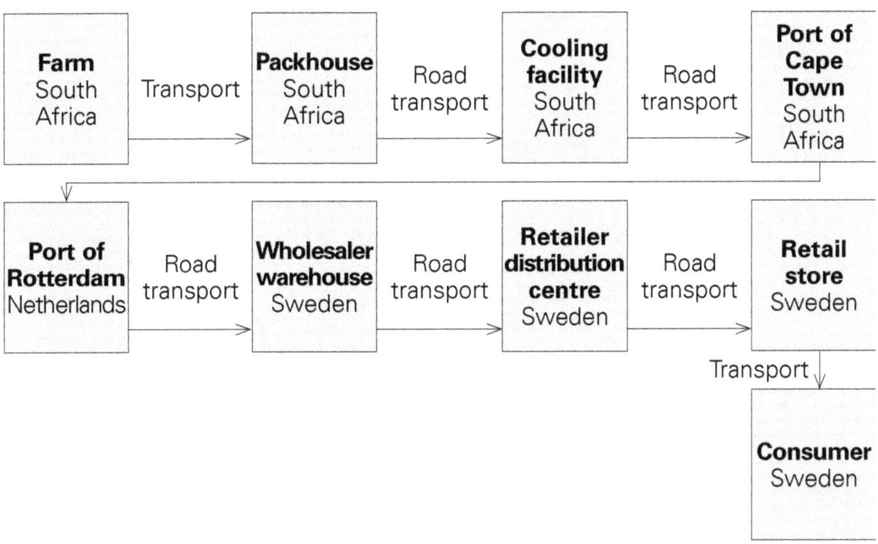

loading in a container. When the facility is busy, there is a risk of breaking the cold chain at this point.

From the cooling facility, an exporter manages the transport to Europe, which is paid for by the retailer. This cargo goes in containers by truck from the cooling facility to the port of Cape Town. The total time in the cooling facility and the port should be a maximum of 7 days, but it sometimes takes longer, as Cape Town frequently suffers from strong winds and operations are stopped at a wind strength of 80kph. As an example, 45 days were lost in 2017 owing to strong wind. This negatively affects the quality of the packed grapes, as it reduces their shelf life. Sometimes the grapes are delayed 2–3 weeks in the port, which leads to poorer quality. The negative effect of the delay is compounded by the fact that summer heat can raise the temperature in the container. A 1,000-container vessel takes approximately 30 hours to unload and load. Depending on size, a vessel usually stays in port for 6–30 hours. Containers of grapes and some other products have special instructions. Grape containers are not to be stored on top of a container stack to protect them from the sun.

After loading, the vessel goes to the Port of Rotterdam in the Netherlands, which takes about three weeks. On arrival in Europe, there is a 72-hour quality control before the grapes are transported by truck to a wholesaler warehouse in Sweden, where they are stored and repacked from one tertiary packaging to another tertiary packaging. Thereafter, the grapes are transported to a retailer distribution centre (DC), which stores and repacks them into smaller quantities based on the demand from the retail stores. This is followed by transport to a retail store, where either the secondary or primary packaging is replenished. Finally, consumers buy primary packages of grapes and bring them home.

Packaging system

The primary packaging is a plastic tray made of PET, which weighs 500–540g when filled with grapes. The primary package weighs about 24g and measures 190 × 115 × 80mm. The biggest challenge with the plastic trays is the risk of pressure damage to the grapes. For this reason, the packages must not be filled too high. There is also a risk of getting moisture on the grapes in the primary packaging. The secondary packaging consists of a plastic bag, corrugated board packaging, and a sheet, which slowly emits sulphur to reduce any water on the grapes. Ten primary packages are put into the plastic bag, which then is put into corrugated board packaging. The dimensions of the standard secondary packaging are 400 × 600 × 90mm. The producer also uses secondary packaging measuring 300 × 400 × 120mm, which better protects the grapes from pressure from above. The secondary packages are put on pallets (1,000 × 1,200mm) to a height of 2,400mm. This means that the lowest layer of packaging bears a weight of 90kg. A full pallet has stabilizing material on the corners and straps to hold them together. The pallets are loaded into a container in the cold storage facility. This packaging system remains unchanged until the grapes reach the port of Rotterdam, where the pallets are loaded onto a truck for transport to the wholesaler. At this point, the secondary packaging is transferred to Euro pallets (1,200 × 800mm). In the retailer DC, the secondary packaging is repacked onto yet another Euro pallet.

Packaging-related challenges in the supply chain

The supply chain contains a number of challenges, many of which can be influenced by the design of the packaging system. Packaging waste occurs in several stages of the supply chain – in the filling process, in each repacking process, and when emptying a primary, secondary or tertiary package. The volume efficiency of the packaging system affects the efficiency of the logistics operations and transportation. Primary packaging uses approximately 80 per cent of the volume of secondary packaging, which means that some 20 per cent is not used. Furthermore, there are 10 primary packages in secondary packaging, which affects handling efficiency in the wholesaler DC, the retailer DC and the retail store. If it were possible to include more primary packages in the secondary packaging, it would increase handling efficiency. However, there are trade-offs owing to other supply chain requirements, such as weight restrictions for ergonomic reasons and pallet utilization.

Product waste is a general problem in table grape supply chains (Clarke, 2012). Generally, temperature variations can result in up to 25 per cent loss of table grapes in transportation per day (Kader and Rolle, 2004). This case identified a number of supply chain challenges that can lead to damage and waste. If the table grapes are in contact with, or too close to, the lid of the primary package after the manual filling process, there is pressure damage. This occurs quite frequently. Another potential for pressure damage is on the secondary packaging in the bottom layer on the pallet, which carries 90kg when fully loaded. Further, one of the biggest challenges is moisture in the packaging. If the packaging solutions prevent effective ventilation, moisture can be produced in the primary packaging, which will negatively affect the quality of the table grapes. To prevent moisture, the current packaging solution includes a sulphur sheet. Unfortunately, there is a risk that the sulphur can burn the grapes. Vibrations and shock to containers are other challenges in the supply chain, particularly in the loading process in the port, which can be affected by strong winds. Still, damage to the grapes cannot be tracked to the port, as the containers are never opened there.

The risk of food waste is highly subject to time and temperature. Table grapes should be consumed within about 50 days after picking if they are handled correctly (sometimes longer is acceptable). A time challenge in the case study is that in the peak season, the cold storage facility can be full, and the farmers must store the table grapes in the packhouse at approximately 22°C, instead of cooling them down to –0.5°C in the cold storage facility. This significantly cuts the grapes' shelf life. The effect of temperature on shelf life is such that they deteriorate more in one day at 4°C than a week at 0°C (Thompson *et al*, 2008). Maintaining the cold chain is also challenging in other parts of the supply chain. In the container loading process in the cold storage facility, the temperature is about 22°C, which is much higher than that of the cooled grapes. Usually, this process is fast, but in the peak season it can take more time, leading to a negative impact on the grapes. Further, the placement of pallets of grapes in cargo containers affects the temperature of the grapes. A study by Freiboth *et al* (2013) showed that grapes on pallets closer to the door had higher ambient temperatures than those closest to the refrigeration unit. In the outdoor storage area at the port, the sun can warm the containers. To reduce this effect, cargo containers with grapes in them should not be stored on the top of the stack.

Containers can be delayed in the port because of strong winds and because of delayed vessels, which also affects their temperature. A delayed vessel must wait for a new time slot, which leads to a further delay. Table 7.1 shows the time and potential delays in different supply chain stages. If all potential delays occur, the shelf life in the retail stores is significantly reduced. If such delays are combined with temperature rises inside the packaging, the shelf-life reduction is even greater.

Table 7.2 summarizes the challenges regarding packed table grapes. Based on these challenges, the environmental impact of the packaging can be described in the three areas of packaging waste, logistics and transport efficiency, and product waste. Packaging waste occurs in the packhouse, as excessive material is wasted. After repacking and emptying, there is waste

TABLE 7.1 Time and potential delays in different supply chain stages (grapes should be consumed within 50 days after picking)

Potential delay (days)	Supply chain stage	Time (days)
Packhouse	3	Capacity full in the cold storage facility
Cold storage facility	4	Late notification of shipping need
Port	4	Sometimes 14–21 days Strong winds, vessel misses its time slot
Vessel	21	Bad conditions
Port	3	Vessel misses its time slot
Road transport	1	Congestion
Wholesaler DC	–	Not specified
Road transport	x hours	Congestion
Retailer DC	–	Not specified
Road transport	x hours	Congestion

TABLE 7.2 Packaging activities and challenges regarding packed table grapes in different supply chain stages

Supply chain stage	Packaging activities	Challenges on packed table grapes
Producer	Reusable packaging	Not packed yet
Packhouse	Precooling Packing: primary, secondary and tertiary packaging	High stacks, keep cold chain, shock from movements of packaging
Cold storage facility	Forklifts move pallets from unloading area to cooling area Cooling for 5 days Put into containers	Packages on the lower tiers on pallets are regularly damaged by the forklift operations Risks of broken cold chain in container loading Humidity from rapid temperature changes in container cooling
Port of Cape Town	Unloading of containers, outdoor storage, loading	Strong wind and delayed vessels lead to waiting time, which leads to temperature rise in containers and reduced shelf life Shock and vibrations from container handling

(continued)

TABLE 7.2 (Continued)

Supply chain stage	Packaging activities	Challenges on packed table grapes
Road transport (various types of vehicle)	Loading and unloading (included in the other activities), transportation	Vibrations and shock Temperature Time
Sea transport	Loading and unloading (included in the other activities), transportation	Vibrations and shock Temperature Humidity Time
Port of Rotterdam	Unloading of containers, outdoor storage, quality control, loading	Vibrations and shock Time
Wholesaler	Forklift operations, unloading, storage, repacking, loading	Vibrations and shock Temperature Time
Retailer DC	Forklift operations, unloading, storage, repacking, loading	Vibrations and shock Temperature Time
Retail store	Unloading, storage, replenishment	Vibrations and shock Temperature Time
Consumer	Purchase, storage	Vibrations and shock Temperature Time

and used tertiary packaging at the wholesaler DC, retailer DC and the retail store. Some accidents in the forklift operations in the cooling facility lead to repacking. The secondary packaging becomes waste at the retail store, and the primary packaging at the consumer end.

Furthermore, the volume efficiency of the packaging system affects storage space and transport efficiency in the different road transport stretches. Logistics and transport efficiency as well as product waste are affected by the packaging design and material. It can:

- compensate for moisture by providing sufficient ventilation, which affects the packhouse, the cooling facility, the port of Cape Town, and the sea transport;
- minimize the risk of breaking the cold chain in quality control in the port of Rotterdam by helping to ensure that as little fruit as possible is exposed to the outer environment;

- protect from shock and vibrations in the port of Rotterdam, at the wholesaler, at the retailer DC, in the retail store and at the consumer end;
- increase the stability of the pallets in the cooling facility;
- facilitate rapid loading in the cooling facility to minimize the exposure to a higher temperature.

Furthermore, the design and placement of containers can protect from the sun's heat and cooling technology in containers can compensate for heat in the port of Cape Town. Labelling can minimize identification time through track-and-trace capabilities in road transport, in the wholesaler DC, in the retailer DC, in the retail store and at the consumer end. With the addition of a temperature sensor, it can also indicate whether the cold chain was maintained.

Conclusions

This case presented the potential of packaging logistics for effective and efficient supply chains. It also defined and distinguished between sustainable packaging and packaging for a circular economy. It showed that packaging practices and decisions influence logistics operations, transport efficiency, product waste and the effectiveness of the packaging material. Thus, they influence the financial and environmental performance of focal companies, their suppliers and their customers.

With a focus on environmentally sustainable packaging, the case presented a structured approach for identifying the environmental impacts and the reduction potential of packaging in supply chains. A study of packed table grapes in a global supply chain from South Africa to Sweden illustrated the approach. The study analysed the environmental impacts of the material in the packaging system and the environmental impacts of packaging on logistics and transport efficiency and on product waste.

This case emphasized the importance of understanding the impact of packaging decisions on both specific operations and overall supply chain performance, which can lead to a competitive advantage for the supply chain. A key issue of the approach is to apply a system perspective, which supports holistic decision-making.

QUESTIONS

Based on this case, with a structured approach to identify the environmental impacts and the reduction potential of packaging in supply chains, a number of discussion points should help you to understand the potential of packaging logistics for effective and efficient global food supply chains, and to categorize the environmental impact areas of packaging.

1. Use Table 7.1 to discuss management principles for packaging to manage the effect of the potential delays.
2. Use Table 7.2 and the insights about a circular economy to discuss the impact of packaging on circularity in the case of table grapes.
3. Apply first a circular economy perspective and then a sustainability perspective to the global food supply chain of packed table grapes. What are the similarities and differences in packaging system requirements?
4. Discuss food waste challenges from a packaging perspective in the case of table grapes. Based on Figure 7.1, what can be done to reduce the amount of damaged and wasted table grapes?
5. Discuss packaging material challenges in the case of table grapes. Based on Figure 7.1, what can be done to reduce packaging material waste?
6. Discuss logistics and transport challenges from a packaging perspective in the case of table grapes. Based on Figure 7.1, what can be done to improve logistics and transport efficiency in the global supply chain of table grapes?
7. Table 7.2 describes challenges regarding packed table grapes in different supply chain stages. How can the packaging system address these challenges? What potential trade-offs do you foresee?
8. How should a farmer or producer select a packaging system for table grapes? How can different supply chain requirements be identified and included? How should costs and benefits be shared when sustainable packaging is accomplished?
9. In what way can a packaging system for table grapes add competitive advantage?
10. Use Figure 7.1 to describe in what way the packaging system for table grapes can be developed to become more sustainable and support a circular economy.
11. Present 10 supply chain decisions that are affected by packaging.

Answers on page 227.

References

Clarke, G (2012) South African table grape industry, Gerber Fresh (Pty) Ltd

Freiboth, H W *et al* (2013) Investigating temperature breaks in the summer fruit export cold chain: a case study, *Journal of Transport and Supply Chain Management*, 7 (1), pp 1–7

Geissdoerfer, M *et al* (2017) The circular economy: a new sustainability paradigm?, *Journal of Cleaner Production*, **143**, pp 757–68

INCPEN (2009) [accessed 24 July 2019] Table for One: The energy cost to feed one person, *INCPEN* [Online] www.incpen.org/table-for-one/ (archived at https://perma.cc/LRB7-9GZP)

Kader, A A and Rolle, R S (2004) [accessed 4 July 2019] The Role of Post-Harvest Management in Assuring the Quality and Safety of Horticultural Produce [Online] www.fao.org/3/y5431e/y5431e00.htm (archived at https://perma.cc/Z9WG-XPHD)

Lewis, H (2005) Defining product stewardship and sustainability in the Australian packaging industry, *Environmental Science and Policy*, **8**, pp 45–55

Nordin, N and Selke, S (2010) Social aspect of sustainable packaging, *Packaging Technology and Science*, **23**, pp 317–26

Pålsson, H (2018) *Packaging Logistics: Understanding and managing the economic and environmental impacts of packaging in supply chains*, Kogan Page, London

08

Organizational conformance and recognition systems

GRAEME HERON AND ERICA BALLENTYNE

(1) (2) (3) (4)

Knowledge

You will be able to:

- better comprehend the reality of modern road freight transport operations as lynch pins in supply chains, which can deliver organizational leanness;
- envision how extended distances → time compression → increased flexibility → smaller batches → higher frequency → lower inventory → commoditization of data from within the organization can act as opportunities for efficiency and optimization in order to meet the needs of policymakers by challenging their own incumbent systems and looking to maximize the value of assets and colleagues;
- realize that policymakers are charged with interpreting directives for sustainability and air pollution, which can be delivered as cleaner air → fewer peak-time flows → better traffic and vehicle management → reporting and sustainability;
- assimilate current organizational abilities, legislative requirements and scheme types within the contexts of short- mid- and long-term development strategies;
- prioritize the identified conventions in order to maximize benefits.

Action

You will be able to look inside their organization and identify where tacit knowledge can become explicit knowledge. The wider research literature to date commonly regards knowledge and quality as separate entities rather than as component parts of an overarching paradigm of continuous improvement and colleague development. Organizational knowledge and knowledge management have the ability to deliver and sustain quality management. This case does not call for wholesale change and capital investment; it calls for freight transport organizations to review their human capital and assets in order to further commoditize and add value to their outputs. To this end, the case introduces a set of sectoral conventions as benchmarks for the participants to commence their journey.

The organization will be able to decide which type of recognition scheme is most suitable for them, or whether they believe a system adapted to their own needs, designed and managed internally, offers greater value. The eight conventions for extending organizational efficiency can be flexed and prioritized to best suit local conditions and the requirements of commercial customers and legislative customers alike.

Introduction

This case study considers and examines the scenarios through which an organization can continue to satisfy its forward-facing customers while complying with the requirements set out by legislative bodies. In particular, we explore two types of conformance and recognition schemes with differing objectives. We also introduce a set of conventions as a third option for freight transport, storage and distribution organizations to be able to identify customer requirements and undertake a series of colleague-driven incremental steps to drive both engagement and continuous improvement. We address the benefits and potential dilemmas of each scheme as well as reviewing the potential for an organization to extract benefits by taking an independent approach to extracting implicit knowledge, engaging colleagues and utilizing knowledge management to meet its customers' requirements.

There are several attributes to this inquiry and analysis which extend beyond scheme membership. These include colleague development, skill acquisition and engagement, which are important factors in the logistics sector where there are currently significant concerns related to skills gaps, shortages and an ageing workforce. The operationalization of an organization's strategy through scheme membership lies in a widely agreed sector acknowledgement of high staff turnover and shortages (Freight Transport Association, 2016, 2018; Road Haulage Association, 2017) that can significantly increase operational risk as colleagues, particularly drivers, leave an organization, taking implicit knowledge with them (Haas and Hansen, 2007; Ragab and Arisha, 2013).

Case methodology

The research for this case adopted a mixed methods approach, with an industry-focused survey and qualitative interviews with operators, local government officers and scheme representatives. Purposive sampling was applied as an appropriate approach (Easterby-Smith *et al*, 2015), commencing with an examination of existing schemes, membership demographics and fixed time periods. Those holding operational and strategic roles participated in the data collection as they are of equal and critical importance in relation to scheme adoption by commercial organizations. The role and influence of tacit knowledge in scheme adoption choices is also important in relation to organizational scale. An example of this would be a small commercial organization which, unable to overhead the costs of a full-time transport manager, share the services, experience, skills and tacit knowledge of a freelance transport manager with several other small organizations. At the opposite end of the scale, a well-connected senior manager or director may gain significant social and sectoral capital through networking at freight partnership forums and professional institute/industry body events where they have the opportunity to counsel the thoughts of others or 'keep an ear to the ground'. A purposive sample was drawn from current, lapsed and aspiring scheme members, scheme administrators, local authority policymakers and other industry stakeholders based in the UK. These criteria were driven by the need to comprehend 'same but different' operational scenarios in the road freight transport sector. Initial primary data were gathered via an autonomous self-administered survey. The semi-structured interviews were based on *a priori* themes extracted from mixed literature sources and used to supplement the quantitative survey data, to allow recording of particular occurrences, phenomena and underlying constructs (Jonsen and Jehn, 2009). The semi-structured interviews provided a source of information gathering for rich, textual data (Silverman, 2015). The interviews enabled our research to explore relevant topics while not conforming to a rigid set of questions (Easterby-Smith *et al*, 2015). In particular, the interviews gathered views to examine the perceived benefits and disadvantages of freight and commercial fleet operator schemes, helping us to determine potential areas for scheme improvement and generate recommendations for increasing the uptake and wider impacts of schemes in relation to skills acquisition and knowledge sharing. In total there are 60 surveys and 15 interviews in the data set.

Comparison and historical contexts of the schemes

Freight and commercial transport operators must comply with legislation introduced to tackle air quality and congestion. At local levels these are mandated and controlled through local transport plans, clean air zones and so on. There is a common perception, confirmed by our data analysis, that this requirement to comply is regarded as punitive by commercial operators. The two schemes reviewed recognize and commend operators who comply with, or exceed, baseline expectations. It is easy to understand the unfavourable reaction from operators facing daily challenges to meet customer requirements. However, wider supply chain management research has led to the emergence of customer and supplier relationship theories underpinned by a common thread of continuous improvement and mutual benefit. An example of this latent commonality that lies between some of the awkward and sometimes adversarial stances between commercial organizations and policymakers is that, for instance, proposals to tackle congestion on a strategic road network are not wholly at odds with the needs of commercial organizations across the freight transport sector to have faster transit times and improved journey time reliability.

Each existing scheme is organized slightly differently, and the principal drivers behind their creation have usually been one or a combination of the following objectives: to address political targets around air quality and sustainability; to improve the operational efficiency and performance of commercial vehicle fleets; to improve road safety; and to adhere to industry best-practice standards.

The most prominent membership accreditation schemes targeted at vehicle fleet operators include Scheme 1 (S1 hereafter) and Scheme 2 (S2 hereafter). While there are other smaller schemes developed by industry bodies, this research focuses on S1 and S2. Since their inception, both S1 and S2 have widened their participation to be more inclusive of fleet operators more generally, including the bus and coach sectors and licensed taxi firms. Interest in such schemes and their potential benefits is not wholly confined to the UK; there are S1-type schemes operating in various European locations, serving as evidence of local interpretations of EU directives, for example the EU Transport Commission's role in promoting mobility that is efficient, safe, secure and environmentally friendly (EU Commission, 2011). S1 and S2 have their genesis in initiatives such as the Operator Compliance Risk Scores programme (DVSA, 2006), the Sustainable Urban Mobility Plan (SUMP), the Sustainable Urban Goods Logistics Achieved by Regional and local policies (SUGAR) (Interreg 2013), as well as the Reward and Recognition Scheme (EU EUROPA RECODRIVE; European Commission, 2010) and the Auditing & Certification Scheme (EU EUROPA ADVANCE; European Commission, 2014).

S1 was devised by four local authorities in 2009, as part of a regional Air Quality Initiative to promote best practice in fleet operations and improve engagement between local and regional governments and commercial fleet operators. Unlike S2, the S1 scheme continues to remain free for operators to join and aims to help them improve efficiency, reduce fuel consumption and emissions, and achieve cost savings. S1 has been adopted by numerous local authorities across the UK, including extensive take-up throughout Scotland, and is open to fleet operators of HGVs, buses, coaches, vans or taxis that are either based or operating in an area with a local S1 scheme. S2 was initiated for transport operators to be able to respond to the newly introduced London Low Emission Zone. Originally S2 was a free, voluntary accreditation membership scheme that aimed to improve the delivery of freight across central London, where it formed part of the wider London Freight Plan. Although no longer a free scheme, it remains voluntary and the benefits of membership have been made more widely available to fleet and freight operators nationally across the UK. S2 still aims to assist vehicle fleet operators to improve all aspects of their operations, including, *inter alia*, road safety, fuel efficiency, reducing emissions and cutting costs.

The remainder of this case seeks to demonstrate the potential for compliance and recognition schemes targeted at commercial freight and fleet transport operators to act as business readiness tools. It will also discuss how the establishment of such schemes in specific geospatial zones has the potential to further align the needs of local government around clean air zones, and consider how schemes could promote the integration and adoption of continuous improvement within commercial organizations as part of their strategies.

Analysis

Several themes emerged from the data analysis that have an influence on commercial fleet transport operations and the adoption or integration of compliance and recognition schemes to address colleague development, knowledge management and competitiveness. The investigation revealed clear geographic dominance based on scheme adoption, in particular the legacy factors around S2, which has retained a significant population of members in the South East of England who tend to operate within the London controlled zones. Some of the interviewees recorded that being an S2 member was now being mandated into contracts and presenting as anti-competitive. S1 has grown its presence outside these aforementioned areas, in particular extending beyond the region in which it was originally developed, and into Scotland. The identified geographic scheme hotspots are not necessarily a hindrance to achieving the goals of sustainable road transport and addressing the wider air quality agenda. The findings from interviews with industry practitioners support the hypothesized view that operator schemes can indirectly benefit best practice. This is achieved through the geographic migration that naturally occurs within the freight transport industry as vehicles cover large distances and optimize direct routes. Therefore, as commercial operators seek the most direct and convenient routes available to them, they disseminate best practice both within and beyond a specific region, across the strategic road network and neighbouring transport corridors.

There was much anecdotal evidence of growing concerns around skills and driver retention from both scheme and non-scheme members interviewed. This reflects a wider national industry problem where there are currently 40,000 driver vacancies (Road Haulage Association, 2017; Freight Transport Association, 2018). The next Driver Certificate of Professional Conformance (CPC) round is due, and there are fears that there will be a repeat or worsening of the 2013 phenomenon where 9 cent of drivers left the industry. It is also important to acknowledge that at the time of publication, 11 per cent of the current driver workforce in the UK are non-UK citizens (Freight Transport Association, 2018), and for a sector that has been characterized by the government as low-skilled, this creates a significant barrier to recruitment and retention in itself. This further compounds the issue of an ageing population of drivers in the UK road haulage industry (Freight Transport Association, 2018; Road Haulage Association, 2017; Transport for the North, 2019). The UK is not alone in this predicament, with Germany reporting very similar issues.

A unanimous view among our respondents indicated that knowledge management is key to organizational performance; however, it is commonly overlooked. One particular overlooked aspect of knowledge management is digitalization, which has resulted in large amounts of autonomously generated vehicle data. A clear example of this is the regulations on drivers' hours and tachographs for goods vehicles; in Great Britain, 'GV262' gives general guidance about drivers' and tachograph rules for lawful compliance with the current enforcement policy for goods vehicles (DVSA, 2016). Among our respondents, the digital tachograph regulations are generally seen as onerous compliance and monitoring, rather than a data-gathering opportunity that could deliver benefits regardless of scheme membership. An example of this is data being used to earn recognition, where vehicle operators prove they meet driver and vehicle standards by regularly sharing performance information with the Driver and Vehicle Licensing Authority (DVLA), irrespective of scheme membership.

Given the analysis, this case investigation reasonably presupposes that recognition and compliance schemes are more valuable tools for cross-cutting sustainability agendas and delivered in partnership for wider stakeholder good; to proffer for, rather than profit from. This further positions the importance and potential benefits of considering the role of quality and continuous improvement cycles of plan → do → check → act within operator schemes for driving continuous improvement, both within organizations and externally in the geographic areas where members' vehicles are operating. Thus, quality management influences on an operator are not negatively influenced by scale, but rather improved upon by skill recognition and data optimization of the organization regardless of scale.

Additionally, this case reveals that a 'one size fits all policy' approach such as demonstrated by S2 is counterintuitive towards achieving innovation and continuous improvement. Further, industry interests are not practically addressed at both extremes of scale in S2; here, a homogeneous approach does little more than deliver imitation rather than the innovative approaches required to improve customer satisfaction and deliver continuous improvements and colleague development. To this end, there are alternative government-funded schemes that derive more value from colleagues' implicit knowledge being made explicit, by recording shared data and implementing performance indicators. This can lead to the aforementioned 'earned recognition' and positive profiling. Relatively low-cost initiatives can also autonomously generate performance data on a periodic basis to 'report upon'. This would suggest that extensible enterprise data sets developed through colleague development provide more value in real terms to an organization than more expensive commercialized schemes. Our case analysis reveals that many memberships are at the first or introductory level, and they have been sought to satisfy customer and construction project requirements, as opposed to seek perceived added value and benefits associated with scheme membership.

This case has addressed transport and freight movement perspectives within the contexts of skills, employee retention and business readiness of operators for competitive advantage and as part of an organization's strategy. Notwithstanding scheme choice, this investigation concedes that to reap the benefits of a scheme requires a high degree of commonality in approaches to business-friendly local transport plans, transport corridors and seamless access for freight. This can only be achieved under a general consensus that is willing to overlook bipartisan attitudes and local political imperatives.

Business readiness and conventions

To deliver sectoral advantage, the research in this case study posits that a holistic approach, based upon a set of conventions, encourages inclusive and equally participative colleague development.

Conclusions

While there is competition for membership across S1 and S2, there is no limit to the number of schemes an operator can join. The predominant deciding factor for operators is often the economic limit set by organizations regarding the affordability of maintaining multiple scheme memberships, and the potential benefits of levels of accreditation. Notwithstanding this economic decision factor, our analysis reveals the benefits of a continuous improvement paradigm over simple compliance with a level of membership criteria, whereby a commodity or service increases customer satisfaction and economic viability. This can engender a change in organizational culture in the freight transport sector, whereby operational performance is more stable and proactive with regard to service variability, reporting and compliance activities. However, in respect of this, it is important to acknowledge that adaptation of operational practices will likely lead towards a more holistic organizational benefit than pure adoption of generic management tools. Successful adaptation will likely lead to a better comprehension of customer needs and identification of who the customer, internal or external, actually is. Our call for adaptation of the organization to the best-fitting scheme, rather than simple adoption of a particular scheme to address a short-term problem, is central to a successful and more sustainable outcome given the nature and peculiarities of the sector and the lack of certainty in the near to mid-term future that the freight transport industry faces.

QUESTIONS

1. *Discovery:* How would you undertake an organisational analysis as you decide which scheme would be best for your organisation?
2. *Identification:* List all of the external and internal customers that the organisation must satisfy.
3. *Choice:* Which approach would you take, Scheme 1, Scheme 2 or your own independent approach. As a result of your choices, how would you rank the conventions hierarchically and what would be your reasoning behind these rankings?
4. *Inclusion, quality management and customer satisfaction.* Quality management and customer satisfaction is a philosophy, a paradigm (set of beliefs). Scheme membership as such, drives inclusion, quality and customer oriented successful fulfilment. This is broadly derivative of Feigenbaum's concept of total control:
    1. Quality is a company wide process
    2. Quality is what customer says it is
    3. Quality and costs are a sum not a difference
    4. Quality requires both individual and team zealotry
    5. Quality is a way of managing
    6. Quality and innovation are mutually dependant
    7. Quality is an ethic
    8. Quality requires continuous improvement
    9. Quality is most cost-effective
    10. Quality is implemented with a total system connected with customers & suppliers.

Answers on page 232.

References

Driver and Vehicle Standards Agency (DVSA) (2006) [accessed 24 July 2019] Operator Compliance Risk Score (OCRS), *DVSA* [Online] www.gov.uk/operator-compliance-risk-score

Easterby-Smith, M, Thorpe, R and Jackson, P R (2015) *Management and Business Research*, SAGE, Thousand Oaks, CA

EU EUROPA (2010) [accessed 24 July 2019) Rewarding and Recognition Schemes for Energy Conserving Driving, Vehicle Procurement and Maintenance (RECODRIVE), *European Commission* [Online] https://ec.europa.eu/energy/intelligent/projects/en/projects/recodrive (archived at https://perma.cc/KGN8-923H)

European Commission (2011) [accessed 24 July 2019] Roadmap to a Single European Transport Area – Towards a competitive and resource efficient transport system, White Paper, *European Commission* [Online] https://ec.europa.eu/transport/themes/strategies/2011_white_paper_en (archived at https://perma.cc/B8EN-89GA)

European Commission (2014) [accessed 24 July 2019] Auditing and Certification Scheme to increase the quality of sustainable urban mobility plans in cities (ADVANCE), *European Commission* [Online] https://ec.europa.eu/energy/intelligent/projects/en/projects/advance (archived at https://perma.cc/V2ME-7P5S)

Freight Transport Association (2016) [accessed 5 July 2019] FTA Driver Shortage Report: Analysis Highlighting Reliance on EU Nationals, *FTA* [Online] https://fta.co.uk/press-releases/20161027-fta-driver-shortage-report-analysis-highlights-reliance-on-eu-nationals (archived at https://perma.cc/52MG-MAKX)

Freight Transport Association (2018) [accessed 5 July 2019] Addressing the Skills and Labour Shortage, *FTA* [Online] https://fta.co.uk/campaigns/driver-shortage (archived at https://perma.cc/89B3-7Y4R)

Haas, M R and Hansen, M T (2007) Different knowledge, different benefits: toward a productivity perspective on knowledge sharing in organizations, *Strategic Management Journal*, **28** (11), pp 1133–53

Jonsen, K and Jehn, K A (2009) Using triangulation to validate themes in qualitative studies, *Qualitative Research in Organizations and Management: An International Journal*, **4** (2), pp 123–50

Ragab, M and Arisha, A (2013) Knowledge management and measurement: a critical review, *Journal of Knowledge Management*, **17** (6), pp 873–901

Road Haulage Association (2017) [accessed 5 July 2019] Driver Shortage – RHA Sets the Record Straight, *RHA* [Online] https://www.rha.uk.net/news/press-releases/2017-12-december/driver-shortage-rha-sets-the-record-straight (archived at https://perma.cc/2GXS-6NJ4)

Silverman, D (2015) *Interpreting Qualitative Data*, SAGE, Thousand Oaks, CA

Transport for the North (2019) [accessed 5 July 2019] Strategic Transport Plan, *Transport for the North* [Online] https://transportforthenorth.com/wp-content/uploads/TfN-final-strategic-transport-plan-2019.pdf (archived at https://perma.cc/WZ5V-ERP4)

09

Protecting supply chains from counterfeit products

MARK MANNING AND DANIEL STANTON

① ② ③ ④

Knowledge

Many companies are discovering that counterfeit, unapproved, and unlicensed versions of their products are having a significant impact on their business. These products flow freely through black market and grey market channels around the world, and often find their way back into legitimate supply chains. This issue has traditionally been the responsibility of the corporate legal and brand protection departments. But it is fundamentally a supply chain problem, and supply chain managers are increasingly being asked to implement countermeasures in the form of new processes and technologies.

Action

This article presents a strategic framework that aligns brand protection techniques with supply chain processes. This framework enables supply chain management professionals to evaluate potential security options, identify gaps, and integrate an effective brand protection strategy into their supply chain.

Introduction

Many companies are discovering that counterfeit, unapproved and unlicensed versions of their products are having a significant impact on their business. These products flow freely through black market and grey market channels around the world, and often find their way back into legitimate supply chains. This issue has traditionally been the responsibility of the corporate legal and brand protection departments, but it is fundamentally a supply chain problem. Supply chain managers are increasingly being asked to implement countermeasures in the form of new processes and technologies.

This chapter presents a strategic framework that aligns brand protection techniques with supply chain processes. This framework enables supply chain management professionals to evaluate potential security options, identify gaps, and integrate an effective brand protection strategy into their supply chain.

Counterfeit products can create serious problems for a supply chain, including lost profits, increased warranty costs and brand erosion. In extreme cases, counterfeit products can cause personal harm to customers. With today's global marketplace, it is difficult for brands to secure the supply chain for their products from thousands of miles away, often in production facilities and distribution nodes that are less than transparent.

The goal of the case company was to secure their supply chain to ensure that the third-party factory was unable to produce additional product that is identical to the licensed and contracted product being shipped to the brand. This required the introduction of technologies that enable the brand to guarantee the authenticity of the product they have in the field, and to track each individual product back to the assembly partner and the production line that produced it.

Counterfeit products: a growing problem for supply chains

The global market for counterfeit goods is estimated to be $2 trillion (ICC/BASCAP, 2011). Many of these counterfeit and grey market products today are indistinguishable from the genuine articles. One of the biggest contributors to this challenge is unauthorized production overruns, known as **third shift operations**, where products go out the backdoor of a third-party manufacturer that has been contracted to make legitimate products.

To prove to a court that a sample purchase of a suspected counterfeit or diverted product was the fault of a diverter or counterfeiter, the brand first must prove their own factory is secure and unable to ship additional genuine products of their own. Many defendants are using this element of doubt to fight legal cases against them.

So how can a brand secure the production of their products from thousands of miles away in a production facility that is less than transparent?

This is the challenge facing many companies today and one that we're going to focus on within the fashion accessory industry. We'll look at the case of fashion watches that ship in large volumes, produced overseas, with an average retail price of €100–200. The supply chain for these products is certainly not unusual. They have many small parts suppliers delivering components to a final assembly partner that ships finished product to distributors around the world. They need to secure the product at production and throughout the supply chain, so that they can ensure the integrity of their prosecutions and legal cases against brand infringers.

Different types of counterfeit products

Counterfeiting is a multifaceted problem. There are several sources of fraudulent products, but these can be grouped into general categories. We'll start by looking at four different types of counterfeiting so that we can better highlight some of the issues with fighting these types of product fraud, and why securing the manufacturing supply chain is essential.

Blatant counterfeit products

Many people think of high-end watches and fashion items when 'counterfeit products' are mentioned. In this case, a counterfeit is normally defined as 'a copy or replica of a brand's product being sold by an authorized or unauthorized seller'. This is fake product that has likely been produced outside the brand's factory in substandard conditions with far less attention to quality and safety. In addition to watches, other products that are frequent targets for counterfeiting include apparel, footwear, electronics, pharmaceuticals, computers and toys (CBP, 2017).

Grey market and diversion

This is normally genuine product that has been sold into a low-price market or region and is then 'diverted' by a distributor or retailer into a higher-price region, at a discount. Diversion disrupts the pricing structure in the region where it is sold, creating artificially low-cost competition that cannibalizes sales from authorized local retailers. This leads to price erosion and a loss of profits. Diversion can also lead to longer supply chains, increasing the risk of product damage, expiration and obsolescence.

> RETAIL PRICE EROSION
>
> An Italian manufacturer of high-end bicycle racing tyres suffered significant impacts from product diversion. They ignored the problem of grey market sales for so long that they were eventually unable to sell any of their products into retail stores. Retailers refused to stock their products, because the grey market for the tyres was so well established that the retail price for the product was almost the same as the wholesale price. This undermined the brand's growth strategy in the very markets that should have been their most profitable.

Third shift or production overrun

Production overruns are made on the same production line as the genuine item, from the same materials and by the same workers. This is often referred to as 'third shift' production, implying that these parts are made at night, when no one is looking. For all intents and purposes, it is the same as a genuine item, but the brand owner never receives any revenue for it. There is no way for the brand's investigators to determine if this is genuine or unlicensed and, therefore, counterfeit. This unlicensed but 'genuine' product can easily feed both the counterfeit and grey markets.

Blacktopping and remanufacturing

A common problem in the electronics industry is the resale of used electronic components as new, and the intentional mislabelling of low-value components as high-value components. The process of repainting or relabelling a fake as a high-value component is called 'blacktopping'. The systems into which blacktopped components are placed suffer from performance and reliability issues that are often difficult to diagnose and repair. This can lead to high warranty and repair costs, as well as brand erosion. In the case of systems such as aeroplanes and weapons systems, blacktopping has the potential to cause extensive damage and lead to loss of life.

Evaluating countermeasures

When working with third-party manufacturers, two of the most difficult brand protection challenges are:

1. Ensure that the factory is unable to produce additional product that is identical to the licensed, contracted product being shipped to the brand owner.
2. Enable the brand owner to guarantee the authenticity of the product they have in the field and track each individual product back to the assembly partner and production line that produced it.

In recent years there has been a rapid growth of technologies that act as countermeasures against counterfeiting. These technologies can largely be broken down into five categories. Some of these technologies use unique characteristics of the product as individual identifiers. This is similar to the use of biometrics in identifying people. But most of these technologies focus on marking, serialization, data storage and the prevention of tampering.

Marking

Standard track-and-trace solutions leverage open source technologies such as barcodes, DataMatrix and QR codes to provide the logistics and security for their products. Unfortunately, open source solutions may be quick and cheap to implement, but they provide little security for the product, as these solutions are easily defeated or reproduced by counterfeiters and diverters. Some of counterfeiters use these open technologies to create their own versions of tracking solutions for their counterfeit products, setting up fake websites that can authenticate their own QR codes or reproducing the brand's serialization on counterfeit or diverted products. In fact, some of these implementations are a boon for counterfeiters as they allow them to provide simple and cheap authentication for their fake products.

Other common approaches to marking include the use of security inks, etched codes, and electronic tags such as Radio Frequency Identification (RFID) devices.

SECURE THE ACTUAL PRODUCT, NOT JUST THE PACKAGING OR THE LABEL

Many brands today are still using holograms, barcodes and QR codes to provide some form of product security. We still see many examples of the flashy and expensive holograms on hang tags and labels. Unfortunately, there are over 200 hologram manufacturers in Shenzhen alone that will be happy to make a copy of any hologram that you bring them, and to the naked eye these holograms will look identical. Diverters can easily remove serial numbers and packaging, and change labels to hide their identity. The goal for the brand is to make this much more difficult, and to break the business model of the counterfeiters and diverters. This can only be achieved by securing the actual product itself, not the packaging or the expensive label. Even implementing a blockchain is pointless if the actual product inside the box is not secure. Otherwise you're just securing a cheap cardboard box to the highly secure blockchain ledger.

When a brand takes a suspected counterfeiter, diverter or grey marketer to court they need to present irrefutable evidence that the product being presented as counterfeit was not produced in their own factory, or that the diverted product took a known path through the supply chain to the diverter. A defendant would ask the brand owner to prove that the product is not from their own factory or diverted from their supply chain. If a company is unable to secure their supply chain back to the factory, then they are unable to determine if the suspect counterfeit product is genuine or fake. This creates reasonable doubt for the defence in counterfeit or grey market cases, and a victory for the defendant. But if the brand can show that their production process is secure, and additional product is unable to ship through the backdoor, then there is a much greater chance of success at shutting down counterfeit, diversion and grey market operations.

MARKETING FAKES WITH SECURITY FEATURES

One of the authors was at a conference in Dubai during 2018 where an attendee told him that they had found QR code authentication on fake versions of their products, while these were never implemented on the genuine article. Having a QR code that could authenticate to a fake website gave the fake

> product legitimacy in the marketplace. Sometimes the counterfeiters deliver solutions that the brands haven't even thought of. We've seen examples of counterfeiters creating box sets of multiple brands' products complete with the logos and branding of both companies.

Serialization

Assigning serial numbers is a critical step in tracking individual products. But it's generally easy for counterfeiters to rerun serial numbers or even make up their own number ranges. In practice, many manufacturers do not track serial numbers outside the initial production. To have an effective serialization solution, you have to track the serial numbers beyond the machine that originally applied them, which requires a company-wide supply chain effort.

Data

The information about the provenance of a product needs to be stored in a database. The more information that can be captured, the more securely the information can be recorded, and the more widely the information can be accessed, the more valuable this provenance can become. While there are common examples of products being tracked in spreadsheets and SQL databases, the current focus is on creating blockchain systems to store, share and secure these data.

Anti-tampering

Authentic packaging is often used as a disguise for counterfeit products. Therefore, part of securing the physical products is the use of anti-tamper packaging, labels and coatings that make it difficult for counterfeiters to alter products and to reuse packaging.

Case study: iTRACE implementation

Acme Watch Company (name changed) is a global fashion brand based in Europe that is well known for its high-quality watches. Acme outsources the manufacturing of its watches to third parties in China and distributes them throughout the world. Acme watches are sold exclusively by authorized resellers. Given their concern about third shift operations and grey market sales, Acme engaged iTRACE to help secure their supply chain.

iTRACE is a technology firm that uses a suite of tools to secure the supply chains of global brands. iTRACE has integrated a proprietary print and scan technology into production laser systems that can be installed in any production process. The laser system is used to create a secure feature that acts as a covert or overt authentication token when applied to the final product, or to any component (Manning, 2019).

iTRACE provides 'secure part marking as a service' within China to deliver securely marked parts to the brand's assembly partners. This 'security as a service' approach takes implementation of the brand's security out of the hands of the product supplier.

ITRACE implemented a solution in which the security begins when the watch manufacturer issues a purchase order (PO) to their assembly partner. Each PO is accompanied by a secure, encrypted licence key. This key enables the laser system to produce only the exact quantity of codes that match the quantity of units ordered on the PO.

The assembly partner imports the secure licence key into the laser machine and starts to apply the serialized codes onto the selected component to create the authenticated part for the final assembly. Every code that is applied to a product or component is registered in the database transaction log or blockchain digital ledger.

Once the final product is assembled, it is packaged with a standard logistics tracking code that contains the matching unique identifier as part of the track-and-trace mechanism. This can be an RFID tag, barcode, DataMatrix or QR code.

The product is then scanned and tracked through the logistics chain using the iTRACE web-based unit tracking system and the standard scanning infrastructure in the supply chain. All of these tracking data can be stored in a traditional database or pushed through the iTRACE blockchain gateway onto a digital ledger. With each scan, the database is updated with the relevant transaction tracking information. When the product arrives at the distribution centre, it is received and placed into inventory as normal.

When a sales order (SO) is received by the distributor, the pick and pack process starts to fulfil that order. The packer selects all the various products and scans them into the iTRACE tracking database against that SO number, updating the database with the unique identifier (UID), European article number (EAN), Originator ID, Destination ID and operator username. Each manual barcode scan done by the picker takes approximately 1.4 seconds per item for both UID and EAN.

Delivering iTRACE codes as a covert and proprietary layer of security alongside the standard logistics technologies allows the brand to leverage the strengths of both technologies, without the compromises that occurred when trying to use a logistics technology for security.

Acme's goal is to make the effort for the counterfeiters so high that it no longer makes business sense to engage in counterfeiting. By using a proprietary technology for the product security, Acme has created a much higher barrier for the counterfeiters. iTRACE prevents the counterfeiters from spoofing the brand's own authentication solutions owing to its proprietary implementation.

Many brands use marketplace monitoring solutions that are able to identify the sellers of grey market or diverted goods. This approach allows the brand owner to play Whack-A-Mole with the online listings, but it does little to actually solve the problem, because they can't tell if the product came from their factory, a distributor selling into another market, or a retailer pushing excess product into another region. A more effective solution is to identify the source of the diverted product, so that you can cut off that supply and prevent future sales.

When the online monitoring systems identify a suspicious seller of Acme watches, they perform a sample purchase of the product (which will contain the iTRACE covert security). The product is analysed by the brand's investigator, who uses the covert tracking technology and the tracking database to identify which customer that product was originally intended to serve. They are then able to identify who the product was shipped to, investigate with the legal team and take the appropriate action against the diverter. This gives them strong evidence that can be used to support their case and be more successful with their prosecutions.

Conclusions

Almost all successful brands face the issues of counterfeiting, including blatant counterfeits, diversion, and unauthorized production overruns. Production overruns can occur at any point in the production supply chain, from single component providers to packaging and finished goods assembly. Securing the products in the entire supply chain allows the brand to ensure the integrity of their products and will make it much harder for any supplier to create unlicensed product without the brand knowing about it.

Many companies complain about counterfeiting and diversion of their products but place a low priority on implementing any form of real product security. In other words, they are opting to be reactive by using expensive legal resources, as opposed to being proactive with lower-cost technology solutions. Creating a secure supply chain takes vision and requires involvement from almost all parts of the organization: product, legal, operations, sales, production, purchasing and logistics.

The scale of counterfeiting and diversion has grown from a $1.7 trillion global industry in 2009 to a $2.4 trillion global industry in 2017 (International AntiCounterfeiting Coalition (IACC, 2017)). It's very clear from these numbers that the traditional approach of holograms, barcodes and QR codes is not working and that new, integrated security technologies need to be implemented in the global supply chains to defend against the threat of counterfeit products.

QUESTIONS

1 Which part of a company is responsible for dealing with counterfeit products?
2 What are the financial impacts of counterfeiting on a brand owner?
3 What happens if the brand protection strategy is incomplete, or does not align with the realities of a company's supply chain?

Answers on page 234.

References

International Chamber of Commerce/BASCAP (2011) Estimating the Global Economic and Social Impacts of Counterfeiting and Piracy 2011, ICC [Online] https://iccwbo.org/publication/estimating-global-economic-social-impacts-counterfeiting-piracy-2011/ (archived at https://perma.cc/DT87-U7UT)

U.S. Customs and Border Protection, Intellectual Property Rights: Fiscal Year 2017 Seizure Statistics

International AntiCounterfeiting Coalition (IACC) (2017) [accessed 5 July 2019] Counterfeiting Statistics: Counterfeiting Adds up, *IACC* [Online] https://www.iacc.org/resources/about/statistics (archived at https://perma.cc/WR8R-X2KF)

10

The same but different

A comparative analysis of common reverse logistics and closed-loop supply chain issues in the UK multiple retail sector

GRAHAM HERON AND ERICA BALLENTINE

1 2 3 4

Knowledge

Participants can clearly identify the missed opportunities that can be afforded through simple adoption of earlier queuing management, and recognize the benefits that this can bring to an organization and its various actors by creating a more efficient RL/CLSC.

Action

Participants are now able to map forward flows and overlay reverse/closed-loop flows in their supply chain, so that they can clearly identify the issues at play among the various actors and the impacts of laissez faire or 'let do and mend' attitudes that are common in these systems.

Organizations are driven by activity-based cost and accounting models which drive repeatability rather than innovation. By understanding how forward flows are driven by execution, time sensitivity and high degrees of data certainty, it is possible to apply these concepts in reverse flows and closed loops to drive efficiencies and leanness, in order to address the aforementioned legislative, transport, operations, relationship management and governance issues to deliver better systems efficiencies.

Introduction and context

This case investigates the issues of complexity and efficiency in reverse flows of multiple-trip packaging systems and recyclable materials from retail units back to points of distribution. Academic literature around reverse logistics (RL) is abundant in theoretical and conceptual modelling identifying efficiencies of scale and scope. This case aims to identify practicalities, feasibility and readiness for multiple retailers to incorporate or adapt these principles of best practice. We augment this case by reviewing the combination of just-in time (JIT) and a lean philosophy within RL systems. We address whether implementation of JIT is feasible within a multi-trip system and what the possible performance implications of such an implementation might be, especially for information availability, flow and use.

A case study methodology provides a comparative analysis of two UK multiple retailers. The systems deployed by these retailers are described in relation to gaps that emerge between what may be theoretically or conceptually possible, according to the literature, and what was actually observed. We reason why these gaps might occur in a real-world setting, synthesizing the primary data with the extant literature to suggest improvements that could realistically be made to the systems observed. We conclude by suggesting how real-time data may be better employed for RL systems in order to enjoy improved operational effectiveness. Finally, through further synthesis with the literature, this case offers a set of options for improved lean reverse logistics systems and the introduction of an inclusive tripartite 'walk through' model to create action that will address system sub-optimization and drive sustainability.

Case methodology

Selection of the retailers examined was driven by a need to comprehend 'same but different' supply scenarios, whereby a comparative analysis could determine to what extent advantage, if any, is gained in the management of reverse flows that result from higher levels of vertical integration being present in Retailer A. The adoption of case study research enabled the comprehension of practices present within the daily operations of both organizations A and B, as well as understanding the perspectives of internal stakeholders (Cassell and Symon, 2004; Stake, 2000; Yin, 2003). This case presents four operational levels of analysis, these units of analysis being the small, medium and large retail units and distribution/logistics sub-units of both organizations.

A purposive sampling technique was utilized (Easterby-Smith, Thorpe and Jackson, 2015; Saunders, Lewis and Thornhill, 2009), commencing with a 'bottom-up' retail sub-unit activity, back up the supply chain to the point of distribution. The retail units studied were indicative of common store footprints, ranging from small convenience store to large supermarket. Three managers from each retailer would offer sufficient depth of perspective, and these included both logistics and warehousing managers from the distribution/logistics sub-units as they were of equal and critical importance to the case. Table 10.1 shows the themes explored during interviews.

Comparison of the case study retailers

It is common practice for multiple retailers to utilize returning vehicles (the retail backhaul) for the purpose of collecting recyclables and offloading them within a dedicated recovery area within their regional distribution centres (RDCs). Notwithstanding this, it is apparent that system differences can emerge at this distribution node and at the retail unit nodes. Industry initiatives in these areas include: improving space utilization and fuel usage,

TABLE 10.1 Themes explored during interviews

Key theme	Semi-structured question areas
Retail units as suppliers' service	• Tracking of performance and return categories, volumes and condition/suitability • Root-cause analysis of DC/driver pinch points
Composite DC colleague efficiency levels	• Tracking of performance in relation to reverse flows/ bidirectional flows • Impacts on colleague performance/task progression
Availability and visibility	• Maintain strong performance during 'plinth change-over' • The degree to which loads are amended and runs created to reflect store retrieval requests • Track returns by types/volumes/routes
Process management	• Identify causes for 'driver waiting' dock blockage, stock build-up – both clean and dirty RPC units etc • Tracking unacceptable quality/return standards by route and retail unit
Development strategies	• Relationships with recycling firms and development of KPIs through agreements and planning processes • Challenging DC planning by linking RL to colleague availability rather than agency 'top ups'

optimizing road transport, including vehicle design, engine type and fuel type, as well as developing inter-modality and the ongoing building and retrofitting of warehouse facilities to improve sustainability. In the organizational analysis between Retailers A and B, the key similarities between their distribution and fulfilment strategies include continuous 24-hour cycles to minimize stocks and maximize network efficiencies for 'in store' fulfilment, while managing access restrictions borne of unitary authorities' local transport plans.

A and B differ significantly in that there is a higher degree of vertical integration within A. The key characteristics of A and B are detailed in Tables 10.2A and 10.2B.

TABLE 10.2A Comparative summary of retailer A and retailer B

Characteristic	Retailer A (more vertically integrated)	Retailer B
Operating partner: logistics	In-house and third-party logistics partner	In-house only
Product types managed at distribution centres	• Fresh • Chilled • Ambient • Frozen	• Fresh • Chilled • Ambient • Frozen
Regional distribution centre (RDC) design	Composite: receipt, storage and handling of products occur across a range of chamber areas in the RDC, each operating under a specific temperature regime	Composite: receipt, storage and handling of products occur across a range of chamber areas in the RDC, each operating under a specific temperature regime
Composite RDCs	10+	15+
IT systems	Single overarching: several legacy systems still to be incorporated; low interrogative levels with queries being channelled through central order office	Single overarching: legacy systems are minimal; interrogative portals allow vertical and horizontal visibility
Returns protocols	Part formalized; local sortation driven by store size, on-site storage space. Returns driven by availability/vehicle type/local transport access conditions	Part formalized; local sortation driven by store size, on-site storage space. Returns driven by availability/vehicle type/local transport access conditions
Throughput peak	Thursday	Friday

(continued)

TABLE 10.2A (Continued)

Characteristic	Retailer A (more vertically integrated)	Retailer B
Picking regime process	Pick to store: single or multiple store orders picked in a logical sequence, gradually accumulating and aggregating products in multiple-trip packaging systems for wave delivery patterns	Pick to store: single or multiple store orders picked in a logical sequence, gradually accumulating and aggregating products in multiple-trip packaging systems for wave delivery patterns
Recycling strategy	Near: relationships with recycling companies located close to RDCs	Market driven: end point and location unimportant

TABLE 10.2B Continuous supply and distribution summary based upon averages of Retailers A & B excluding extraordinary peak demand

Post-order lead-time (hours)	Fast-moving goods	Slow-moving goods	Beers, wines, spirits	Produce	Temperature controlled
Supplier deliveries to composite RDCs	Typically 0.5 to 4.5 days	Typically 4 to 8 days	Typically 0.5 to 4.5 days for beers and spirits. Wine up to 16 weeks	Dependent upon type, typically 0.5 to 4.5 days	Typically 1.5 to 4.5 days. Plus time-sensitive direct store deliveries (milk etc)
Composite RDCs' receipt, store/pick and delivery to store targets	6 to 24 hours	48 hours	12 to 36 hours	6 to 24 hours	6 to 24 hours, withdirect store deliveries driven by EDI targeted at 4 to 18 hours

Case findings

Process dynamics

On arrival at the RDC, the packaging systems, RPCs, full roll cages and empty roll cages are collected at a central point for deconsolidation/first stage disposition, commonly referred to across the sector as 'De-Kit' areas.

Here, packaging systems, RPCs and recyclables are sorted and recyclables are baled, while packaging systems/reusable containers typified by roll cages and crates are sorted; some types are also cleaned before being redistributed to support forward flow operations. Differing levels of sortation and sortation quality occur depending upon the size of the retail unit, with larger units baling recyclables and smaller units storing recyclables in roll cages.

Differences of opinion emerged between DC and retail interviewees. The retail level considered the quality of baling and sortation to be of low priority, having no relevance to performance evaluation metrics, whereas at DC level it is considered a key process, although this is not reflected in the forward-facing strategy of the DCs despite the necessity of retrieving reusable systems equipment and reducing driver hours, both critical to store replenishment activities.

Low priority being given to return flows from retail units relating to sortation, quality, quantity and integrity of materials returning to the DCs is twofold in impact. First, it is difficult to plan effective deconsolidation as varying levels of sortation are present but may also change on a daily and/or route basis. Further, this lack of RL management is also evident in the analysis of interactions between the DCs and recycling companies, more so with Retailer A, where the main focus is reducing moisture penetration in card bales and identification of contaminated plastic bales. This has led to opportunistic practices by recyclers, for example recyclers declining payment for, but continuing to process, contaminated bales (plastic bales with evidence of cardboard contained within them) on an individual bale-by-bale basis. Where short-term improvements in bale quality emerged, recyclers then started to decline payment for entire loads if just one contaminated bale was found. Such opportunistic behaviour overlooks vested 'win–win' sustainable relationships and would be quite unthinkable in forward flows.

Characteristics of materials acquired for upstream disposition

Multi-trip systems and packaging waste differ from unit to unit; waste and returns were influenced exclusively by replenishment activities. Common to both retailers is the apparent limited or lack of control at the retail level with regard to deciding the amount of packaging systems and recyclable materials to be returned, as this is dependent on available vehicle capacity.

Capacity

There are two main capacity issues common to both A and B. Storage capacity by design is intentionally limited at retail units in order to drive stock replenishment and inventory throughput. This naturally leads to limited storage space for returns, resulting in reverse flow materials commonly being stored outside and thus impacting paper and board quality. The other capacity issue common to both is related to excess capacity at the DC baler, which is not optimized as flow velocity and volumes are dictated by driver availability, dock availability and staff availability. Consequently, this also leads to inefficiencies, such as excessive 'slack' in the system at certain times of day, queues at other times, and a degree of empty running across the network. Holistically this creates an unbalanced network, whereby DC capacity is both greater than the total demand placed upon it, and significantly impacted by the peculiarities of forward- flow optimization.

Dynamics of ownership and capabilities

Prevailing process conditions at both A and B's retail units and DCs are characterized by task/time orientation; this stifles dynamic task orientation in support of RL and can be clearly linked to the low priority of reverse flows at the retail level. At DC level, lack of flexibility to support dynamic responses to RL peaks can be clearly evidenced through regular usage of agency staff within 'De-Kit' areas.

Inhibiting factors and potential system improvements

The principal issue that emerges for enhanced RL efficiencies in a leaner system is related to cost control in relation to duplication of vehicle movements. Other issues recorded as potential barriers included:

- internal focus on the day-to-day activities;
- lack of support for existing projects;
- upstream RL not seen as a priority in servicing customer-facing flows;
- limited internal collaborations, lack of holistic insight and poor legacy management/swift 'post-project death' where RL initiatives have been trialled;

TABLE 10.3 Summary of inhibiting factors and system potential

Inhibiting factors	System potential
Capacity imbalance at DC	Reduction in queuing leading to increased availability of fleet and drivers for forward flows
Storage at retail units	Increased system visibility
Lack of ownership and attitudinal concerns	Removal of constraints/imbalances at the DC
Underutilized IT infrastructure	Improved communications for data management, directives compliance and recycling collaborations
Communication channels	Acculturation of system from current 'afterthought' to a core function
Local government access/time restrictions	Prompts focus and analysis of fleet profiles and metrics

- reactions to reverse flows rather than generation of simple, extensible data to allow anticipation to influence demand planning and collaborations;
- non-sustainable and opportunistic behaviours by recyclers.

Table 10.3 summarizes inhibiting factors and system potential.

Case discussion and actions

Measuring success factors

As with forward flows, the basic requirements to have the right materials in the right places at the right time are compelling factors for network efficiency. Any RL system improvement allowing for efficacious development needs to commence with the retail unit as supplier. This issue can be considered as a compelling need for supplier development and supplier relationship management. The overriding need to ensure customer satisfaction means that there remains a primarily forward focus on movement, whereby RL remains as non-value-adding from the retail perspective. Nevertheless, this attitudinally driven behaviour and mindset at the retail unit end could be considered as 'low-hanging fruit' and an easily attained win within the paradigm of the theory of constraints (Mabin and Balderstone, 2003).

Imbalances between staff availability and dedicated tasks at DCs hinder system change, with teams needing to react rather than proactively manage both forward and reverse flows. This is a shorter-term attitudinal/operational

TABLE 10.4 Six step conceptual road map for measuring success

Conceptual road map for RL increased efficiencies, internal and external collaborations	
Prerequisites: Agreed ownership, common XML data standards, agreed structures, cross-functional teams	
Step 1	Tripartite 'walk through' of common problems in the current systems and agreement on goals
Step 2	Education programme and development of common-access extensible data
Step 3	Pilot programme to test and embed KPIs and agree common performance criteria
Step 4	Root-cause analysis of failures and corrective actions similar to CPFR protocols
Step 5	Continuous improvement cycles and steady rollout underpinned by meaningful engagement and hybridized Kaizen methodology
Step 6	Collaborations become embedded, longer-term strategic tools, leading to vested and sustainable 'win–win' collaborative relationships

constraint rather than a longer-term operational reality. To this end, this case introduces a conceptual road map, based upon the prioritization of issues emerging from the primary data analysis to drive collaboration between supply partners from retail, logistics and DC operations sub-units, presented in Table 10.4.

Networks

Access to retail units for planned retrieval beyond simultaneous drop-off and pick-up is currently restricted by both local authority time and access restrictions imposed on some of the retail units. This issue is only relevant to smaller retail units (in urban and residential areas) and makes assumptions around current fleet type/fleet availability. Nonetheless, it negatively affects both the retail unit as supplier in its ability to feed the system as well as other critical factors such as network design and supplier delivery timing, as local conditions create levels of unconditional inflexibility within an existing network and fleet. While there are differences in provision of logistics service ownership between A and B, there are prevailing characteristics that can act as facilitators in each of the current networks; these include current empty running and excess capacity at certain times of the day.

The networks and systems investigated in this case are internal, part of the same organizations, enabling collaboration between retail units and DCs driving system viability. This leaves DCs in an operating environment where they must anticipate retail unit RL demand and manage that demand by behaving with a degree of flexibility, albeit in a closed network system.

The role of supporting elements

Centralized communications prevalent within both systems work against direct articulation between retail units and DCs. However, this indicates that the essential IT infrastructure is present in both organizations but is not currently utilized for RL. In considering the possibility to 'do more with less', current information systems can support both RL development in the short term and JIT-RL practices in the longer term, providing efficiency benefits without an incremental escalation in current node and network complexity.

There are obvious lessons to be learnt from the boom in online retail and the challenges successfully overcome by these organizations and third-party logistics service providers. An example of this is given anecdotally by online fashion retailer ASOS, who report a return rate of 56 per cent of downstream being returned by customers, with all returns requiring central collation, 100 per cent inspection, repacking, relabelling and reassigning to a central stock control system. Our investigation revealed that each retail unit has the ability to 'write on' and 'write off' stock at store level, thus it would seem remiss not to simply identify empty packaging systems and recyclable wastes as types of stock with a zero value stock keeping unit (SKU) descriptor but a variable SKU component value. Each retail unit would thus create dynamic visibility for DCs and vertically integrated suppliers within systems, allowing for dynamic planning to supplement stable material flows back to DCs as well as providing valuable information, informing disposition strategy and execution further on in the RL supply chain.

Case consequences, creating actions and options

Separate JIT systems flowing forwards and backwards utilizing the same vehicle and driver pool would appear to contradict two of the seven classic *muda* wastes: unnecessary movement and waiting. Running two JIT systems can largely remove pick-up requirements in forward flows, significantly shortening delivery times and increasing dock availability while reducing turnaround/route fulfilment times and increasing route planning options in an integrative system, allowing for increases in RL efficiency pursuant to forward flows. Further, the use of real-time data on types and volumes of recyclables at retail units would in turn allow for load maximization and levelling of process capacity for RL flows into the DCs, ensuring more efficient employment of DC and driver staff. Medium- to longer-term benefits

TABLE 10.5 Lean RL model options

Proposed model options		
Common to all three will be the ability to generate and share real-time data/create 'reverse flows as stock' at retail unit level		
Option 1	**Option 2**	**Option 3**
In-house development of JIT/ Little JIT to address system inefficiencies/traffic and DC operations/sub-optimization, which will allow for greater availability, better management and sight of multiple-trip food packaging systems, other RPCs and secondary/tertiary packaging	Development of a collaborative system that places reverse-flow management in the hands of a 3PL, thus freeing up forward-flow fleet for increased factory gating etc, benefiting fleet reductions/re-profiling. Third party to manage retail unit – DC communications for reverse flows	A fully embedded 3PL organization managing reverse flows, dedicated DC areas, dedicated dock availability, retail unit communications, cleaning, sortation, placement decisions, recycler contractor management, scheme compliances and value generation

potentially extend to re-profiling vehicle fleets (size and type) and a reduction in DC operational running costs (ie agency staff), while increasing throughput (Table 10.5).

Conclusions

This case assesses the feasibility of increasing RL efficiencies to benefit positioning of packaging systems and recyclable materials. Our analysis of the RL systems prevailing in retailers A and B reveal commonality in 'same but different' network systems. While no definitive conclusions are stated for either A or B in relation to their current systems, it is beyond doubt that there are sufficient indicators of RL system sub-optimization to act as a barometer for change through RL system adaptation.

The case does not suggest that wholesale investment is required, since there is evidence of excess capacity in the networks. RL systems are borne of historical development of store replenishment, in which retailers' reuse and recycling practices are present, formalized but informally managed. Both A's and B's systems lend themselves to increased RL efficiency through facilitating IT infrastructure elements already embedded across operations to generate and mine extensible RL-relevant data from forward flows.

Increased accountability of materials flowing back up the supply chain can also address opportunistic behaviours; for example, it is possible for A and B to develop a more sustainable, integrated RL system where queue management begins at retail units, not at often congested DCs.

This case reveals a low priority of packaging system/recyclable materials/ RPC ownership regardless of retail unit size or concerns over 'dead hauling' common across both retailers. Notwithstanding these issues, and critical to the case, there is a consistent throughput and a great degree of commonality in DC fulfilment practices, indicating the predictable volume and low combinatorial complexity typical of 'lean' flows and JIT. What is missing from both is locally generated and extensible exported/mined data which would reposition queue management, occurring earlier and more efficiently (Figure 10.1).

Under traditional lean paradigms, demand generates processing, which provokes supply to meet demand. This stands counter to the RL systems revealed here, in which capacity imbalances exist and outstrip supply, amassing multi-trip packaging systems leading to stockpiles in the wrong place at the wrong time.

Revealing RL sub-optimization, barriers to increasing RL efficiency and potential benefits of lean/JIT-type RL system adaptation, this case indicates that extensive and sweeping changes to current network structures are not always required. Alternative overarching systems and strategies can be developed to allow better decisions utilizing existing infrastructures.

Alternatively, an independent third-party system provides a potentially complementary strategy (refer to Table 10.5) if the 'low-hanging fruit'

FIGURE 10.1 Alternative queuing system

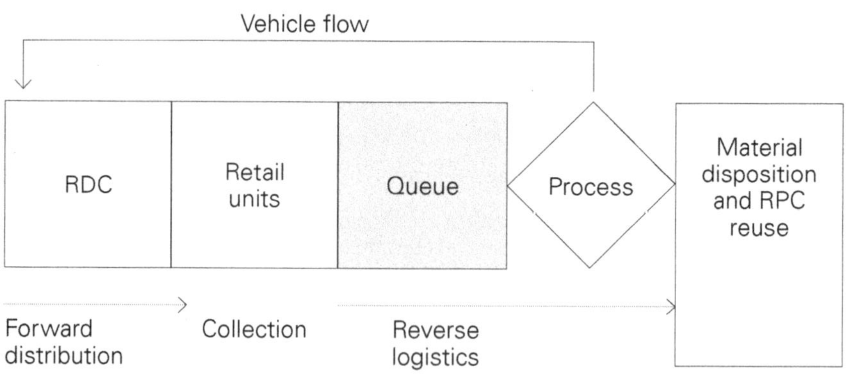

prevail, or when there is already a degree of third-party integration in logistics and DC activity. This would allow either retailer to continue to focus on forward flows, while inviting third-party logistics providers to build value into RL systems. Forward distribution's transport and warehousing operations are highly visible parts of the multiple retailer supply chain, key to delivering system efficiencies for multiple retailers. Therefore, in this regard it is lackadaisical not to investigate areas of RL optimization to extract further value from these networks.

We acknowledge that this case is not beyond circumspection in its relatively narrow analysis of two multiple retailers in a geographically defined area of the UK. However, the method of analysis lends itself favourably to creating improvement actions and generalizable applicability to other sectors where RL flows are relatively deterministic and consistent. Such possible future research applications could be reasonably tested among other retailers, food service organizations and third-party logistics providers managing forward and reverse flows. We believe that this novel comparative analysis case advances RL system comprehension beyond conceptual mathematical models, serving to stimulate further actions and investigations into the operational management of RL systems, to the point where RL is an efficient, reciprocal phase in a circular logistics system where last-mile logistics criteria can prompt mimicking in first-mile recovery decisions.

Discussion points

1. Which of these knowledge insights are applicable to you?
2. Which learnings from the past discussed in this action insight have future implications?
3. What action could be taken from utilizing this knowledge by you personally or by an organization?

QUESTIONS

1. *Priorities and strategies:* The research identifies several barriers as well as opportunities. How would you prioritise these barriers and address them in the short, medium and long term?
2. *Choice:* The three models proposed can be seen as options in relation to complex adaptive systems. As such, overall complexity results from all of the inter-relationships, inter-actions and inter-connectivities of elements within

a system and between a system and its different environments. What do you think that In mapping out the systems that this case researched can you identify where more complexity of less complexity may benefit organisational efficiencies?

3 *Sustainability.* The research in this chapter presents a unique and novel approach to the application of JIT systems, not only showing that it is possible in operational contexts, but also that JITRL systems may offer significant benefits beyond these organizations, to distribution networks in operations within a similar environment to that of these organisations ie relatively high volumes of demand certainty and relatively low complexity of the materials under management. With these factors in mind, which of the proposed models would you adopt, and why? How would this choice be influenced by sustainability?

4 *Decision.* Based on the research in this chapter and your wider experience / organisational knowledge, which option would you choose?

Answers on page 235.

References

Cassell, C and Symon, G (2004) *Essential Guide to Qualitative Methods in Organizational Research*, SAGE, Thousand Oaks, CA

Easterby-Smith, M, Thorpe, R and Jackson, P R (2015) *Management and Business Research*, SAGE, Thousand Oaks, CA

Mabin, V J and Balderstone, S J (2003) The performance of the theory of constraints methodology: analysis and discussion of successful TOC applications, *International Journal of Operations and Production Management*, **23** (6), pp 568–95

Saunders, M, Lewis, P and Thornhill, A (2009) *Research Methods for Business Students*, 5th edn, Prentice Hall, New York

Stake, R E (2000). Qualitative case studies, *The Sage Handbook of Qualitative Research*, 2nd edn, ed N K Denzin and Y S Lincoln, SAGE, Thousand Oaks, CA

Yin, R K (2003) *Case Study Research: Design and methods*, 3rd edn, SAGE, Thousand Oaks, CA

11

Supply chain disruption

Ad omnia paratus: prepared for anything

STEVE O'SULLIVAN

(1) (2) (3) (4)

Knowledge

The complexity of supply chain management has been compounded by globalization along the dimensions of replenishment, time and distance (Christopher and Towill, 2002), and vulnerabilities to disruptions have increased as supply chains 'become more lengthy and complex due to globalization and vertical integrations' (Rajesh and Rao, 2015), forces that are accelerating 'beyond our ability to adapt', together with technology advancements and climate change (Friedman, 2016). This has led to a volatile operating environment, 'fraught with greater demand uncertainty, higher risk, and increasing competitive intensity' (Roh *et al*, 2014), and 'increasingly, organizations are finding themselves at the center of un-plannable events that interrupt and threaten their global supply chains' (Gattorna, 2015).

Such disruptions can include attacks from purposeful agents, escalating natural events, uncertain customer demand, quality issues, transportation delays, poor supplier performance, equipment malfunctions, inventory and capacity issues, technology breakdowns, increasing competitive intensity, and human-centred issues from strikes to fraud (Kleindorfer and Saad, 2005; Roh *et al*, 2014; Roberta Pereira, Christopher and Lago Da Silva, 2014). These result in severe stock and operating underperformance and should be a high priority for senior management and shareholders (Kleindorfer and Saad, 2005), 'with costs and other consequences even more challenging than terrorist acts, as they have a greater cumulative effect over time' (Roberta Pereira *et al*, 2014) and have a disproportionate effect on demand (Sheffi, 2001). We have come to understand that disruptions can come from practically any source and appear unexpectedly over the horizon like *Exocets*. However, I have dug deeper than this, and have come to the conclusion that *policy*, be it at government (and in this case) military or business levels, is the underlying source of disruption to contemporary supply chains. If this insight is true, it implies that human behaviour at all levels and locations along supply chains has become distorted through the cultures embedded in the guilty organizations. And one of the biggest influences on the formation of internal culture is organization design, the structure that we put people to work in.

Actions

My research makes little or no distinction between the type of organization caught up in supply chain disruptions, be it business, military or humanitarian. While acknowledging that each of these spheres can learn lessons from each other, I focus on the common cause, people in organizations making policy, consciously or unthinkingly, that in effect sets up conditions for a major or minor disruption to take place. If we can understand how to make better policy in the future, cognizant of the potential impacts on the supply chains which are omnipresent in our lives, then the effort and corresponding cost of retrieval will reduce significantly, which is a good thing in an operating environment already punctuated with high levels of volatility.

The first action we must take is to broaden supply chain management to an integrated perspective across top management teams so that we are involved in the strategic formulation and renewal process. A second action, *in the interim*, engaging in the process of dynamic organization to supply chain strategic alignment, is the mechanism to reduce the gap of pain in response to supply chain disruptions. Enablers include supply chain management (SCM) education of top management teams, use of SCM data and metrics, SCM simulations to remove emotion, and use of soft skills such as encouraging, coaxing, cajoling and persisting.

Introduction

This chapter introduces empirical research to demonstrate that supply chain disruption is not confined to the external taxonomy of crises, disasters and breakdowns, but is sourced from internal strategic forces, the mitigation of which *must be* alignment of organization and supply chain goals. Two cases are explored. In the first section, Ireland's role in the Nordic Battle Group is contextualized through historical reference, prior to an examination of how the logistics branch operationalized a service level agreement, both a governmental and senior management directive, to overcome significant challenges leading up to and during deployment. The second section concerns the United Nations Interim Force in Lebanon. Commandant (Major) Robert Moriarty, Collins Barracks (Cork), articulated the supply chain disruption that he encountered and resolved, as officer in charge of logistics of both missions.

Nordic Battle Group: historical context

The Nordic location of Finlandia Hall in Helsinki during the summer of 1975 appropriately sets the scene for Ireland's contribution to the pursuit of global security. Attended by then Prime Minister Liam Cosgrave, the Conference on Security and Co-operation in Europe resulted in the signing of the non-binding Helsinki Accords aimed at reducing tensions between the Communist bloc and the West. European Union members subsequently signed the Helsinki Headline Goal 1999 in accordance with the Common Security and Defence Policy, which created a Helsinki Force Catalogue to enable the completion of so-called Petersberg Tasks (Petersberg Declaration 1992). These included humanitarian and rescue, peacekeeping and crisis management tasks. Primarily, it was considered that it took too long to raise a United Nations reactionary force to deal with global disruptions and crises, and from this, an EU Battlegroup was established, now comprising 18 sub-groups of small, independent, self-sufficient, rapid-response units capable of deployment in a theatre of operation.

One such unit is the Nordic Battle Group (NBG), which has been active since 2008 and has a force of 2,500 troops. NBG members include Sweden, Finland, Norway (despite non-EU membership), Republic of Ireland, Estonia, Latvia and Lithuania. This is not a permanent unit, rather it is mobilized on a rotational basis and was headquartered in Enköping, Sweden, for NBG 2015-1, the focus of this study. A modular organization with a mechanized infantry battalion is at the core of the unit, but since 2011 a framework has existed for the integration of additional resources ranging from artillery, air defence, and intelligence, to additional logistical support. The Republic of Ireland, with the second largest troop count behind Sweden, is the eyes and ears of the Battlegroup, providing an ISTAR component: intelligence, surveillance, target acquisition and reconnaissance. However, another vital Irish element has been the afore-mentioned logistical support, the execution of which has met with and overcome many challenges, both strategic and tactical.

NBG: Irish Defence Forces rotation

The Irish Defence Forces operational rotation of the NBG (NBG 2015-1) spanned 18 months, with training taking place between January and December 2014, before a six-month 72-hour on-call period from January to June 2015, followed by the German Battlegroup who stood-to for the next six months, followed by the British Battlegroup in 2016, and so forth. From an Irish perspective, the mission statement, a memorandum of understanding (MOU) signed by the Deputy Chief of Staff (D-COS) of the Irish Defence Forces, mandated the Director of Logistics of the Irish Defence Forces HQ in McKee Barracks, Dublin, to have the capability to set up a theatre of operation anywhere in the world within a 72-hour notice period from its base in Collins Barracks, Cork.

To develop this capability, an expeditionary logistics concept was initiated to integrate with the Swedish Armed Forces and set up within a greenfield site in Skillingaryd on a one-month deployment. This concept derived from the commanding officer for this operation, Lieutenant Colonel Paul Carey, who issued a commander's intent of operation to Commandant Robert Moriarty to lead tactical deployment, supported by Commandant James Hourigan at strategic procurement level. This outlined the purpose, method and end state of the mission. Finalizing the method was subject to constant, and at times innovative, group training and integration, known also as training, tactical and procedures. The MOU adopted a non-traditional all-arms approach that facilitated cross-organizational support to the battle group, such as knowledge and equipment sharing.

Commandant Moriarty was issued with Armaments and Equipment (AAE) and CS-41 documents that outlined the available resources to meet the mission objectives, together with the empowerment, through D-COS support, to internally 're-distribute' equipment as needed. Supply, sustain and maintain were the tenets applied to developing a self-sufficient unit of excellence, food and hygiene being at the forefront of considerations, using a front-load policy that meant positioning all personnel and equipment in Sweden at the start of the operation. By contrast, militaries such as Sweden used a push policy, whereby strategic air support was used to sustain units as needed. Future deployment would necessitate integration with the Swedish push policy as there are limitations to front loading. The AAE and CS-41 made certain provisions from which certain challenges arose within a broad categorization of 'constraints, restrictions, freedoms':

- Fifty-one personnel, including four officers, medical and signals (communication) detachments, three engineers, three ordnances to maintain equipment such as weapons (valued at €1.6 million) and catering systems, and transportation, which included two DAF 6 × 6 trucks, each with two drivers.
- Nineteen containers (660 CBM and 164,400kg, with a combined value of €3.8 million), carried tents on two units, 3,000 pack rations within a 20' reefer (refrigerated shipping container), capable of sustaining the brigade for 20 days in a remote environment as a form of redundancy, dry goods which complemented the Irish policy of purchasing fresh produce from the local community, fuel pod, ammunition, pyrotechnics, which needed to be in a separate container and thereby not completely utilized, weapons systems, together with dangerous goods certificates, and generators.
- Owing to the front-load policy and for security reasons, the Irish moved ammunition, baggage, a fuel pod, generators, weapons and communications to the brigade assembly point in Skillingaryd, Sweden, in advance of the exercise. This included a C2 container housing the Tactical Operations Centre which became the epicentre of the site from which all other elements developed.

The main strategy, or NBG logistical concept, was to conduct operations, regardless of environment, from 30 to 120 days, characterized by a high level of flexibility, modularity and endurance. A statement of requirement provisioned the use of host nation support, contractor support to operations, third-party logistic support and other multinational (including unconventional) solutions to minimize challenges. Supply chain disruptions are contextual and environment specific, and despite the availability of an After-Action Review from a previous exercise (NBG 2011), which was certainly beneficial, a number of challenges arose at various stages of operational preparations.

For example, in advance of the exercise in August 2014, Commandant Moriarty attended a SOR (statement of requirement) coordination conference in Sweden and discovered that an MOU signed between the Irish and Swedish governments did not legislate for electricity maintenance, which it was assumed (as with standard deployment policy) would be provided by the Swedish forces. The Defence Forces (DF) cannot have more than 850 troops overseas at any one time, and a subset of the SOR, a Raise and Concentration Order, did not permit additional electricians and so on. The Irish needed a solution. One option was to secure site generators for the exercise, but the challenge was that these were all deployed on other missions, and had to be transported in pairs, each one in a 20' container, necessitating an unplanned additional sealift with an engineering detachment. Instead, an improvisation was made to transport smaller generators and lighting systems within the allocated 19 containers on the manifest.

The mission readiness exercise, which commenced in June 2014, giving clearance to build all systems, identified further challenges. An example in the corporate world would be a pilot product launch. An initial problem concerned the newly purchased HP 508 tents, which were not fit for purpose owing to the fact that they were not previously integrated into the DF, and this resulted in damage (note: visualize substantial marquees housing a large contingent of troops, kitchen, dining hall, sleeping quarters and so on, hence their criticality). While the tents were erected through power from vehicles, there were three topside struts that needed to be secured manually and the troops simply could not reach these without potential injury. Therefore, A-frame ladders were added to the manifest and these were placed neatly to the rear of the tent racking systems during transportation to Sweden.

These systems were themselves not without challenges, in particular with regard to optimization of container space, for which an outsourced solution was sought. Standard state procurement legislates the tendering of three RFQs (requests for quotation) to vendors. Timeframe was a key component to NBG tenders, coupled with the vendor listening to very specific needs. Certain suppliers offered generic storage units for the transport of tents, whereas the successful company invested time and resources into designing a bespoke racking system with significantly improved utilization. The additional engineering cost of this was offset by:

- Additional space to take an armoured vehicle, thereby increasing troop safety.
- One less (soft-skin) truck, meaning one less driver, enabling one additional specialist to support the maintenance of the site. In addition, one less 'soft-skin' means less protection needed from a security perspective.

- One less container on a ship or aircraft, meaning less weight, resulting in greater fuel efficiency, and by default, incremental cost savings on subsequent DF missions.
- Maximum return for the taxpayer by co-coordinating procurement, engineering and operations. Commandant Moriarty was particularly proud of this triangular alignment.

Other adjustments to the manifest were the inclusion of tent repair kits and clip flooring to prevent floor damage. The tents simply were not soldier-proof and needed specialist assembly. Generators for the mission were also found to be temperamental, but this was resolved through specialist training and maintenance. The DF were burning 60 litres of fuel per day per heating system (VAM), a problem for both cold and hot climates, twice as much as the Swedes, who used built-in thermostats and lagging systems, which not only reduced fuel usage but also evenly distributed heat throughout the tents. This was identified as a need after the mission but did not materialize during MRE (mission readiness exercise). Food portion sizes and storage of plates was resolved by securing stackable and sectioned prison service plates.

The Raise and Concentration Order also did not provide for cooks, and it was recognized that the field kitchen should be part of exercise/certification training in Ireland. Both the provision of a pot wash facility (hygiene being so critical), since procured as part of the capability development of the NBG, and the leasing of local sanitation equipment (dropped on site) were also identified. In addition, ordnance technicians needed to be co-located with the field kitchen in order to maintain the VAMs. In terms of information systems, the Tactical Operations Centre enabled increased situational awareness, range of operation and capabilities when delivering orders, a significant increase in data transfer rate, and the provision of live streaming. However, the satellite communications link was intermittent, and additional equipment was needed, such as batteries, laptops and phones. Constant training in all communication and information systems (CIS) was essential.

Movement of vehicles also presented challenges and it was immediately evident that a low- loader would be extremely beneficial for future rotations. Bulk collection was arranged for all MOWAGs (armoured military vehicles) and six Nissans, which resulted in significant time and labour savings. By contrast, the collection of five infantry LTAVs (light tactical vehicles) was not as coordinated, owing to other mission needs, and this caused minor delays. This strategy was later adopted for the transfer of vehicles to the German BG. Another consideration was the training of drivers and fitters to enable licences and qualifications in fuel pod operation and LTAV/MOWAG maintenance. In the absence of military aircraft, a 3PL (third-party logistics) ocean freight solution was needed.

Equipment was loaded at Ringaskiddy Port using LIFO (last in first out), bound for Halmstad Port in Sweden. The loading concept of choice was RO-RO (roll on/roll off; 8-hour operation) but LO-LO (lift on/lift off; 20-hour operation) was the procured system owing to 3PL availability and sailing schedules. This presented another immediate challenge in that it would have required two drivers moving four containers at a time from Halmstad to the brigade assembly point 141km away in Skillingaryd. Commandant James Hourigan expertly negotiated with the Swedish forces and secured their assistance to move 13 of the Irish containers using seven of their trucks. Another challenge was that these movements necessitated weapons declarations and thereby the availability of specialist weapons inspectors at specific points along the route to Sweden. This needed to be factored into the transit time. Finally, there were planning considerations such as parking space for 20 containers, stores requirement for 660 cubic metres, and storage bays for the MOWAG and LTAV fleet, including a provision for trickle charging.

United Nations Interim Force in Lebanon

An Israeli-Palestinian conflict from 1968 to 1977, in which the Palestine Liberation Organization (PLO), strengthened by 3,000 returning militants from the Jordanian civil war, established a quasi-state in southern Lebanon, a Lebanese civil war (1975–1990) between the Maronite Christians and Druze, and Muslims, and an Israeli bombing in November 1977, killing 70 mainly Lebanese, provide a simplistic background to the tensions that led to the Irish Defence Forces' presence in this region. In March 1978, Khalil Ibrahim al-Wazir, founder of the nationalist party Fatah, and an aide of PLO Chairman Yasser Arafat, planned to take control of a hotel in Tel Aviv and hold hostages in exchange for Palestinian prisoners in Israel, and also to disrupt Israeli-Egyptian peace talks between Menachem Begin (Israeli Prime Minister) and Anwar Sadat (Egyptian President). Fatah did not reach the hotel because of a navigation issue, and instead hijacked a bus, having first murdered an American tourist on a nearby beach, and 38 Israeli civilians were subsequently killed in what was named the coastal road massacre. The response was operation Litani, an invasion of south Lebanon by the Israeli Defence Forces, and the death of 2,000 Lebanese and Palestinians.

United Nations Interim Force in Lebanon (UNIFIL) was immediately established to supervise the withdrawal of Israeli forces and restore peace and security to the area. The Irish Defence Forces had a continuous infantry battalion in Tibnin on a six-month rotation from May 1978 to November 2001, patrolling an area of approximately 100 square kilometres. A mobile mechanized infantry company returned on 31 October 2006 for 12 months alongside a Finnish engineering company as part of a joint Irish-Finnish battalion. A mechanized infantry battalion of 440 personnel again deployed in June 2011, manning two posts along the Blue Line, a border demarcation between Lebanon and Israel established by the United Nations on 7 June 2000. The unit was equipped with MOWAG Piranha III APCs (armoured personnel carriers), Light Tactical Armoured Vehicles (GR32), heavy machine guns, anti-tank guns and Javelin missiles, heavy and medium mortars, and reconnaissance surveillance equipment. In November 2013, the DF changed operations to a 336-personnel 'high visibility, low profile' infantry group.

Together with a contingent from Finland and a platoon of 38 Estonian soldiers, they form(ed) IRISHFINBATT based at UNP 2-45 in UNIFIL Sector West (Irish Defence Forces, 2018). This sector is also supported by Ghanaian, Italian, Korean and Malaysian battalions. The east sector consists of Indian, Indonesian, Nepalese and Spanish battalions. Seven Brazilian naval vessels provide a maritime task force, and the total mission strength is 10,490 uniformed troops. Ireland is the largest per capita troop contributor (Lawrence *et al*, 2016). On 1 November 2017, Commandant Robert Moriarty deployed for six months. With four decades of peace support operations, you would assume a degree of internal stability to this current mission, and that the only supply chain disruption would come from the external forces of Hamas, Hizbullah, Fatah, Israel or Syria. Not so in this case. In December, the Finland mandate expired (this was renewed annually) and they withdrew from the mission. This came as a complete surprise – a sudden unplannable change.

Both forces have had a history of strong collaboration since the establishment of UNIFIL and developed joint operating capability through regular overseas pre-deployment training, alternating between Irish and Finnish installations, and of course through active duty together. Each quarter they formally held joint meetings at national headquarters (J-level) in the format of a bilateral military coordination group. In these meetings, issues reported by battalion staff (S-level) from the area of operation (AO) were resolved. It could never have been envisaged at an operations level that such a harmonized partnership would not continue. This significant disruption presented two major challenges to the mission:

- Loss of serious operating capability:
  - A mechanized company of 130 Finnish personnel, including an integrated Estonian platoon of 38 soldiers. This provided a manoeuvring element that conveyed presence in the AO.
  - Fifteen-tonne APC fleet of 11 vehicles, a critical capability in the event of threat levels increasing, weapons systems (including ammunition and storage) and ancillary equipment.
  - Infrastructure, barrack services, welfare facilities to keep up morale, and a SEPURA communications system with 99% coverage of the AO.
- Force protection had to be maintained:
  - Security could not be compromised and in the immediate aftermath of the Finland withdrawal, the DF troops had to work twice as hard to fill the void within significant budgetary restrictions.
  - A further impediment was that a major refurbishment programme was in progress to send the DF fleet of MOWAGs from the previous six-month rotation to Switzerland.
  - The Finnish fleet of APCs needed to be replaced with utility vehicles (SUVs) that now became mission critical but did not have the same capability. This put significant strain on mechanical fitters to keep these vehicles operational and there was a much greater demand on spare parts. Further challenges included water and NATO-mandated diesel, a fuel that is restricted in Lebanon, and diesel engine parts are consequently difficult to source. Sixty thousand litres of water are used daily, and SUVs that cannot have water access will not function. Two water trucks are used, each drawing 10,000 litres, and so the DF lifts 20,000 litres three times per day.
  - Fleets are positioned as contingent owned equipment under a United Nations wet- lease. The United Nations in turn perform quarterly checks of all vehicles and reimburse annually.

'Outputs simply could not fall' and fall they did not. In particular, the Finland withdrawal of the mechanized company, APC fleet, weapons systems and other ancillary equipment potentially had the most direct impact on operations. Therefore, to assess the gravity of the situation, an analysis system taught in the DF military college and known as the military decision-making process (MDMP) was initiated, involving the operations officer (S3) and the logistics officer (S4). According to Comdt Moriarty (S4), 'this is a thought process that we apply when presented with planning issues and can take several hours, it can be laborious and time consuming, but it ensures that no areas are missed'. In terms of strategic alignment and response to supply chain disruption, this process is a lesson for all domains in our profession. This analysis (including here, Comdt Moriarty comments and some MDMP actuals) considers:

- *What is your higher commander's intent?* In this context, the intent (also called the factor) stated that Finland would not renew its current MOU, indicating that it would withdraw significant quantities of assets to Finland and UNP 9-1 (another deployment) but was prepared to leave some infrastructure in UNP 2-45 (DF post in Lebanon) for sale or lease to the DF. Comdt Moriarty (S4) was requested to conduct analysis of FINCON (Finland contingent) equipment and the implications of its withdrawal, and to provide costing to national headquarters (J4). The deduced disruption was that the withdrawal of FINCON would mean a reduction of one-third of IRISHFINBATT operating capability. Mitigation of this reduction was an examination of the specific shortfall in equipment and the means by which Ireland needed to increase its contribution, or alternatively if it required a new strategic partner. Comdt Moriarty was the main effort in this task, a task and purpose that needed to be achieved. Success was dependent on obtaining a costed inventory of FINCON equipment to be withdrawn and analyses of the impact of its withdrawal to IRCON (Irish contingent). All information obtained at the tactical level was to be forwarded to the strategic (J4) level in order to inform the strategic decision-making process.
- *What are your specific tasks to achieve?* The main (superior officer-issued) task was for S4 to conduct analyses of the impact on IRCON of the FINCON withdrawal. This required clarification from higher headquarters (but in other contexts and cases could also be directed at subordinate staff) on whether Ireland's intent was to move to full battalion strength or whether a new strategic-level partner was to be sought. Planning guidance (PG) tasked the operations officer (S3) to advise the S4 on the operational imperatives of such a withdrawal, with emphasis on combat support requirements (namely APCs) to ensure credibility in DF posture. PG tasked the S4 to liaise with FINCON Logistics to obtain a complete

inventory and cost of the contingent owned equipment (COE) to be withdrawn in order to provide a cost estimate to J4 and subhead managers. This was anticipatory combat service support. S4 was also tasked under PG to identify critical infrastructure required by IRCON if it increased its battalion strength, such as vehicle servicing and logistics storage tents. A final task was to liaise with UNIFIL HQ on developments. The main purpose of these tasks was to prevent a reduction in Ireland's capability to provide a safe and secure environment in its area of operation and to provide efficient combat service support planning on the FINCON withdrawal. The PG was the S4 instrument to communicate all needs to the battalion commander.

- *What are your constraints (must do) restrictions (cannot do) and freedoms (can do)?* Assets available (personnel/equipment), acceptable risk (on United Nations operations, the DF must accept some level of risk but mitigate it), TEST (time, opposing capabilities, size of AO, terrain), actual (Finns are pulling out) or likely changes (new partner nation) in planning, and are there any 'implied' tasks not specifically mentioned by higher HQ but required? For example, a specific task is to 'repatriate vehicles' but implied tasks arising from that task are liaison with customs and shipping agents and the movement of the vehicles, essential tasks (specified tasks with possible vital implied tasks added in).

One can observe that this approach ensures that the supply chain division does not breach the boundaries of the organization's core competencies and suggests that the role of our profession is execution. Perhaps this should be applied to all 'stable' situations to reduce potential disruption and thereby the gap of pain in strategic implementations. For the DF, this process of analysis resulted in a 'restated mission for the unit', from which a number of papers were constructed at a tactical (ground) level, to inform the strategic (decision-making) level. One very positive outcome of the PG was a capability development in the form of a DF investment in a communications system similar to SEPURA, for which a budget allocation has been secured, and a tender has been initiated. This is categorized as COE and therefore the Irish government will be reimbursed by the United Nations under a wet-lease agreement.

The remaining Finnish losses of infrastructure, barrack services and welfare facilities are under negotiation for purchase but again the DF have reshaped this to their benefit. For example, when factoring in the cost of disassembly, transport to Finland and depreciation of maintenance vehicle servicing tents (MVSTs), Comdt Moriarty secured this equipment for less than the standard purchase price. The DF have secured additional combat support capability at an absolute cost to the Irish tax payer of less than 18 per cent of market value. This is supply chain resilience in action, a demonstration of an organization with the ability to 'evolve to a new and more desirable state after being severely disturbed' (Yang and Xu, 2015)... by Policy.

Supply chain disruption: Irish Defence Forces

The source of the supply chain disruption described here is Policy. For the combined NBG and UNIFIL missions I am going to dispense with a preparatory phase so as not to absorb into the discussion the purpose of the one-month joint exercise in Skillingaryd, Sweden, or indeed the mission readiness exercise prior to deployment to Sweden, as this was a clearance to build all systems, or the coordinated Irish and Finnish pre-deployment training. While Skillingaryd unearthed further supply chain friction, this was not caused by the mission itself, but by the AAE and CS41 strategic documents. I say this because the literature informs of a phased response to disruption. In equal measure, I found recovery to be consequential to the response. One could argue that an after-action review forms part of the recovery. However, it seems that this instrument is based on conditions that are too contextual and conditional, and do not influence improved organization to supply chain strategic alignment. This viewpoint is strengthened by a 2016 joint report from the International Centre for Defence and Security, and the Irish Department of Foreign Affairs and Trade, in relation to Ireland, Finland and Estonia in UNIFIL, which concluded that: 'there does not appear to be a high-level process for identifying the strengths, weaknesses, successes and failures of each rotation. There is certainly no such exercise involving all three states, nor has the United Nations undertaken a substantive and critical appraisal of the UNIFIL mission' (Lawrence *et al*, 2016). This indicates that supply chain challenges and successes (operational and financial) are not factored into the strategic renewal process. This is what we need to change as a profession.

So, what exactly do we want to change as a result of these and further case studies? First, we must increase our understanding of supply chain managers' engagement in the process of dynamic organization to supply chain strategic alignment, within the context of supply chain disruption, and second, as suggested by Wu *et al* (2014), contribute to the broadening of supply chain management to an integrated perspective across the top management team rather than a unidimensional and dichotomous view. Extending from these aims are specific objectives:

- *Determine how supply chain managers operationally identify, predict, cope with and recover from supply chain disruptions.* The NBG and UNIFIL disruptions could not have been identified or predicted in the absence of organization-to-supply-chain strategic alignment. Therefore, Comdt Moriarty had to respond to AAE and CS-41 strategic documents that needed to be reshaped to situational needs, while staying inside the core competencies of the DF, and to the sudden change of the UNIFIL withdrawal of Finland after a partnership that dated back to May 2012. The Logistics Branch needed to cope with the non-provision of electricity, HP 508 tent equipment that was not fit for purpose, a troop profile that did not sufficiently resource the mission, an inadequate heating system, the absence of the most efficient ocean vessel loading concept, and the loss of a mechanized company, APC fleet, weapons and communications systems, infrastructure, barrack services and welfare facilities. The coping mechanism applied in each case by Comdt Moriarty resulted in recovery that was an evolution to a new and more desirable state. On a general note, it is important to acknowledge that the DF pre-positions (prepares) redundant supplies based on average consumption to mitigate supply chain risk. According to United Nations standard operating procedures, at least 14 DOS (days of supply) must be held in reserve. For instance, the average daily consumption of diesel is 2,000 litres and therefore 28,000 litres are maintained. This can only be consumed with the authority of Comdt Moriarty in the event of an emergency, or for stock rotation. The commanding officer must be informed any time stock levels go below the required DOS.
- *Identify which phases in the supply chain disruption process require engagement with top management to implement strategic solutions aligned to organization goals.* This objective will develop throughout the case investigations. In the case of the DF, engagement came during the response phase of the sudden disruptive events, the nature of which was impossible to predict and identify (prepare for) in advance. This response demonstrated a supply chain that was both agile and fully flexible.
- *Consequently, determine whether a categorization of supply chain strategy exists, such as a tier consisting of strategies that can be implemented autonomously by the supply chain division, and a tier(s) that requires*

'negotiation' across the top management team prior to implementation, to collaboratively mitigate risk. Yes, it was found that negotiation across the top management team was needed to reshape the troop profile for Skillingaryd, such as the provision of cooks and ordnance technicians, or to secure a gross investment to the value of €820,000 for combat capability developments in Lebanon. The absolute cost of this investment was €150,000, and this value creation was largely due to the expertise at S-level, comprising price negotiation and wet-leasing.

- Fully flexible. A sub-tier of autonomous tactical response was found in the context of supply chain friction, such as solutions to electricity provision, robust tent infrastructure, improved container utilization, vehicle movement in Skillingaryd, provision of SUVs, the efficient use of mechanical fitters, and provision of petrol and water.
- Agility. This autonomous tactical sub-category also demonstrated value creation that transcended the contextual and situational elements of the mission at hand.

- *Determine how supply chain managers engage with the top management team in the process of aligning organization and supply chain strategies, thereby identifying key enablers and inhibitors.* Reynolds and Yetton (2015) said that there is little guidance on *how* to build and sustain alignment. Therefore, the MDMP is a valuable tool. This analyses supply chain capabilities and tasks while simultaneously aligning with top management team strategy (the foremost consideration) and respecting the boundaries of core competencies (restrictions and TEST). Even in such a directed environment as the military, I suggest that this is a tool that should be applied to all formal strategic situations at the formulation stage, to reduce the gap of pain in responding to disruption. This is especially true of an organization that repeatedly demonstrates sustainable value creation (when coping with, and triumphing over, sudden change events), compounded by the fact that Policy itself is a source of disruption. Strategic alignment does not diminish top management team (TMT) authority.

As this chapter concludes, I wish the Irish Defence Forces a safe journey in all their endeavours. It has been my privilege to have been given a small glimpse into such a highly professional organization. My message is simple. Policy is a source of supply chain disruption. Alignment of organization and supply chain strategic goals will have a significant impact on reducing the gap of pain in response to external disruptive events.

QUESTIONS

1 The two DF case studies outline various disruptions to supply chain operations and these can be generically categorized as breakdowns. However, given that all logistical challenges were in the absence of enemy engagement, can you identify the true source of supply chain disruption? Consider supply chain disruptions experienced in your own organization. Perhaps poor supplier performance has impacted operations. Can you search for clues as to what may have caused these situations at a deeper level?

2 Supply chain management has been described as a *sub*-discipline of operations management (Holweg and Helo, 2014), and the two DF case studies demonstrated that the Logistics Corps were not included in the strategic formulation process, despite the suggestion that *supply chains compete, not companies* (Christopher and Towill, 2002). How can we elevate supply chain management to the TMT?

3 Until such time as supply chain management is a regular member of TMTs, how can we negotiate changes in our supply chain networks with the policymakers? What is the threshold in your organization for such negotiation?

4 Policymakers must acknowledge the existence of supply chain friction and factor this into the strategic renewal process so that it can be triumphed over. Can you categorize the DF logistical challenges into events that required strategic negotiation with the TMT, and those that could be autonomously and tactically responded to by the Logistics Corps? For any autonomous actions, what is the main consideration?

Answers on page 238.

References

Christopher, M and Towill, D R (2002) Developing market specific supply chain strategies, *International Journal of Logistics Management*, **13** (1), pp 1–14

Friedman, T L (2016) *Thank You For Being Late: An optimist's guide to thriving in the age of accelerations*, Farrar, Straus and Giroux, New York

Gattorna, J (2015) *Dynamic Supply Chains: How to design, build and manage people-centric value networks*, FT Press, London

Holweg, M and Helo, P (2014) Defining value chain architectures: linking strategic value creation to operational supply chain design, *International Journal of Production Economics*, **147**, pp 230–38

Irish Defence Forces (2018) [accessed 8 July 2019] Home | Defence Forces, *Irish Defence Forces* [Online] http://www.military.ie/home/ (archived at https://perma.cc/7BDY-4J2L)

Kleindorfer, P R and Saad, G H (2005) *Managing Disruption Risks in Supply Chains*, John Wiley & Sons, Hoboken, NJ

Lawrence, T, Jermalavičius, T and Bulakh, A (2016) *Soldiers of Peace: Estonia, Finland and Ireland in UNIFIL*, ICDS, Tallinn

Rajesh, R, Ravi, V and Venkata Rao, R (2015) Selection of risk mitigation strategy in electronic supply chains using grey theory and digraph-matrix approaches, *International Journal of Production Research*, **53** (1), pp 238–57

Reynolds, P and Yetton, P (2015) Aligning business and IT strategies in multi-business organizations, *Journal of Information Technology*, **30** (2), pp 101–18

Roberta Pereira, C, Christopher, M and Lago Da Silva, A (2014) Achieving supply chain resilience: the role of procurement, *Supply Chain Management*, **19** (5/6), pp 626–42

Roh, J, Hong, P and Min, H (2014) Implementation of a responsive supply chain strategy in global complexity: the case of manufacturing firms, *International Journal of Production Economics*, **147**, pp 198–210

Sheffi, Y (2001) Supply chain management under the threat of international terrorism, *International Journal of Logistics Management*, **12** (2), pp 1–11

Wu, L *et al* (2016) Smart supply chain management: a review and implications for future research, *International Journal of Logistics Management,* **27** (2), pp 395–417

Yang, Y and Xu, X (2015) Post-disaster grain supply chain resilience with government aid, *Transportation Research Part E: Logistics and Transportation Review*, **76**, pp 139–59

12

Defence support chain performance dashboard development

Copyright © 2018 by The Performance Organisers Limited

ALLEN WOODS

(1) (2) (4)

Knowledge and action

The purpose of a case study is to explain how a particular problem was solved, draw conclusions from the solution and then suggest actions that may be carried out to mitigate the problem itself. There were many lessons learnt during the course of the exercise, many of them specific to the circumstances the author found himself working in; however, there were five key lessons that can be identified as being significant, which are general but significant in nature in that it is likely that all organizations will benefit from addressing them. They are:

1 Develop a meta or canonical model data dictionary that contains standard definitions of data attributes, their scope, value and aliases. Time spent on the kind of exercise being recommended will never be wasted. Once completed, the meta data dictionary will become a key standards definition document for any subsequent architectural enterprise.

2 Given that IT tends to focus on process and given that eventually some means of collation will be attempted, one of the key gaps in respect of alignment of data sources is a reliable and robust description of organization form, function and purpose that is 'joined up'. It is quite common nowadays for there to be a drawing or mapping tool in use that provides the means to map process flows, organizational interaction and so on, with the diagrams following some form of UML schematic symbol set. In the author's opinion, using the diagrams as just that, without understanding the underlying database that provides the means to recall and redraw such diagrams, is a mistake. The aim for all such diagram production should not be for them to end up in a repository, but instead to be in a position to 'change the diagram, change the data flow', with the diagrams acting as living documents in their own right. The organization mapping tool described as being used in this case study supports that operating concept.

3 Finally, the importance of carefully defining performance metrics, as a data collection and information delivery specification of requirements, cannot be underestimated. In exercises in which performance reporting is a key end product, in the author's opinion, treating performance metric profiling in the way suggested gives the organization the means to direct, authoritatively and accurately, what their IT and software development staff are supposed to be building. In short, performance metric profiles are information engineering documents that the business side of the equation should be the masters of.

4 Concepts like significance, inversion of control and inferential distance have a definite impact on the validity of supply chain reporting and can, in extremis, skew any analytical effort. The kind of dashboard developed on the third iteration gave the means to identify the impact of those concepts and, given that it was easy to modify the dashboards, they could be mitigated against relatively easily.

5 Financially, a key lesson to learn was that it was and remains perfectly feasible to develop a sophisticated reporting capability in-house that would be free of commercial licensing. While the programming skill required to produce such a reporting capability might be expensive, it is not as expensive as ongoing and annual licensing costs of commercial-off-the-shelf (COTS) business intelligence packages.

At the time of writing, the CEO of Facebook was giving evidence to the US Congress on matters related to a significant breach of trust. The ins and outs of the exercise are neither here nor there in respect of this case study. What is relevant, however, is that the kind of architectural approach described in this case study lends itself to being able to plug in diverse data sets and use them in composite form. The reverse is also true, in that data sets can be kept separate, and in the current IT operating climate, in which privacy legislation in particular is being imposed, means that the approach has clear business advantages.

- In closing, the exercise the author took part in was unusual and the opportunity to do something like it will probably never happen again. That said, the task generated a unique set of software development problem-solving experiences that have been to the benefit of the author personally.

Introduction

This case study describes an exercise in information delivery carried out by The Performance Organisers as a proof of concept project to determine the feasibility of providing contextual multi-perspective multidimensional performance reporting across the UK Defence Support Chain. The case study has been produced as a submission to an anthology of similar exercises to be published in the UK by Cranfield University.

What is to be gained in terms of new knowledge by reading this case study?

Historically, information technology and supporting data collection has focused on process. But focusing on process is parochial and tends to produce data silos. Supply chain management reporting capable of providing coherent decision support across the command and management chains, however, tends to be dynamic, viral and organic and requires the application of different programming styles and logical forms as a consequence. By reviewing this case study, the reader will gain insight into the nature of the issues data silos present in terms of collation and a method of resolving those issues using elements of general systems theory to do so.

Background

At the end of August 2015, the author was tasked with developing, as a proof of concept, a performance reporting platform for the UK Defence Support Chain. The aim of the exercise was to establish the feasibility of building a corporate reporting capability to be used by all three services and Defence Equipment and Support (DE&S) from which a 'single source of truth' view of the Defence supply chain and its efficiency and effectiveness could be derived. The aim was to identify major data management issues that would need to be resolved and to test possible solutions. The proof of concept work was to take six months and was to be completed by the end of March 2016. (See Figures 12.1 and 12.2.)

The scale of the Defence Support Chain in terms of scope of business is, quite simply, huge. The UK MoD has a worldwide (and beyond) presence covering land, sea, air and, increasingly, space operations. In financial terms, the Defence Support Chain, forward and reverse supply, supports a logistics business with a turnover of (at the time) £8.5 billion and includes the need to manage a catalogued inventory of some 16 million separately identifiable items covering every aspect of military supply both on operations and in barracks.

Like the scope of the business, the Defence Support Chain's information management architecture is complex and, at the time, contained within it several hundred separate logistics support systems that used just about every computer operating system, software language and database form then in current use. It may give some indication of the nature of the complexity that some six years ago, the MoD outsourced much of the information management infrastructure referred to under the banner 'Future Logistics Information Systems' (FLIS), which, on its own, resulted in a single source contract costing the Defence budget £800 million over 10 years.

In support of the project, policy and governance documentation for the management of the Defence Support Chain was provided in the form of a series of Joint Service Publications (now replaced by the Defence Support Network) that covered all aspects of Defence logistics management from information security to inventory management. The most significant from the perspective of logistics management was JSP 886, which set out the processes and standards by which the MoD supply chain was expected to operate and the performance standards it was expected to meet.

Needless to say, the operating environment was dynamic, with the Defence Support Chain being responsible for the delivery and subsequent

FIGURE 12.1 Request for stores throughput

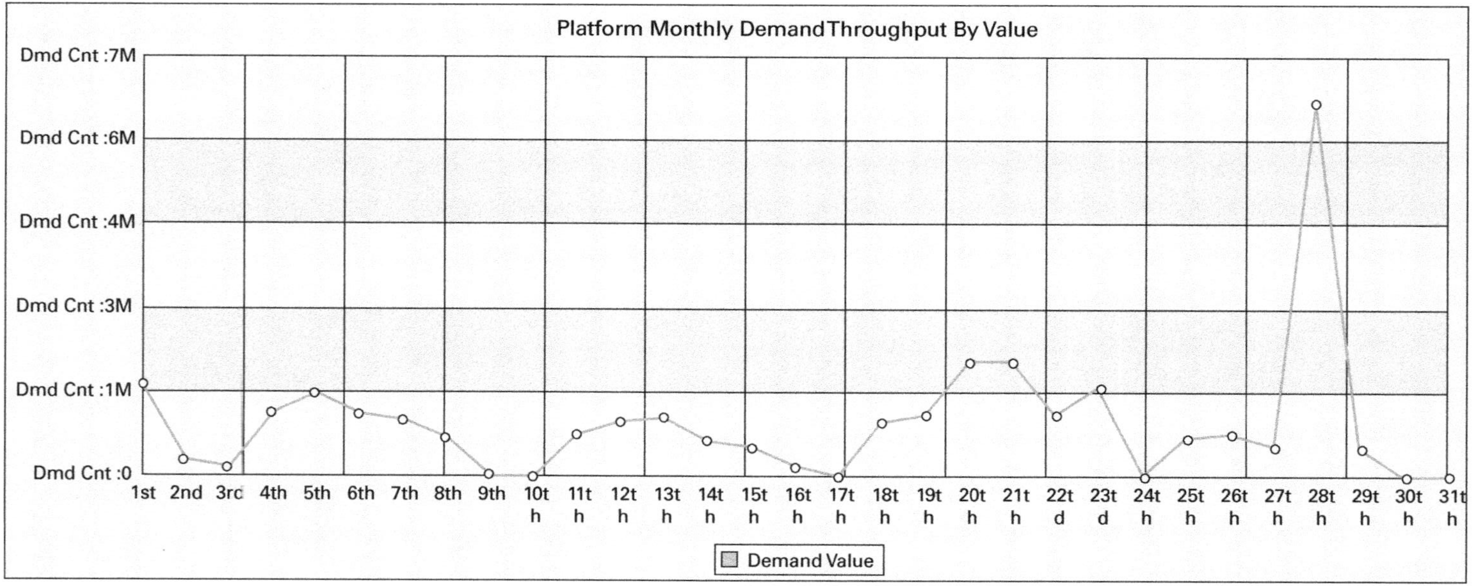

FIGURE 12.2 Request for stores composite chart

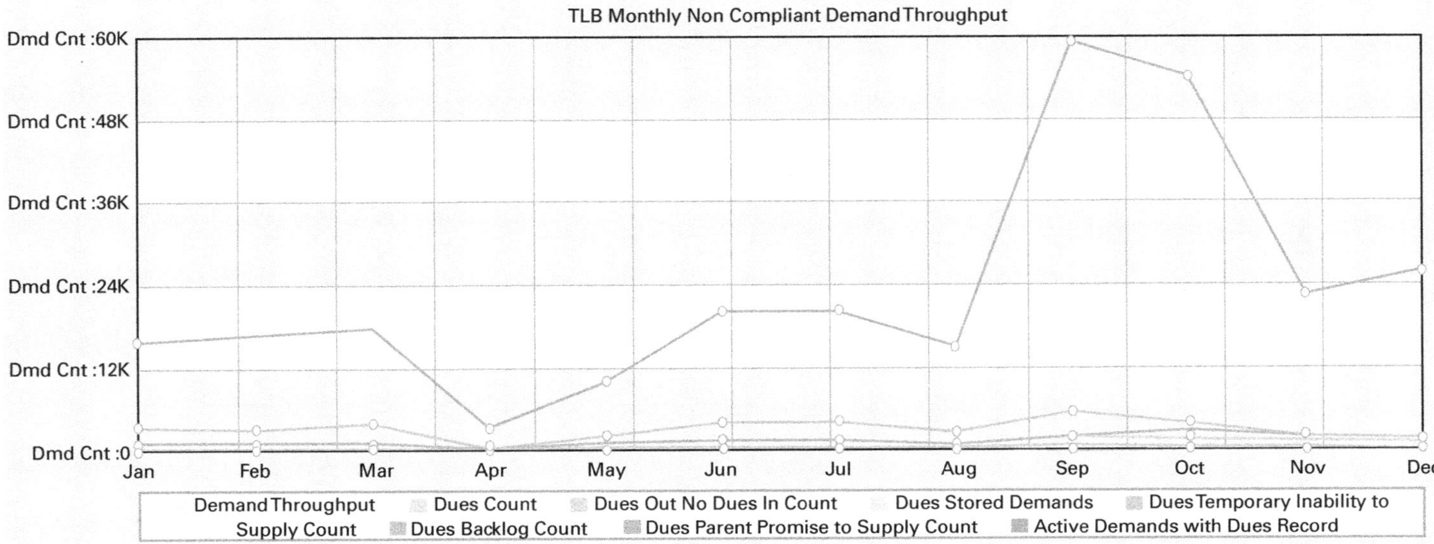

return of military stores for several operations (Op Herrick in Afghanistan being perhaps the most well known) and for less warlike activities in barracks both in the UK and elsewhere. At the time of the project, the MoD had recently completed deployment of a single forward, or front line, logistics management system, known as 'Management of the Joint Deployed Inventory' (MJDI), to all three services as a single common-use frontline logistics information system to all operational units. It should be noted that MJDI had taken more than 10 years to develop, test and deploy and its user population was somewhere in the region of 20,000 logistics personnel of all ranks and grades, again across all three services worldwide. One of the features of MJDI that made it a game changer was that it provided the means to make any frontline stores management facility a node in what was in effect a global supply warehouse. The major operational benefit of that change was perhaps that units operating anywhere could request inventory items locally from other units with a similar role as opposed to referring requests back to the UK, with consequent improvements in general supply chain performance being the end result.

During the course of the case study, there were more than a few policy and governance procedural changes to take into account also. Originally, the reporting emphasis was targeted on 13 primary metrics that were geared towards what was, at the time, standard MoD contractual practice with suppliers. However, changes to contract form, and the introduction of the DefSCOR (Defence Supply Chain Operations Reference model) forward and reverse supply chain methodology, meant that the metric profiles changed or increased in terms of number and scope.

The volumes of data being generated on a daily basis were (and remain) huge. The Defence Support Chain has an electronic data warehouse (EDW) which, at the time of the study, contained some 3.5 Pb (petabytes) of raw data stored in several hundred copies of active operational databases. The data were, with one or two exceptions, stored in their original database structures in a teradata warehouse that had its own sophisticated querying mechanism based on SQL, but with its own product-specific extensions. An associated issue in design and collation terms was that there was no master data dictionary available, and as a consequence the ability to identify data descriptive attributes that were similar in scope, value and meaning but with separate and distinct aliases was dependent on the skill and business knowledge of those querying the data.

A further consideration that had a significant impact on the achievable speed of information delivery was that the EDW was being refreshed and updated with new additional data and database forms on a near-weekly basis; furthermore, it was being used by other teams mining the data for their own reasons from across Defence on a daily, if not hourly, basis. The combination meant that the nature in terms of quantity and functional scope of any Extract, Transfer and Load (ETL) requirement would change as additional data were added. And the impact of those additional data would be felt in many ways, not least in terms of the speed of query response. To give some indication of the impact, it might be worth considering that the first major SQL Select statement (with no joins), tried on an experimental basis for proof of concept extraction purposes on just one database for one year's worth of transaction data, took some 36 hours to execute and download from the EDW in CSV (comma-separated values) form to the author's MoD terminal.

Design considerations

In the light of all of the above, there was a need, in order to meet the requirement, to plan architecturally, from an end-to-end basis, on the principle of accurate and managed data volume reduction. During a number of observational exercises, it was noted that the nature of querying by third parties varied in terms of complexity and that at least one third-party team was regularly disrupting data extraction across the board because of the nature of the query techniques that appeared to be used. The author was therefore obliged to consider an approach that supported relatively simple query building, the result of which was (initially) high-volume data extraction with as much of the subsidiary and supporting processing as possible being carried out on a local MoD terminal. It was imperative that the extraction approach could be proved in a mathematically sound way that would also support the ability to retain provable links to the raw source data.

After careful consideration of alternatives, the author elected to take an approach that applied the principles of cybernetics and communications theory (both constituent parts of general systems theory) with the underlying theme of the 'organization as a system'. The key sources of ideas in respect of the nature of cybernetics were drawn from the following authors:

- Stafford Beer (in particular his Viable Systems Model)
- Ludwig von Bertanalffy (from his seminal work *An Introduction to Cybernetics*
- James Grier Miller (his book *Living Systems* introducing the concept of 'fray out')

- Claude Shannon (his original paper on communication theory being a key source of inspiration)
- *Patterns of Strategy*, by Patrick Hoverstadt
- *Creative Problem Solving* by Messrs Flood and Jackson (both advocating a multi-methodological approach)
- And for a Defence-specific influence, a book called *Power to the Edge* from the US DoD.

There were other books that influenced the development of the design approach, and a full reading list is provided at Annex A, but the ones listed above were the most important. The aim of the design approach was to get away from the traditional focus on process and recognize that the Defence Support Chain is a dynamic living thing, and in doing so to take into account organization form, function and purpose as the basis for the design of a valid report generation capability available on an 'on demand' basis any time of the day or night. The initial focus was to provide a verifiable reporting capability that would meet field force requirements initially with the ability to contextually summarize reports for the benefit of higher-level command authorities at a later date.

As a consequence, in purely practical terms, another consideration taken into account was how the end product might be deployed and used across Defence. The primary operating concept considered as appropriate was the US DoD approach of providing information in a timely, accurate and verified manner to decision takers in the field, summed up by the term 'Power to the Edge'. For that, the three ideas of 'Concept of Operation' (CONOPS; how the resulting application might be used from an operational perspective), 'Concept of Use' (CONUSE; what the end application might be used for) and 'Concept of Employment' (CONEMP; who will use the resulting reporting capability for evidence-based decision support purposes) were applied. It was felt by the author that this kind of focus would meet the reporting needs of forward logisticians.

There was the practical issue of providing a suitable hosting platform, and for that, with permission from the project sponsor, the MJDI portal (written by the author) was selected as a suitable platform given that it had the hard disk storage space and two installations of an industrial-strength database (SQL Server) which, after design consolidation, would support the testing of multiples of near-simultaneous report generation exercises across the defence network.

It should be noted that as the proof of concept was to be hosted on an existing facility, there were no software licensing or usage issues because of the existence of spare capacity on the MJDI portal server and because source code would be written entirely by the author.

In order to support decision taking at both strategic and operational level, a reporting structure or metaphor, based on the balanced scorecard, was selected as the basis for the provision of a multi-perspective gateway, the architectural impact being that it should be possible to design a series of scorecards that in principle could be similar in construction and operation such that each could be used on a 'drill down' or 'drill up' basis, within the constraint of 'need to know' (Figure 12.2). Figure 12.3 illustrates the nature, from a scorecard hierarchical perspective, of the scope of each scorecard level, from the strategic to the operational. This gave rise to the need to assess the architectural nature of the reporting tool set from the following perspectives:

6. the need to resolve any conflict of interest, managerially, between central control and delegated responsibility;
7. the idea of perception of value, as a form of value chain analysis (what may be seen as important and necessary at senior management level may not be seen in the same light at the front line);
8. minimizing risk associated with increasing inferential distance the further away decision takers are from data input;
9. detection of 'inversion of control', or to put it another way, the means to detect the impact of decisions taken at the operating level that may, for whatever reason, impact significantly on strategic intent;
10. that each data set is a filtration of the totality of available information and that therefore in order to provide a comprehensive decision support capability, multiple data sets would need to be collated and combined.

Given the architectural impact of the CONOPs, CONUSE, CONEMP (see Figure 12.3) triumvirate and the five perspectives set out above, the next consideration, given the change in nature of the decision support requirement both up and down the command/management chains, was to recognize that there would be a need for different forms of processing at key transition points in the reporting architecture. At each transition there would be differences in logical form applied (procedural to predication, for example), statistical analysis approach (determinism to Bayesian), collation/summarization of data volumes (from the relational model to fact tables, for example) and finally, the provision of support for alignment of data forms (structured data in databases and relatively unstructured data in document files for example).

FIGURE 12.3 CONOPS, CONNEMP CONUE

For the purposes of the proof of concept, the transitions shown in Table 12.1 were identified as having an impact on the eventual dashboard design:

The next most significant design considerations were related to accurate data targeting on both a Cartesian and Euclidean basis using standard (in military terms) ontological and taxonomical constructs with the aim of

TABLE 12.1 Transitions

Series	Transition	Purpose	Exercise scope
1	Data input	Collection of raw data at the 'desk top'	Out of scope for the exercise, but considered as a possible impact on ETL exercises
2	Initial alignment	Marrying up data where possible after identifying like-for-like data attributes in terms of scope, meaning and value	In scope and key. Basically data extracted from EDW databases and then aligned as far as possible on a like-for-like basis and error corrected

(continued)

TABLE 12.1 (Continued)

Series	Transition	Purpose	Exercise scope
3	First reduction	Reduction of multiple lines of database entries to factual summary	In scope, dependent for completeness of metric definition as information engineering artefacts
4	Second alignment	Application of normalization to fact tables and subsequent integration to the formal military command and management chains	In scope, the end effect and benefit being to use relational analysis to speed up reaction to multidimensional reporting requests
5	Third alignment	Cataloguing of unstructured document content and database content	Out of scope, but achieved on a subsequent exercise – 'lithium test', subject of a separate case study
6	The semantic layer	Application of alternative logic forms to the procedural to predication transition, pattern recognition being the most prominent	Out of scope, but pattern recognition and progress on the application semantic techniques have been successfully implemented post the case study

TABLE 12.2 Three-tier dimensional framework

Series	Name	Purpose
1	Main perspectives, following a balanced scorecard metaphor	Economic (covering financial matters), Efficient (internal, best use of resources), Effective (external, meeting end-customer need) and Evolve (briefly, reaction to change)
2	Primary dimensions	Identification of key classes of capability (equipment platforms, assets, geophysical etc)
3	Secondary dimensions	Based on an adaptation of the Zachman framework ontological approach to relationship definition, adding an additional question 'Who, What, Where, Why, When, How' and adjusting the relationship identifiers to reflect a military supply chain operating environment that lends itself to forward and reverse supply chain reporting

providing a coherent means to filter, accurately, consistently and completely, the volumes of data that were available. To create the kind of targeting framework that was thought to be beneficial, a three-tier dimensional framework approach was applied at each of the data transition points (Table 12.2).

The foundation – master data identification and definition

Having worked out a conceptual design framework, given the number of data sets in the UK Defence Support Chain EDW the first practical step was to define or identify master data elements in common use in the Defence inventory. A focus, for identification of key attributes, was placed on the elements shown in Table 12.3 and how they are described in database terms.

One of the key master data structural gaps that was identified early on in the case study and needed to be addressed was to find the means to describe organization form, function and purpose digitally for both the military command's terms and the administrative management chain's terms such that the end result could be used as a coordinating data source as an additional dimension.

Ideally, any reporting facility should be capable of providing decision support to each class of management activity, the end effect being to more closely link the structure of the enterprise to the structure of its data such that the eventual model dashboard could cope with rapid deployments of people and material but still keep reporting on less warlike static scenarios.

TABLE 12.3 Master data elements

Series	Name	Purpose	Authoritative source
1	Part	Thing at the lowest level of identifiable decomposition	The UK National Codification Bureau, a Defence asset, is responsible for the allocation of NATO stock numbers. Definition of 'part' was taken from their data dictionary
2	Platform	In Defence terms, generally refers to a class of equipment	In UK Defence there were and are multiple definitions of 'platform'; the version chosen, given that it is in widespread use, was the MJDI definitions contained in its data dictionary
3	Demand	In Defence terms, 'demand' refers to a request to supply from the supply chain	The then JSP 886 demand management definitions, covering prioritization, classification etc, as applied in MJDI and the base inventory management systems was applied
4	Unit or Formation	To identify Units in the command and management chains across the military management and financial structures	The definition of 'Unit', in day-to-day practical and data definition terms, varies from service to service and across internal management domain boundaries. Initially, the MoD Unit catalogue was adopted as a stand master data definition

It is one of the many anomalies of information and data management that organization form and function tend not to be described in a structurally sound database form. This anomaly has its origins in traditional IT development effort in that much of it is based on data capture at the level of process and is therefore parochial, relatively speaking. Mapping organization form and function as a database meant the production of a structurally coherent means of describing how the organization as a whole works that became just another part of the architectural metadata. To achieve the mapping, the author used his own organization mapping software and inserted the result into the data-to-information transition structures described earlier in this case study. While the command and management relationship mapping took some time, the end result was that it became possible to use a standard dashboard design to report on a common basis across the MoD budget and command structures transparently.

The further design consideration, as an aspiration, was to incorporate some form of legislative compliance reporting capability. For that, given its sensitive nature, and to further complete the meta model to be used, the author chose the US Arms Export Control Act and decided to prove whether or not it would be possible to demonstrate a means of locating US-supplied inventory using standard ISO country codes and NATO stock catalogue equivalents. This introduced the need for some form of interactive geophysical capability, which too was provided using elements of the author's extensive code base. Figure 12.4 shows the operating circumstances the project would have to support.

FIGURE 12.4 Operating environment

It should be noted that the canonical or master meta model described as 'canonical' provides a rule-based translation service for data attributes and like-for-like value comparison in terms of meaning and scope, on which the organization and operation of the subsequent extract, transform and load exercises at each data transition point could be based. To further streamline query response times, at the third transition point a series of fact tables were created, each implanted with dimension-table primary keys, with the end result being a renormalized set of such tables that follow relational principles and, as such, could be exploited in query terms, in much the same way as more common process-based database applications. The fact tables, in design specification terms, were generated from performance metric profiles specifically written as reporting specifications of requirement. See Annex C for a list of the resulting fact tables.

The primary benefit of the federated architecture was that it became a relatively straightforward matter to provide the basis for sophisticated navigation across diverse data sets on a top-down, bottom-up and lateral basis.

Time, the great constraint

In any major data manipulation exercise, time, the great constraint, is always a factor to consider. The considerations include, but are not limited to:

- the freshness of the data in EDW terms, as a whole and on an individual data set basis;
- the time taken to extract volumes of data, securely, over a network;
- the time needed, once extraction is complete, to reprocess the extraction result as per the transition stages from raw data to (say) the semantic level;
- the time taken to execute queries and deliver the result to the desk top;
- the use of an EDW, for both simple and complex querying, by other agencies.

In the case of the task, the primary time factor was the time taken, at the point of request, to deliver functional reports to the desk top that were verifiable and properly validated. The target time was 30 seconds from request to final formatted delivery, given the potential volumes even after the kind of reduction envisaged was successfully implemented

Other factors that influenced the ability to deliver the kind of reporting capability required included, but were not limited to:

- The Defence Support Chain EDW was and is an MoD-wide asset and as a consequence was a data resource in use by multiples of departments and individuals at the same time.
- The nature of the querying in terms of query complexity (multiple joins across one of more data sets, for example) varied. In extremis, one particular department had a reputation for building complex queries that would take many hours to execute prior to data delivery, which had the detrimental effect of disrupting all data-mining activity.
- The data update refresh rate, which varied in time from 14 days for one of the key databases to a few hours.
- The significance of individual data elements (primary keys, master data reference attributes, for example) that required scope, meaning and context validation for collation purposes.
- Not all key data were, at the time, held in the EDW and would have to be sourced separately, and each data set held outside of the EDW had its own refresh and maintenance cycle.
- The lack of documentation, in the form of a description of physical data structures held in the EDW against those in the active systems.
- The volume of data, which had to be transmitted across the UK Defence network.

All of the factors set out above meant the need for an ETL strategy that was inevitably reductionist in nature. Some statistics that may give some indication of the nature of the reduction effort required may be worth setting out:

- The NATO stock catalogue (the main inventory or asset list) contains some 16,000,000 separately identifiable items each with its own NATO stock number (NSN). It may be of interest to note that the NSN system has its origin in the US Federal stock numbering method.
- Depending on operational circumstances, on a daily basis, there were in excess of 50,000 requests for stores, per day, submitted on an entirely random basis in the deployed inventory space and subsequently, where required, transmitted back to the base inventory systems.
- The footprint of the EDW at the time, containing historical transaction data going back several years, was approximately 3.5 Pb.

FIGURE 12.5 Architecture functional overview

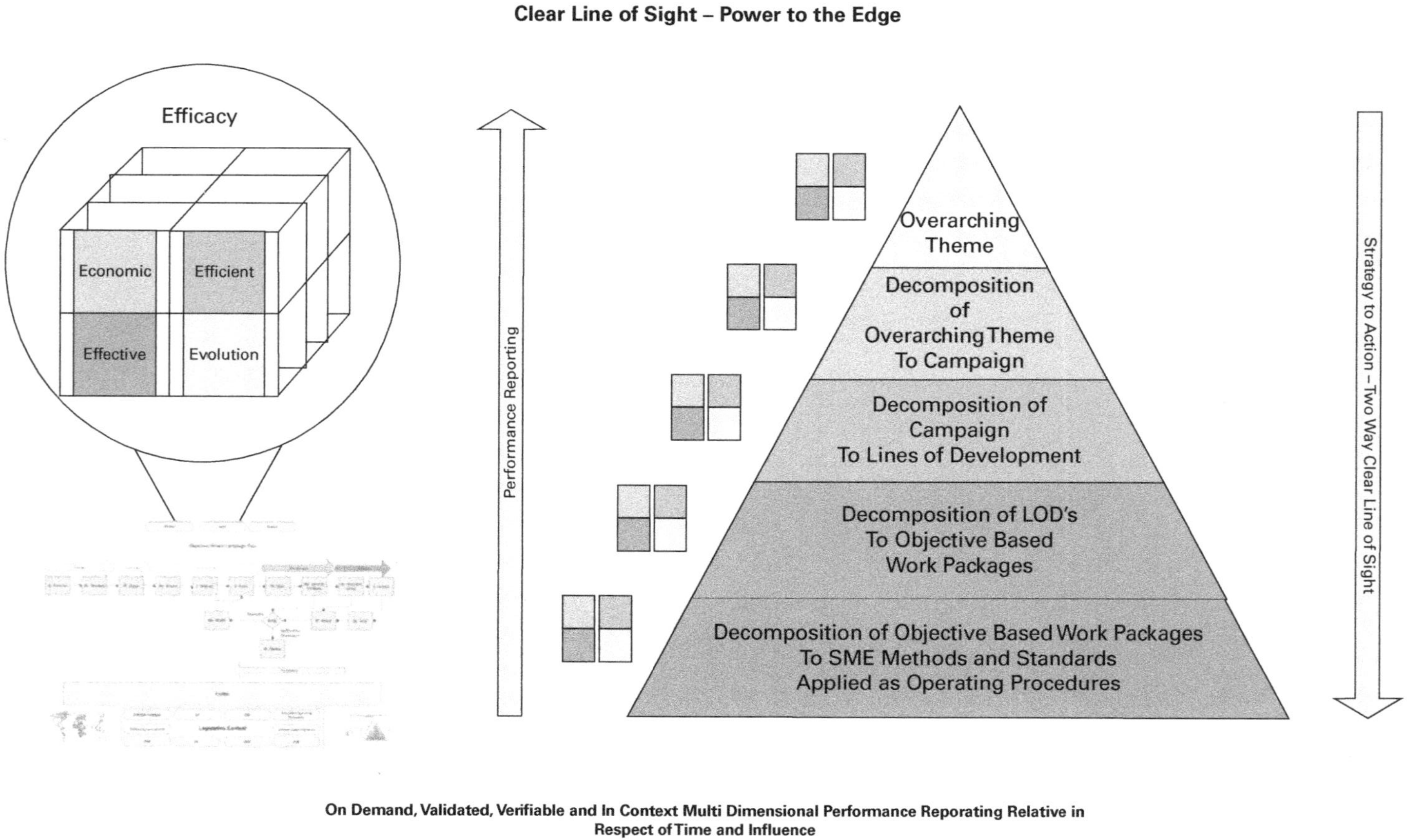

- That reports would have to be delivered to a standard MoD terminal meant that the reductionist design would need to be in the order of 95%, given disk cache sizes and other constraints, principally related to network security and integrity that, quite simply, could not be got round.

With all of the factors set out above in mind, a series of extraction experiments were carried out to test the time taken to extract data from the high transaction volume databases. The first experiment extracted some six months of transaction records, in CSV form, from just one key transaction data set using a single query took some 24 hours to execute. On top of that, of course, there was additional processing time related to cleansing, collation and alignment of multiple data sets and then transfer of the end result into a hosting portal.

Needless to say, it took some time and experimentation to get the extraction sequence correct, but the general approach ended up following the sequence set out below:

- Identify dimension data that were comparatively static and confirm with data owners what the average data refresh period was. For example, the MoD unit location database, SLIM, while subject to frequent changes, did not change radically on a monthly basis and changes could be made for reporting purposes, cumulatively but less frequently than with, say, transaction data. Some 20 data sets that were in the final reporting architecture fell into this category.
- For high-volume transaction data, take an initial download for six months of historical data and then subsequently, on a weekly basis, extract only new or changed status records.
- After six months of transaction inactivity, remove redundant records from the reporting database on a rolling basis, checked per month.
- Summarize, on extraction, the transaction data into fact tables.
- As per the data-to-information transition design principles set out above, summarize the validated and checked transaction data into summarized fact tables and at the same time align the facts with the dimension data and apply standard data normalization techniques, with the end product being a fact-based relational database.

After several test runs and review exercises, the volume of transaction data held in the reporting database could be reliably established as holding six months of data, refreshed in sequence with the EDW refresh rate.

The resulting database container structure was a transaction database containing some 2,500,000 records at any one time, a relational fact database containing some 20 multidimensional fact tables in a referential model database and approximately 20 dimension databases (NATO stock catalogue, MoD Unit Address List, Budget Structure etc) held in a federation with the summarized transaction data and the fact database. Figure 12.6 gives an indication of the nature of the federation.

The net effect of the extraction strategy was that the kind of dashboard that was eventually developed could be deployed for multiples of units and platforms that could be actioned independently and on demand on multiples of standard MoD desktop PCs on a random basis across the MoD intranet.

Process and performance metric profiling

The next design consideration was to place the end reporting capability in the context of the Defence Support Chain end-to-end process. At the time of the exercise, the primary description of process and related performance targets was contained in Joint Service Publication 886; however, during the course of the proof of concept exercise, a Defence take on the Supply Chain Operation Reference model was introduced under the acronym DefSCOR, with the aim of linking supply chain operations with engineering activities (both being symbiotic in logistics management terms), which also made provision for reverse supply management (related to equipment modification programmes etc). The author took the design decision to position the end product in the context of DefSCOR, and the positioning result is illustrated by the red box in Figure 12.7. It may be useful to readers to be made aware that the aim of DefSCOR was to integrate both forward and reverse supply chain management and engineering effort within the context of 'through life' management; given the nature of complex equipment management from acquisition to final disposal, the positioning of the proof of concept reporting capability was a crucial scoping decision.

Once the positioning and scoping described above was determined and approved, the nature of data collection and subsequent reporting could be explained and made relevant to the target audience.

The final design consideration was to provide a means of specifying reports that met a business need, but were fashioned in such a way that they formed an information delivery statement of requirement that also included

FIGURE 12.6 Database federation

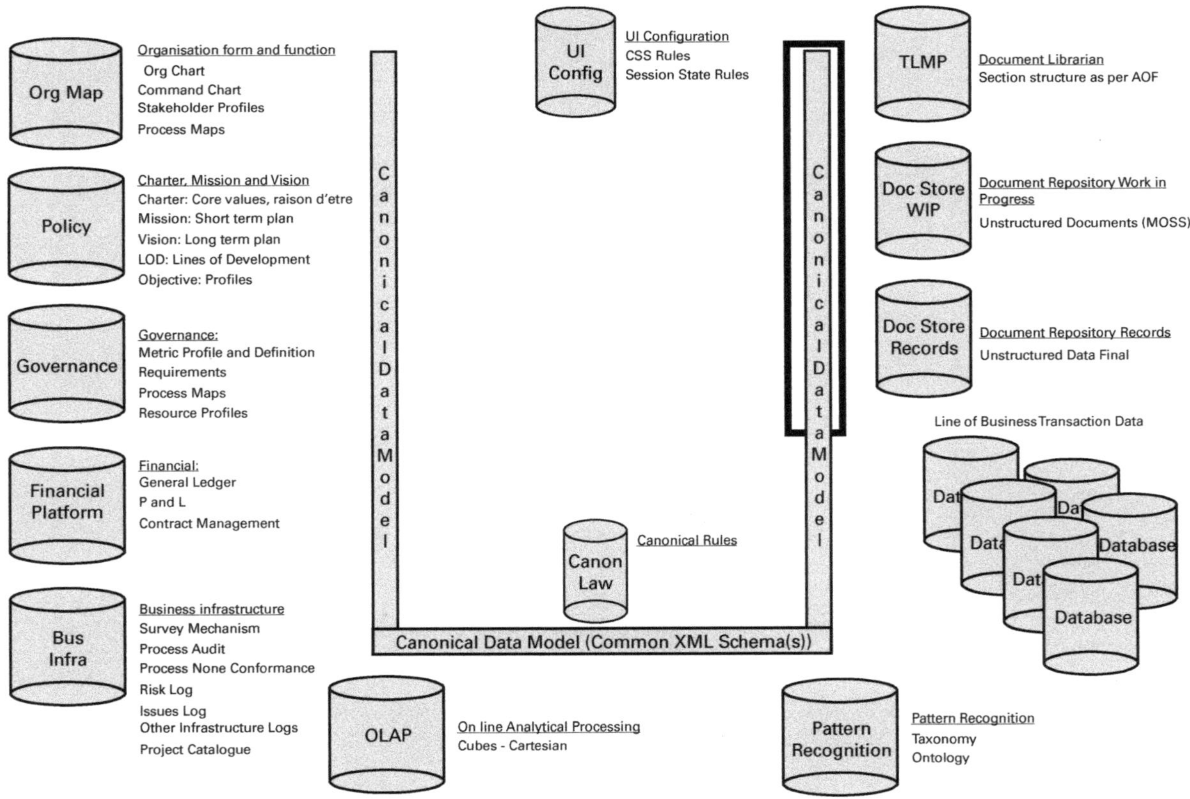

FIGURE 12.7 DEFSCOR supply chain forward and reverse process

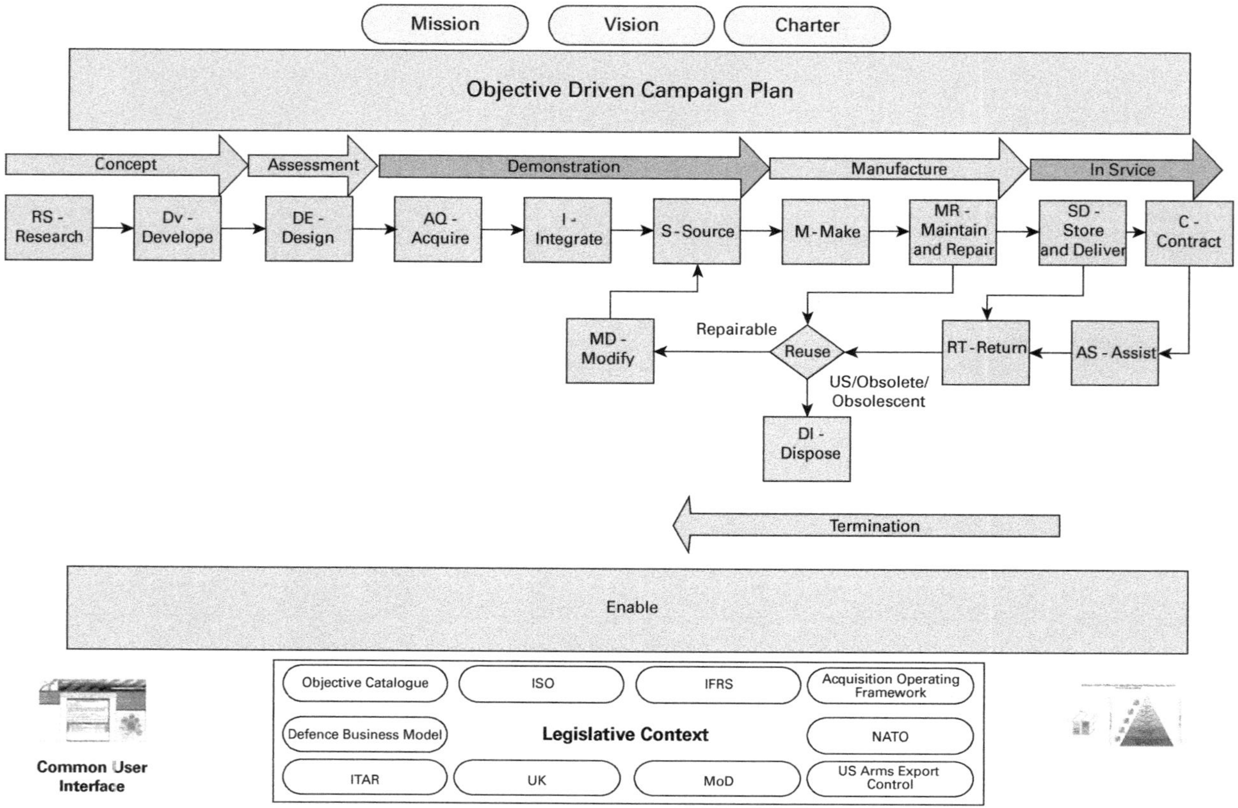

indication of where, in the DefSCOR/JSP 886 process cycle, appropriate data could be sourced, validated and verified using the ETL approach outlined in this chapter.

A key step was to develop a metric profile template that required a definition of measurable transaction points, at the process level, from which data could be retrieved, with the second key step being to identify process parameters on which to apply methods of calculation associated with process inputs and outputs. Given that at the time, DefSCOR was relatively new and undocumented, the primary source of methods of calculation and any influencing parameters were drawn exclusively from JSP 886. The basic calculations were related to request for supply (in military vernacular, 'demands') throughput, followed by constraining issues such as non-availability of requested items from industry (Dues Out, No Dues In – DONDI).

Three measurement approaches were then applied to the basic data collection. The first was to identify tolerance values by which it was possible to identify exceptional behaviour in supply throughput (Figure 12.7). The aim of this measurement technique, usually time driven, was to test the efficiency and effectiveness of the supply chain in terms of process. This aspect is illustrated in Figure 12.8. But a single view (originally total number of demands) was augmented with additional views such as demand throughput by item value and by number of items requested by simple volume.

The second measurement technique applied was to test on the basis of standard deviation against overall supply time targets set out in detail in JSP 886 but with supply priority also taken into account as an influencing factor in determining supply chain exceptions (Figure 12.10).

FIGURE 12.8 Supply tolerances

FIGURE 12.9 Multi view single page charts

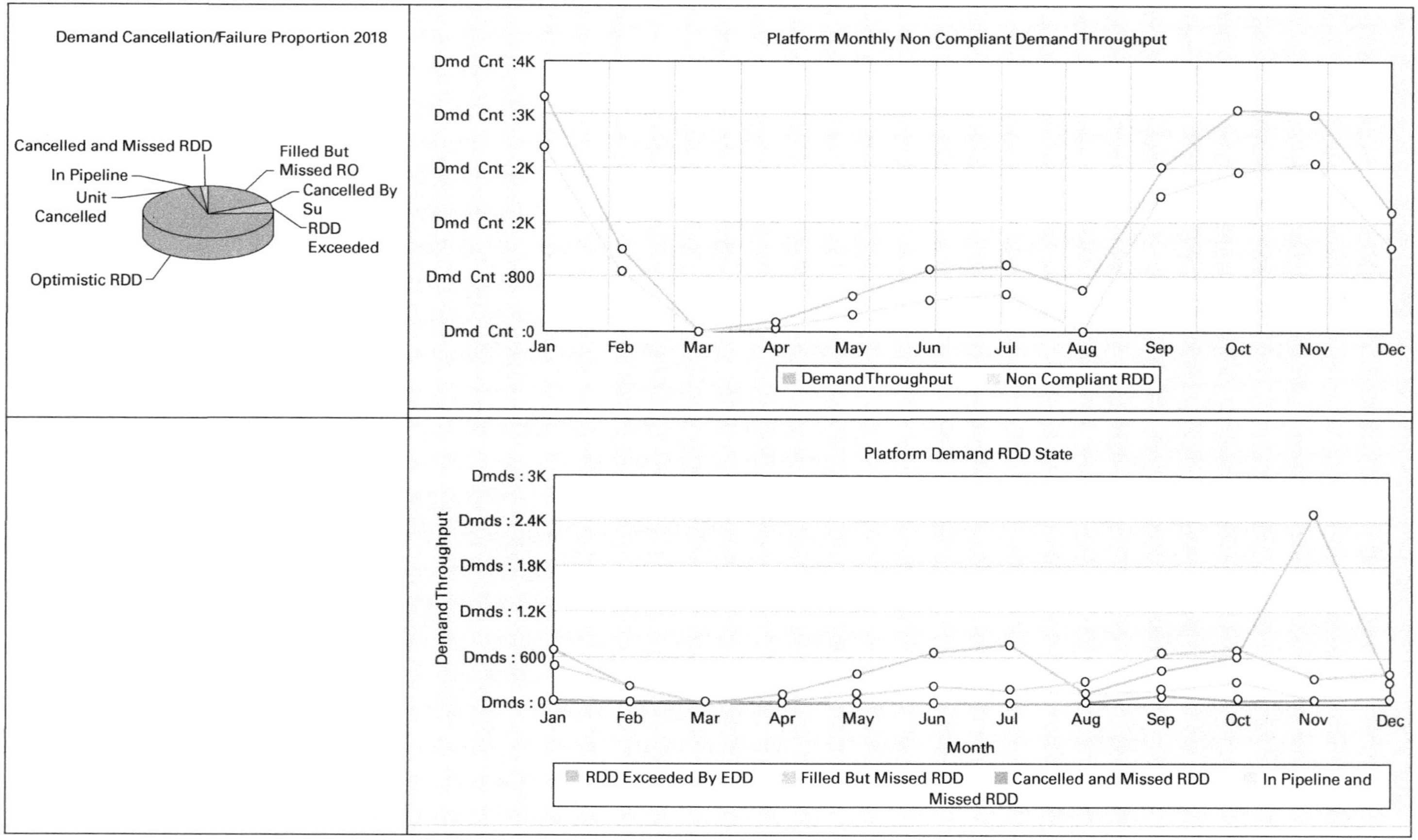

FIGURE 12.10 Measurement by standard deviation

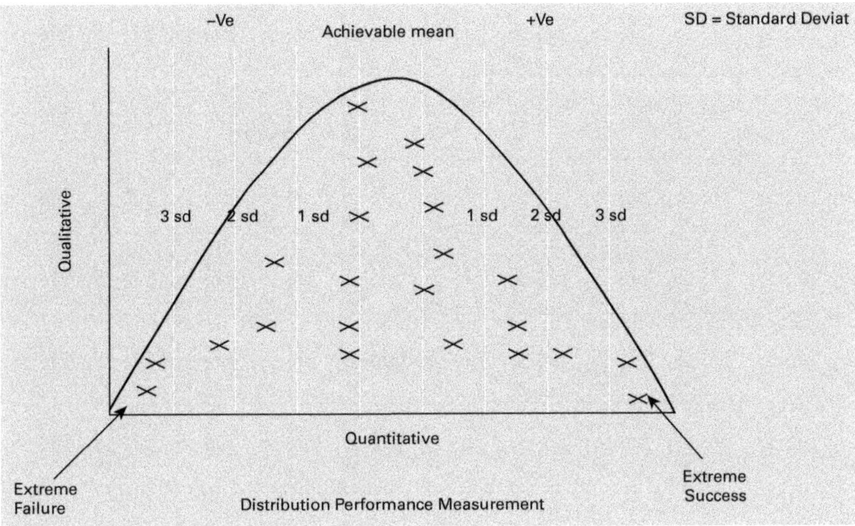

The final statistical analysis approach was that of the maintenance of 'rolling averages' across all statistical analysis forms for trend identification purposes.

The combination of analysis techniques gave the means to provide a sophisticated approach to the application of deterministic techniques that could be, in effect, 'plugged in' to the data-to-information transition cycle described earlier.

The dashboard design

Having determined the main influencing factors that would determine the nature of information delivery, the next step was to decide on presentation. And presentation turned out to be one of the more difficult aspects of the exercise.

The first dashboard iteration, as specified by the sponsor, was to produce a simple tabular interface with the means to connect into simple graphs and charts (see Figure 12.11). The initial design was quickly found to be cumbersome in that it did not lend itself to viewing supply chain activity on a multidimensional basis in a visually appealing and informative way.

The second iteration consisted of a series of Red, Amber, and Green (RAG) dials (see Figure 12.12), again with a simple drill-down capability.

FIGURE 12.11 Dashboard design stage one – tabular information delivery

No of Demand Records on File	No of Demands Met In Full	% 69.79%
1,463	1,201	69.79%

Priority	Demand Count	In Cycle	% Filled Internally	% Filled Externally	View
1	1	0	100.00%	0.00%	
2	5	2	40.00%	20.00%	
3	5	1	20.00%	60.00%	
4	0	0			
5	36	16	25.00%	30.56%	
9	442	107	32.58%	43.21%	
13	847	242	32.70%	38.72%	

FIGURE 12.12 Dashboard design stage two – red, amber, green traffic lights

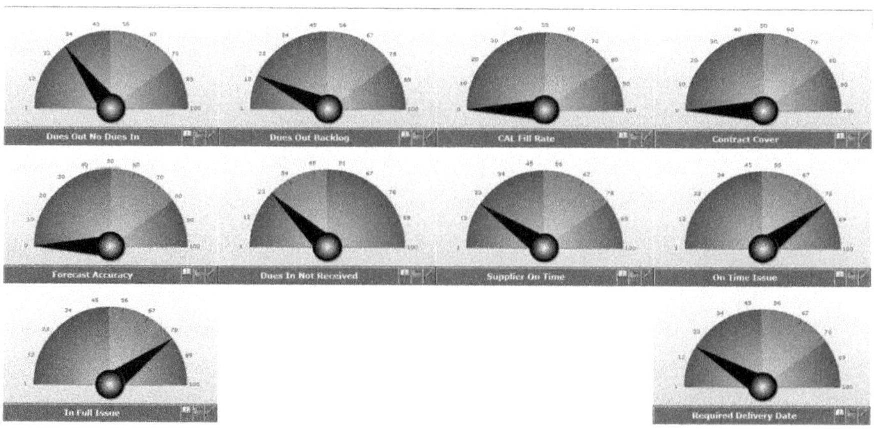

RAG and other traffic-light analogies are common in performance reporting interface design, but with them come problems associated with the polarity of the RAG sequence and the immediate impact of 'actions on' if, for whatever reason, one or more of the dials go 'red' (or 'green'). Furthermore, traffic-light reporting simply indicates current state; they do not give a ready indication of trends or other influencing factors that may indicate mitigating issues that may indicate the reasons for process anomalies. It took some time (six weeks on a short six-month contract) to demonstrate and prove the reporting shortcomings of the project-sponsor-defined reporting requirement based on dials. But eventually a third iteration was designed and built that moved a step further towards the multi-perspective, multidimensional reporting capability, made feasible by applying the principles of managed data-to-information transition coupled with the application of dimensioning in such a way that data could be accurately targeted contextually using the richness of the meta model that had been planned and developed. A screen shot sample of the third iteration is provided in Figure 12.13.

The final interface, consisting of some 14 tab pages (see Annex B), provided a variety of reports (line graphs, stacked bar charts, pie charts, tabular lists). Capitalizing on the underlying meta model, each chart contains an active navigation capability into other reports, charts and lists on (usually) a single-click basis which all (on the live dashboard) lead contextually into detail data (Figure 12.13).

The number and type of graphs on each tab varies, but the aim was to provide multiple but contextually sound views of the perspective implied by the tab title (Figure 12.14).

The architectural effect was that each dashboard (one for each of the primary dimensions) could act as a direct gateway into the wider architecture as, in addition to the dashboards' internal navigation capabilities, provision was also made for hyperlink management and librarianship

FIGURE 12.13 Multiple tabs, multiple views

FIGURE 12.14 Dashboard as gateway

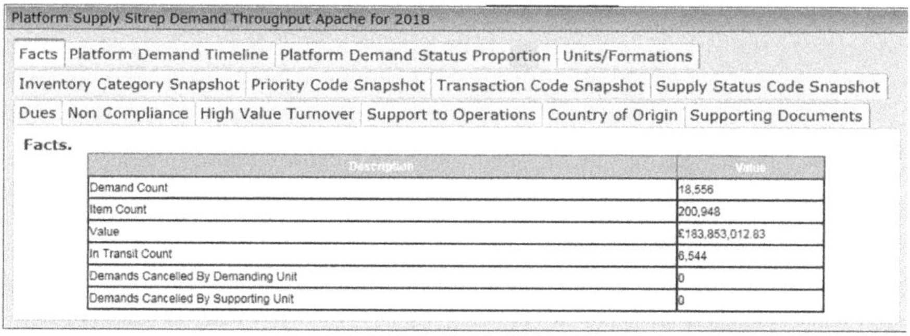
Platform Supply Sitrep Demand Throughput Apache for 2018

Facts | Platform Demand Timeline | Platform Demand Status Proportion | Units/Formations

Inventory Category Snapshot | Priority Code Snapshot | Transaction Code Snapshot | Supply Status Code Snapshot

Dues | Non Compliance | High Value Turnover | Support to Operations | Country of Origin | Supporting Documents

Facts.

Description	Value
Demand Count	18,556
Item Count	200,948
Value	£183,853,012.83
In Transit Count	6,544
Demands Cancelled By Demanding Unit	0
Demands Cancelled By Supporting Unit	0

FIGURE 12.15 Multi-dimension, multi perspective 'fray out'

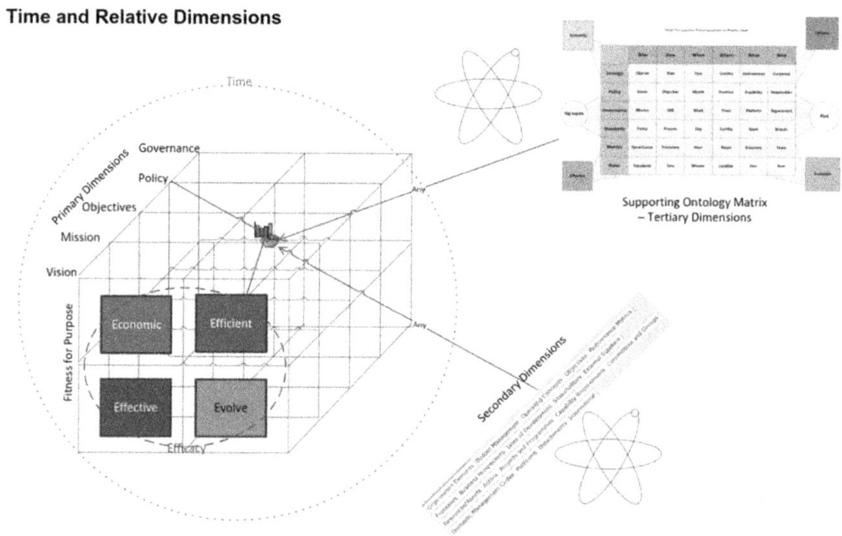

such that supporting evidence could be easily added by non-technical personnel.

Figure 12.15 illustrates in overview the nature of the layered effect the third iteration of the dashboard supported. The long-term impact being to provide the means to view supply chain activity as a 'living system' as per James Grier Millers concept of the system as a living thing.

The follow-on question, though, is: did it achieve the aim of proving the feasibility of multi-perspective, multidimensional reporting across the UK Defence Support Chain? For that question to be resolved, as often happens, opportunity came knocking.

The scenario – admirals, sailors, pirates and soap powder

The first tab of each third iteration dashboard presents several views of demand throughput. The three views, to reiterate, are:

- number of requests to supply;
- the financial value of supply requests;
- the volume, by quantity of items requested.

An illustrative sample of the first of the throughput charts appears in Figure 12.16.

FIGURE 12.16 Original demand throughput chart

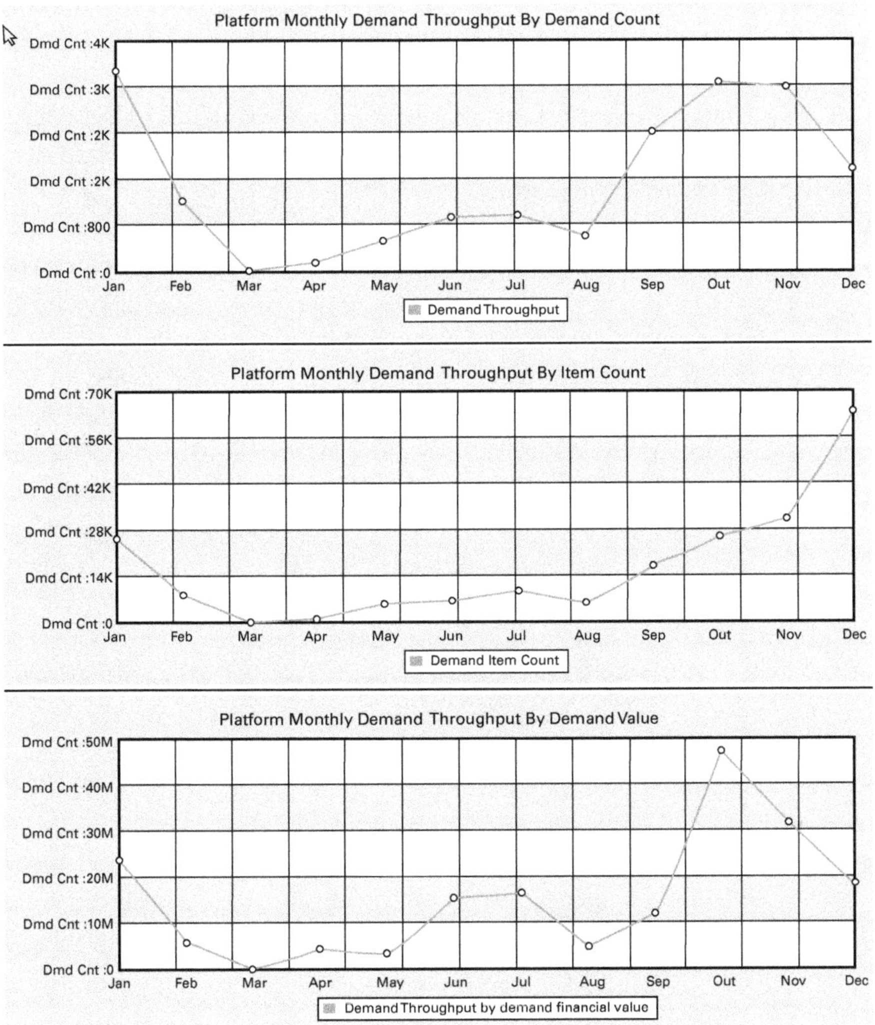

In November 2015, while refining the dashboard on an architectural basis (experimenting with speeding up chart generation and so on), the author was approached by two senior naval warrant officers from the DSCOM organization to ask if a particular class or type of stores request, known as 'Z', could be separated out so that they could examine the end result.

The warrant officers were asked why they wanted the required separation and to seek permission from the project sponsor before anything was done. The explanation for the request, to paraphrase, went something like...

The UK had made the national, strategic decision to acquire two new aircraft carriers as one of the aims of a recent strategic Defence review undertaken by the UK government. For such major procurement exercises, in order for a new ship to be accepted into service, there is the concept of 'first fitting', which is to ensure that on day one of acceptance, whatever is being delivered by industry into active service is as complete, in terms of equipment fit, as possible.

For such large warships, first fitting requires national effort and can have a temproary skewing effect on supply activity as the ships (platforms) near completion. At such times, from time to time, higher demand fulfilment priorities are imposed, with the aim of ensuring that 'first fitting' is as complete as possible. The means of notifying any change of priority in those circumstances is for someone senior to issue an 'order to adjust priority status' that is published across the Navy and beyond. What had happened in the particular circumstances of the aircraft carrier was that just such a re-prioritization had been ordered, but the wording of the order had been left open to interpretation in that it did not specifically state that the re-prioritization applied specifically to the new ships. The order said explicitly that a class of demand known as 'Z' could only be refused or cancelled by a small number of key naval lgistics staff. But it did not say, equally explicitly, that the priority only applied to the new ships.

Meanwhile, 3,000 miles away in the Persian Gulf, there was a warship, one of many on anti-pirate duty off Somalia, which had, because they were on operations, a high demand priority status anyway, but for reasons of distance (3,000 miles away from the UK and several hundred miles away from any coastline where they were operating) they were pre-planning their re-provisioning on return to port. It was noted, by the two naval warrant officers who were monitoring the naval supply chain, that shortly after the 'Z' re-prioritization order had been published, some ships, other than the designated aircraft carriers, were also labelling some of their replenishment requests with the re-prioritized category.

FIGURE 12.17 Z demands, misinterpretation of reprioritization

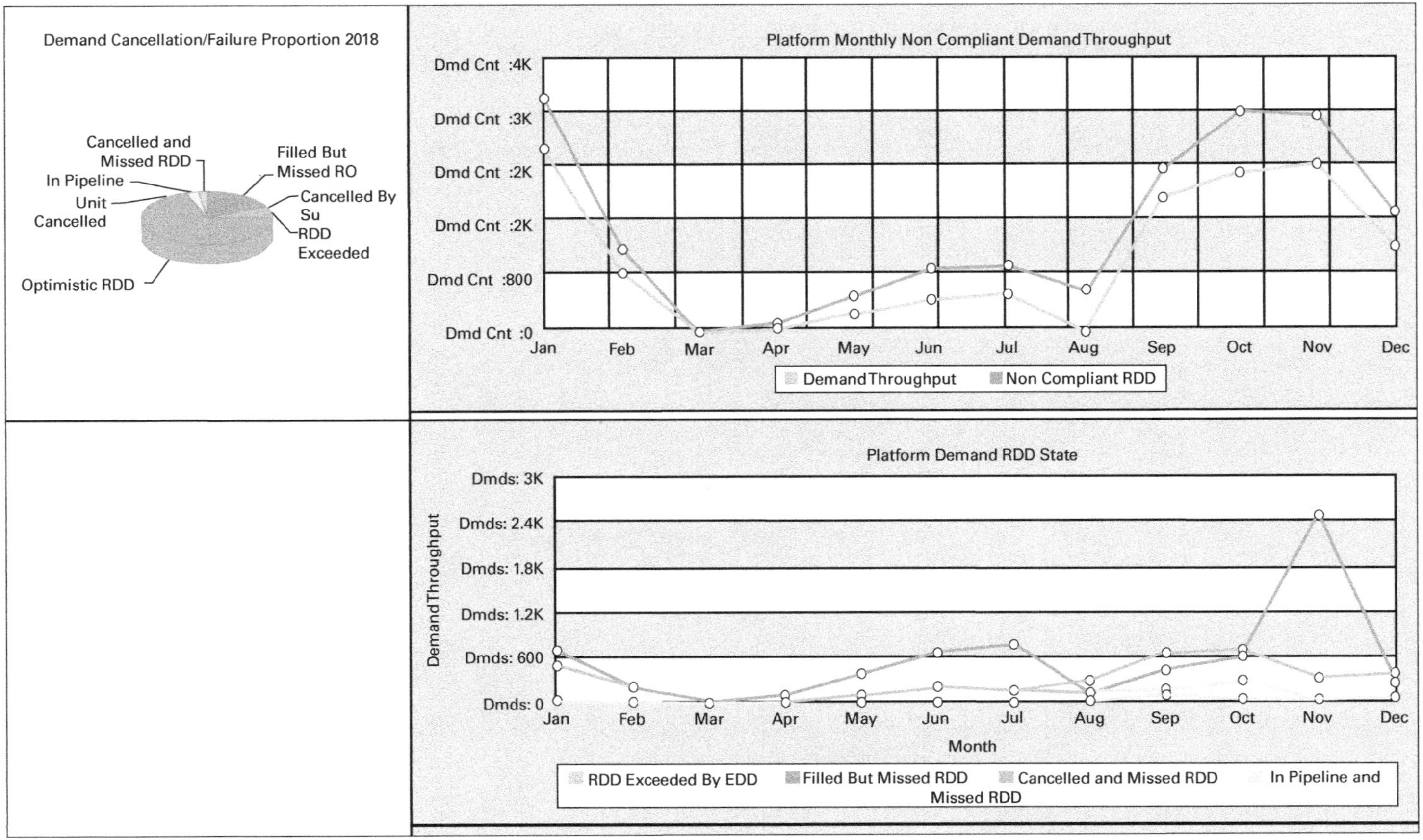

The aim of the logisticians concerned was to do their best in supply management terms for their ship so that it was as well equiped and provisioned as they could arrange. The downstream impact of the misinterpretation, however, was, in part, significant, in that if any frontline unit on operations requests re-supply, quite rightly, the support chain makes every possible effort to make sure that those requests are met. But, while there is usually more than one way to achieve re-supply of non-warlike items (purchasing locally, for example), the impact of the combination of operational priority and the 'Z' classification was that some non-essential stores (and in such circumstances non-essential as a term is open to debate) were being despatched by air bridge to the nearest secure resupply facility in Bahrain. And it was that possibly unnecessay skewing of the supply chain supply effort that concerned the warrant officers.

Once explained, project sponsor approval was given, and a few hours' programming effort with the aim of adding additional detail to the demand throughput graph revealed a rise in 'Z' priority stores requests within hours of publication of the high-level supply prioritization order for the aircraft carriers. Once the evidence proving the concerns of the warrant officers was validated, corrective procedural action was taken and the situation was resolved. In effect, this was an example of 'inversion of control', in that it is often the case that actions taken at the direction of senior decision making by those lower down the management chains can have unexpected impact when decisions taken at the process level are applied incorrectly, either through ambiguity in the direction (in this case) or deliberate action of one sort or another. A good management information system, carefully architected, should be able to reveal that kind of phenomenon. And that can only happen if the concept of data-to-information transition is understood and the nature of the programming and logic applied is built in to the information delivery architecture as a matter of design.

Understanding significance

Among a number of discovery exercises that the project was able to demonstrate was the need to understand the significance of NATO catalogue items in respect of analytical skewing of issues such as performance reporting. A very simple exercise was carried out to determine which items were the most frequently requested in terms of number of demands submitted and the number of items per demand, the aim being to demonstrate that the commonly used 'perfect fulfilment' metric frequently used in the monitoring of suppy chain performance might be influenced by non-essential items. The experiment revealed the most frequently occuring demands and the highest volume per item demands were caused by items that could concievably be purchased locally. The top ten list contained things such as toilet paper and black plastic bags, for example.

While no doubt those items are important, in comparison to, say, a key vehicle spare which may be keeping vital equipment out of operational use, the more significant item is more likely to be the vehicle spare given the specialist nature of military vehicles. It proved difficult to get the senior supply managers to understand that the nature of the business benefit that the kind of reporting that was possible provided might be useful.

What happened next?

The proof of concept was established as viable and the task was terminated at the end of March 2015. Under the direction of the project sponsor, the MoD went on to acquire a sophisticted high-end pattern recognition application suite that was technically more capable than the POC (among other things, it included a server fitted with some 3Tb of memory). The author of this chapter went on to be tasked with acting as the Indpenendent Qualification Body (IQB) for the RAF Voyager (the air tanker fleet) platform transformation programme.

However, the author did not simply 'park' the code and design approach but has gone on to extend the capability to the fourth transition level, writing, testing and proving components that can open, read and catalogue document files and maintain a managing link between content and document location such that document files can be treated as 'just another data source'. The dashboard reporting capability was further expanded to include provision for support of other forms of legislative compliance. In particular, code was written and attached to the final dashboard that is capable of establishing geophysical referential links between point of supply and point of use.

And finally, with the architectural scope of the site, information delivery has been widened to include the use of international reference data such as the financial Global Legal Entity Identifier Foundation (GLEIF) database. The initial exercise, linking GLEIF profiles to NATO Stock Catalogue NCAGE values, provided the means to establish a link between suppliers and detailed financial and other financial status reporting capabilities which, coupled with geophysical links, means that in terms of supplier performance, a more balanced view can be taken of external effectiveness and efficiency.

Conclusions and lessons learnt

At six months, the period of time to demonstrate proof of concept was short and was, for the author, an intensive experience given the level of change that was encountered and the volume of data that was available. It is indicative of the nature of the task that the MoD's subsequent acquisition of an industrial-strength analytical capability took some three years to complete and bring into service at the cost of several million pounds. Nevertheless, the proof of concept was achieved.

There were many lessons learnt during the course of the exercise, and the primary ones were:

- Performance reporting stands or falls by the business having a clear understanding of what it needs to know in order to determine the viability of the organization.
- Performance metric profiling should be treated as the primary means by which the business can specify information delivery requirements.
- No one data set is the totality of available information and, as a result, there will to be a need at some point, as a matter of design, to align numbers of data sets.
- In terms of processing efficiency and effectiveness, alignment of multiples of data sets requires a capability to translate database values from the perspectives of value, scope and meaning.
- Reporting is a viral activity, constrained by 'the need to know', whereas data collection is linear.
- Reporting, in the first instance, is dependent on high-quality data for accuracy.
- A planned 'Extract, Transform and Load' plan can mitigate against many forms of data error but is dependent on the creation of a master or canonical data model.
- The operating environment, at the desktop level (in the MoD's case a standard configuration PC), means that part of the ETL effort is to reduce data volumes where possible, using mathematically sound means.
- Development of the kind of reporting capability envisaged requires specialized knowledge of both technical issues (programming, database design etc) and how normal business is conducted.

- Two key factors that may be used to prove the viability of the end product are to test the stability of the end reporting tool from the perspective of reducing the impact of inferential distance while at the same time being able to detect the impact of inversion of control.
- Finally, and key, the author has some 38 years' worth of experience in Defence both in and out of uniform, some 23 of them writing software for the Defence logistics effort. That level of professional qualification and business knowledge was crucial to one person being able to do what was achieved. While that level of qualification and experience is quite rare, if the author were to make a recommendation, it would be that that rarity is a missed opportunity and if 'data are the oil of the next generation of business form and function', then it makes sense to train staff, both uniformed and civilian, on a formal basis, in the skills and techniques required to exploit the huge reservoir of data that is available to Defence and to sustain them as part of the professional career framework of the UK Armed Forces.

The list of lessons learnt set out above is not exhaustive, but they are the most significant. Along the way there were any number of ups and downs, but the end effect was achieved in that it was feasible and possible to use Defence Support Chain data accurately to achieve the specified aim.

QUESTIONS

1. Of all of the design factors taken into consideration which was the most significant from a business perspective?
2. It would seem that there were multiples of databases/sets included in the exercise, rather than, say, the inventory systems. Why was that?
3. In this document there is one scenario described. Where there any other success in respect of the provision of an ability to investigate or drill down into detail data?
4. The study was quite short in duration, what kind of skills and experience were required in order to attempt it?
5. Was the aim of the study taken further?

Answers on page 240.

Annex A – Reading list

The Puritan Gift by William and Kenneth Hopper
De-facto history of US management from the puritans to just after the Lehmann Brothers crash

The Fractal Organization by Patrick Hoverstadt
An introduction to the Viable Systems Model

The Fifth Discipline by Peter Senge
A description or method explaining how to apply systems thinking to organization design and optimization

My Years With General Motors by Arthur P Sloane
A management masterpiece and classic

Enterprise Architecture Planning by Steven H Spewak
A precursor to Zachman; an enterprise architecture classic

Creative Problem Solving by Robert Flood and Michael Jackson
Describes the application of the concept of 'Total Systems Intervention' related to managed application of multiple design and process-based methodologies

Systems Thinking, Systems Practice by Peter Checkland
The trio of books by Peter Checkland set out the design principles and justification for the Soft Systems Methodology, a key aim of which is to move from the prevalent goal-driven positivism to something more interpretive in nature in the field of information management

Information Systems and Information Systems by Peter Checkland
The trio of books by Peter Checkland set out the design principles and justification for the Soft Systems Methodology, a key aim of which is to move from the prevalent goal-driven positivism to something more interpretive in nature in the field of information management

Soft Systems Methodology in Action by Peter Checkland
The trio of books by Peter Checkland set out the design principles and justification for the Soft Systems Methodology, a key aim of which is to move from the prevalent goal-driven positivism to something more interpretive in nature in the field of information management

All Services, All the Time by Doug McDavid
Takes the view that organizations are living systems and addresses issues related to capability sustainment and development in that context

Functional Decomposition by Paul Kisak
A series of essays on the design discipline of functional decomposition

Creating the Corporate Future by Russel L Ackoff
No book list on enterprise architecture would be complete without naming Russel Ackoff. A classic in the field of organization design

Beyond Alignment Edited by John Gotze
A series of essays on matters related to the application of the Viable Systems Model invented by the pioneering Stafford Beer

General Systems Theory by Ludwig von Bertalanffy
An introduction to general systems theory, its principles and some descriptions of observational experiments proving the validity of the subject area

TABLE 12.4 Annex A

ISBN	Title	Author	Reason
978-1845119867	*The Puritan Gift*	William and Kenneth Hopper	De-facto history of US management from the puritans to just after the Lehmann Brothers crash
978-0470060568	*The Fractal Organization*	Patrick Hoverstadt	An introduction to the Viable Systems Model
978-1905211203	*The Fifth Discipline*	Peter Senge	A description or method explaining how to apply systems thinking to organization design and optimization
978-0385042352	*My Years With General Motors*	Arthur P Sloane	A management masterpiece and classic
089-4354361	*Enterprise Architecture Planning*	Steven H Spewak	A precursor to Zachman; an enterprise architecture classic
0471-93052-0	*Creative Problem Solving*	Robert Flood and Michael Jackson	Describes the application of the concept of 'Total Systems Intervention' related to managed application of multiple design and process-based methodologies
13978-0-471-98606-5	*Systems Thinking, Systems Practice*	Peter Checkland	The trio of books by Peter Checkland set out the design principles and justification for the Soft Systems Methodology, a key aim of which is to move from the prevalent goal-driven positivism to something more interpretive in nature in the field of information management

(continued)

TABLE 12.4 (Continued)

ISBN	Title	Author	Reason
0471-95820-4	*Information Systems and Information Systems*	Peter Checkland	The trio of books by Peter Checkland set out the design principles and justification for the Soft Systems Methodology, a key aim of which is to move from the prevalent goal-driven positivism to something more interpretive in nature in the field of information management
0471-986054	*Soft Systems Methodology in Action*	Peter Checkland	The trio of books by Peter Checkland set out the design principles and justification for the Soft Systems Methodology, a key aim of which is to move from the prevalent goal-driven positivism to something more interpretive in nature in the field of information management
978-1-63157-276-0	*All Services, All the Time*	Doug McDavid	Takes the view that organizations are living systems and addresses issues related to capability sustainment and development in that context
978-1-51777-292-5	*Functional Decomposition*	Paul Kisak	A series of essays on the design discipline of functional decomposition
0471-09009-3	*Creating the Corporate Future*	Russel L Ackoff	No book list on enterprise architecture would be complete without naming Russel Ackoff. A classic in the field of organization design
978-1-84890-116-2	*Beyond Alignment*	Edited by John Gotze	A series of essays on matters related to the application of the Viable Systems Model invented by the pioneering Stafford Beer
0-0876-0453-4	*General Systems Theory*	Ludwig von Bertalanffy	An introduction to general systems theory, its principles and some descriptions of observational experiments proving the validity of the subject area

Annex B – Final dashboard chart types

There is a caveat to this annex. During the course of the post proof of concept refinement, the author produced a supply demand or supply transaction generator that automatically produced pre-transformation records that, in effect, mirrored the behaviour of forward operation of the Defence Support Chain as per MJDI. Screen shots contained in this part of the chapter and elsewhere make use of fictitious data for illustrative purposes. Page 1 is basically, a simple list of summary statistics.

Page 2 shows three annual demand throughput time line charts for:

- number of demands or requests for stores, per calendar month;
- number of items demanded;
- financial value of items demanded.

A 'drill down' capability was provided to support the principle of retrieving a monthly summary of the dashboard.

The aim of the chart shown in Page 3 was to indicate where in the supply process, as per JSP 886, demands were currently situated in process terms and to give an indication of possible supply chain choke points in summary form. As with the throughput charts, the demand throughput chart had a 'drill down' capability

This chart shown in Page 4 provides an indication of which units were requesting a particular type of inventory items associated with classes of major capital assets (in military parlance, platforms). From time to time, this chart would reveal potential anomalies, such as units that did not hold the platform under review requesting items from inventory that they should not need. The majority of such requests, on investigation, were legitimate but, nevertheless, from time to time there was a need for corrective action.

FIGURE 12.18 Page 1: Fact summary

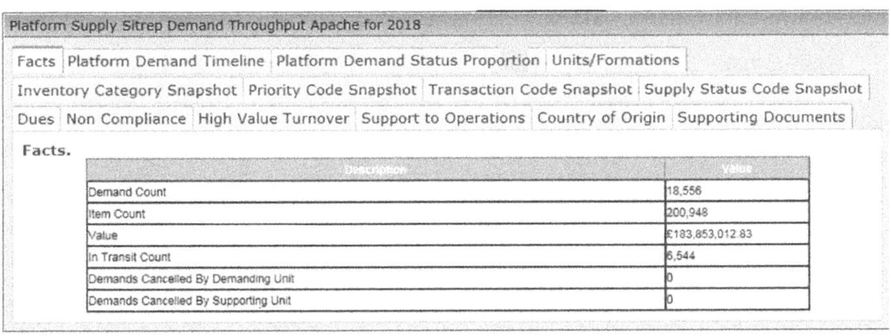
Platform Supply Sitrep Demand Throughput Apache for 2018

Facts | Platform Demand Timeline | Platform Demand Status Proportion | Units/Formations
Inventory Category Snapshot | Priority Code Snapshot | Transaction Code Snapshot | Supply Status Code Snapshot
Dues | Non Compliance | High Value Turnover | Support to Operations | Country of Origin | Supporting Documents

Facts.

Description	Value
Demand Count	18,556
Item Count	200,948
Value	£183,853,012.83
In Transit Count	6,544
Demands Cancelled By Demanding Unit	0
Demands Cancelled By Supporting Unit	0

FIGURE 12.19 Page 2: Demand, or Supply Throughput

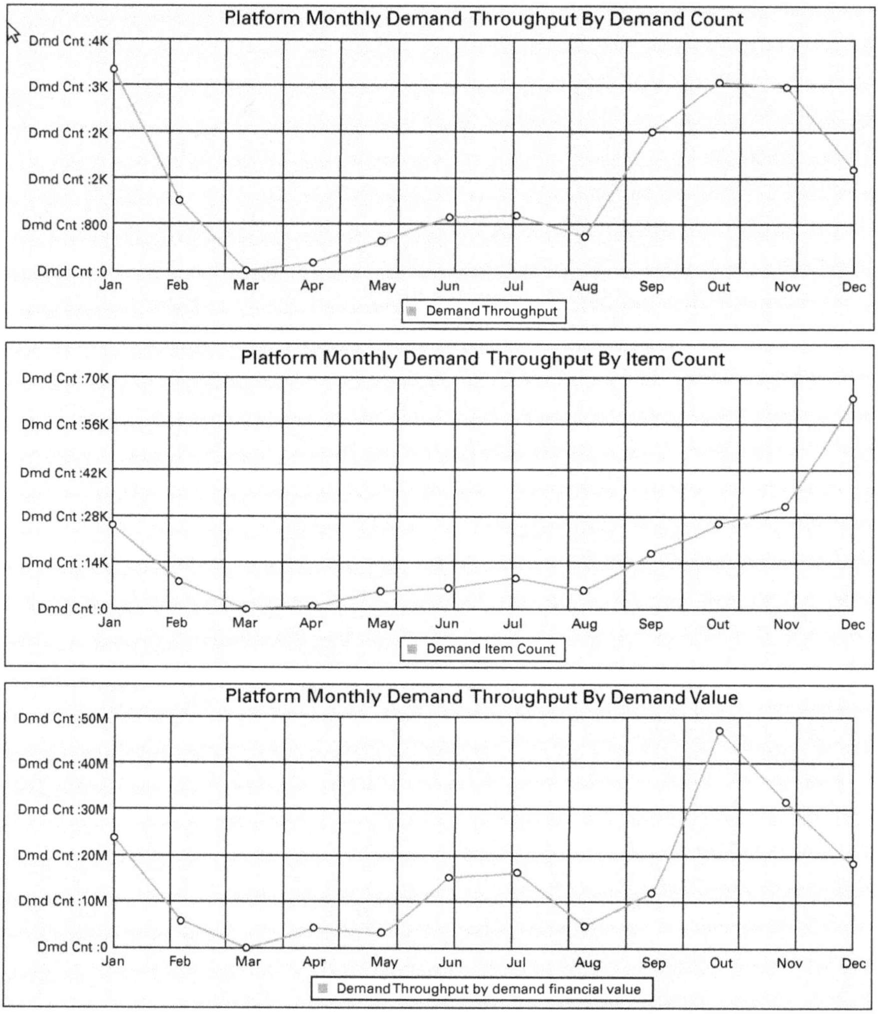

In complex inventory management scenarios like Defence there is need to group part-numbers using a number of categorization classes (Page 5). In this case, the categorization method is related to the equipment programme underpinning the capability development and sustainment of the platform, which may involve multiples of budget streams.

Supply priority, as the name implies, is an indicator of supply importance (Page 6). Frontline operations have a higher priority than rear echelon supply requests.

FIGURE 12.20 Page 3: Demand or supply throughput as a multi-stacked bar chart

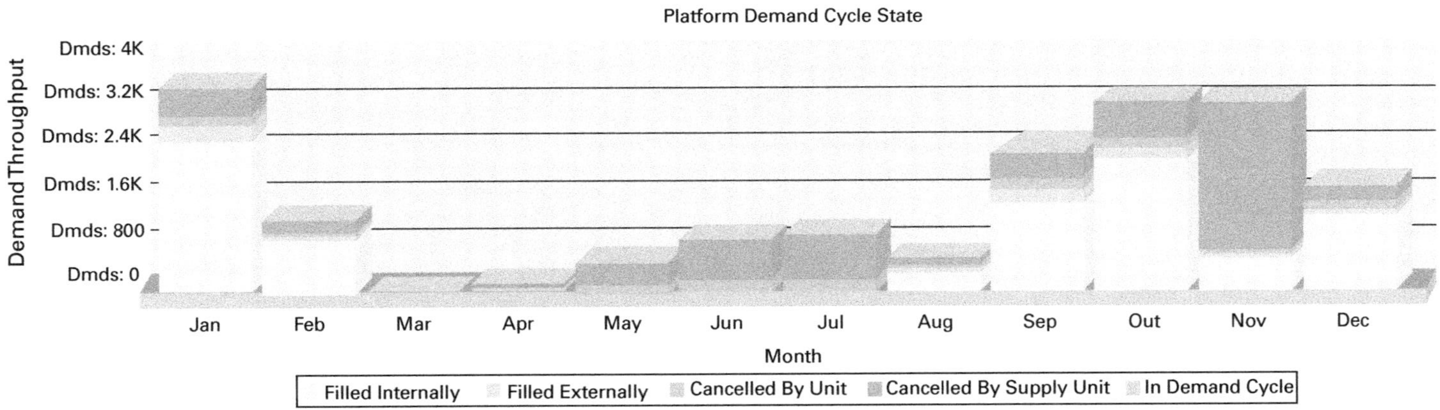

FIGURE 12.21 Page 4: Requesting units

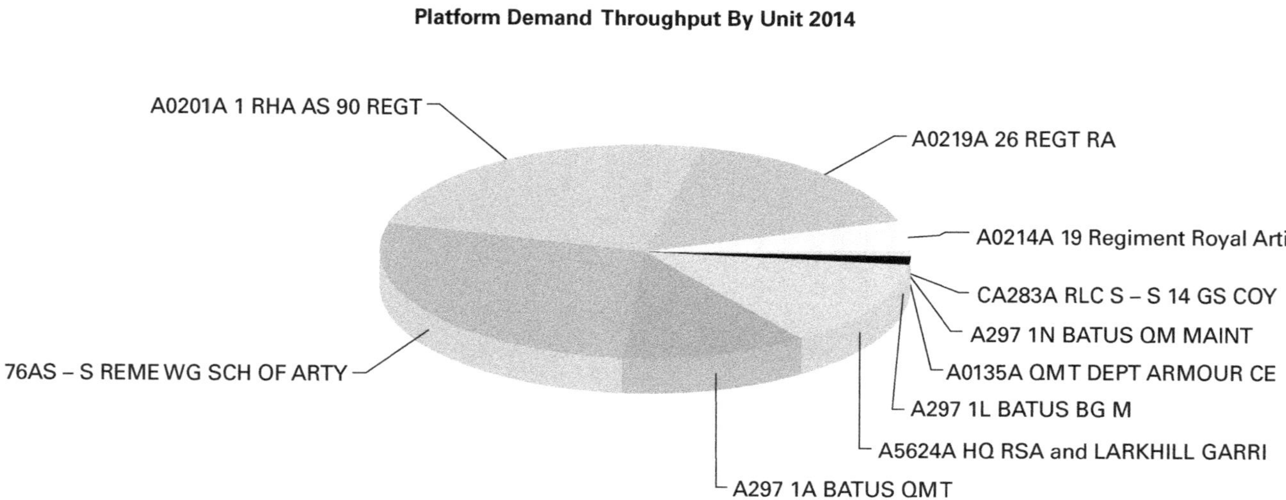

FIGURE 12.22 Page 5: Inventory Category

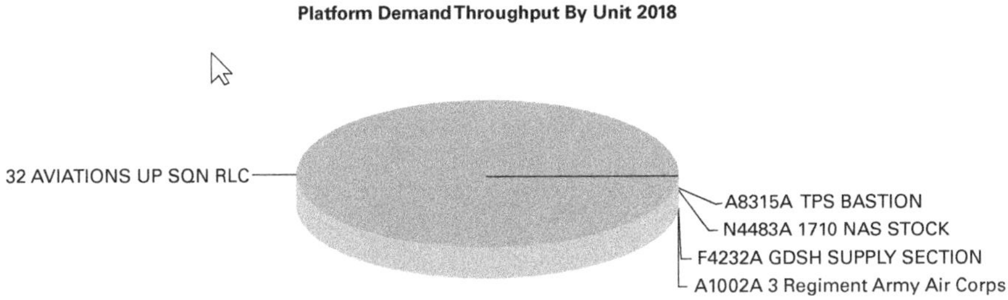

FIGURE 12.23 Page 6: Supply Priority

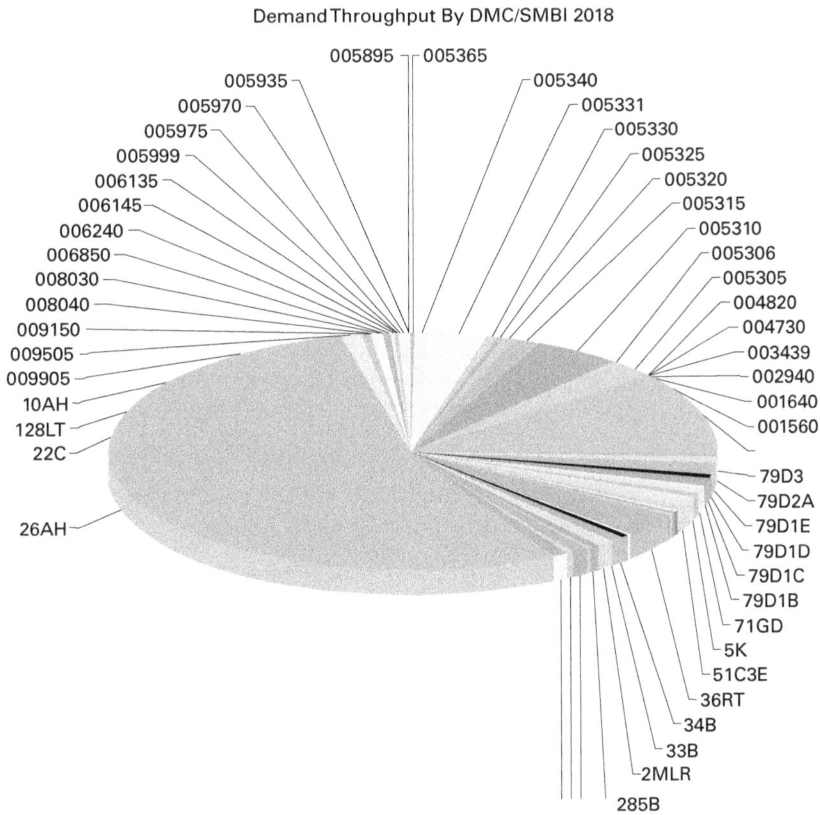

The transaction code report (Page 7) illustrates the nature of the way supply business is done, covering types of transactions such as inter-unit stock transfers, planned replenishment of expendable items and so on.

To give some indication of a request to supply in respect of in process decision taking, the concept of supply status provides the means to identify where in the decision cycle, requests or demands are (Page 8).

FIGURE 12.24 Page 7: Transaction Codes

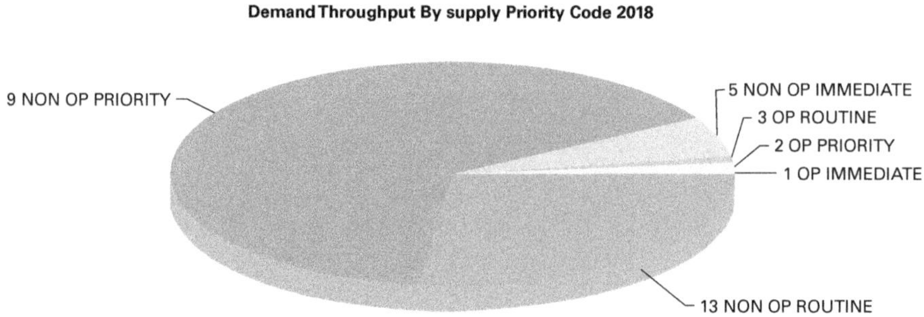

One of the key reports, as it turns out, was built into the dashboard. The report (Page 9) gives an indication of the status of items requested that are awaiting supply from industry, giving some indication of supply chain lag generated by an inability to supply that is not in the control of the military logistics system per se (quite simply, there is none of the items requested in stock).

In much the same vein as the situation that demonstrated the capability of the design approach to detect 'inversion of control', the non-compliance report (Page 10) was used to illustrate situations in which mandated supply chain procedures were not being followed by requesting units. For example, a key date-based performance driver for the supply chain is the 'required delivery date' set by requesting units, but defined, in terms of applicable constraint, by JSP 886; in other words, a unit requesting something in a timeframe that was unachievable, and similar invalid request forms.

Page 11 provided a simple list of high-value items requested by units.

At any one time, UK Armed Forces are often involved in more than one military operation. This report (Page 12) presented a means to gauge the comparative balance of effort required to supply a platform 'in theatre'.

The last two tabs were subsequently added to the dashboard after the end of the proof of concept as experiments on the art of the possible, by the author.

An increasing managerial concern has been to get into a position where inventory could be identified by country of supply origin. The author deconstructed the NSN systems and used national codes to provide the four charts shown on Page 13. On drill down, a country profile is generated for the platform being reported on, which has also been aligned with UK NCAGE codes and the international GLEIF system to identify suppliers by address and financial status where possible.

FIGURE 12.25 Page 8: Supply Status Codes

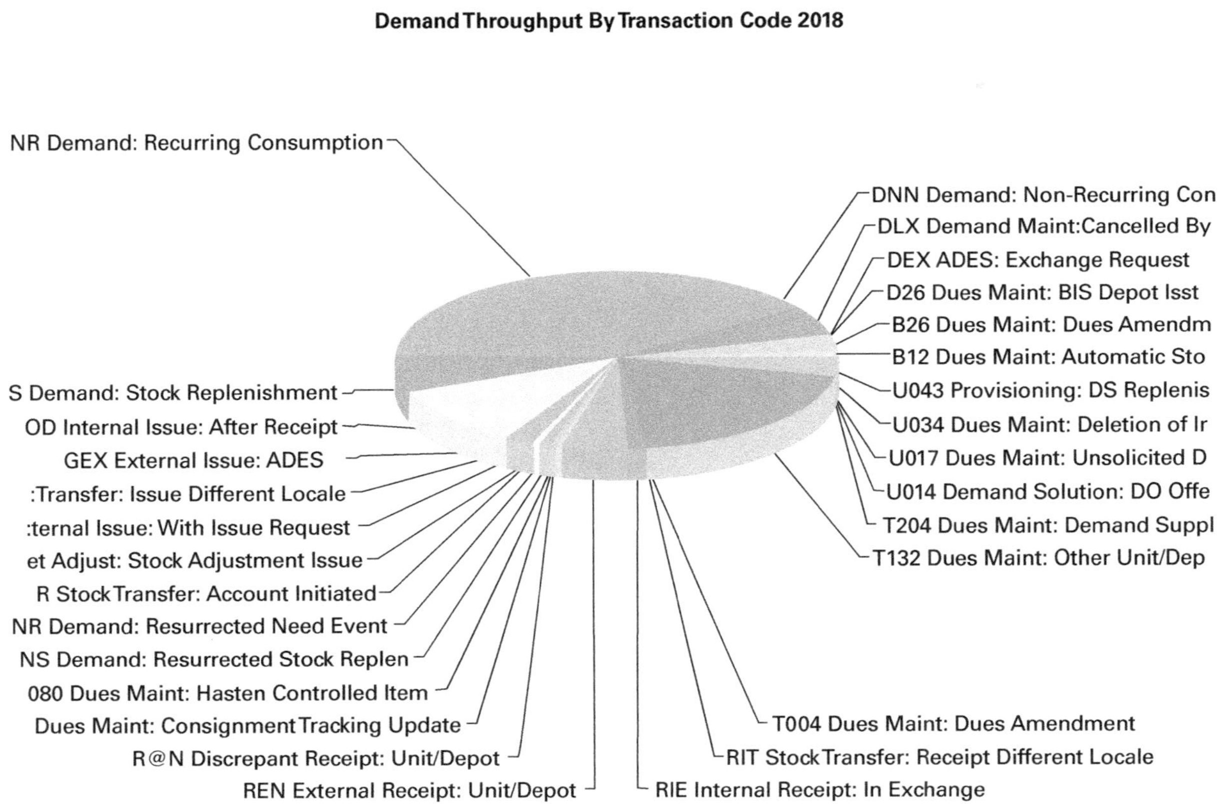

FIGURE 12.26 Page 9: Items due in and out

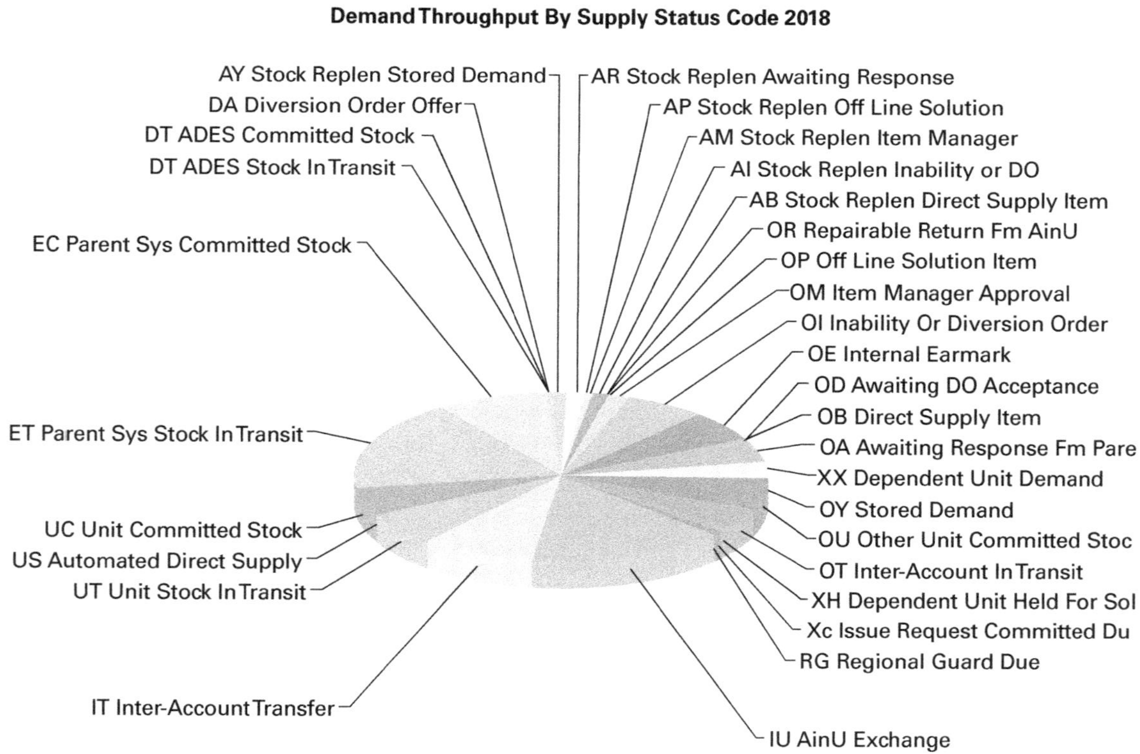

FIGURE 12.27 Page 10: Non-compliance

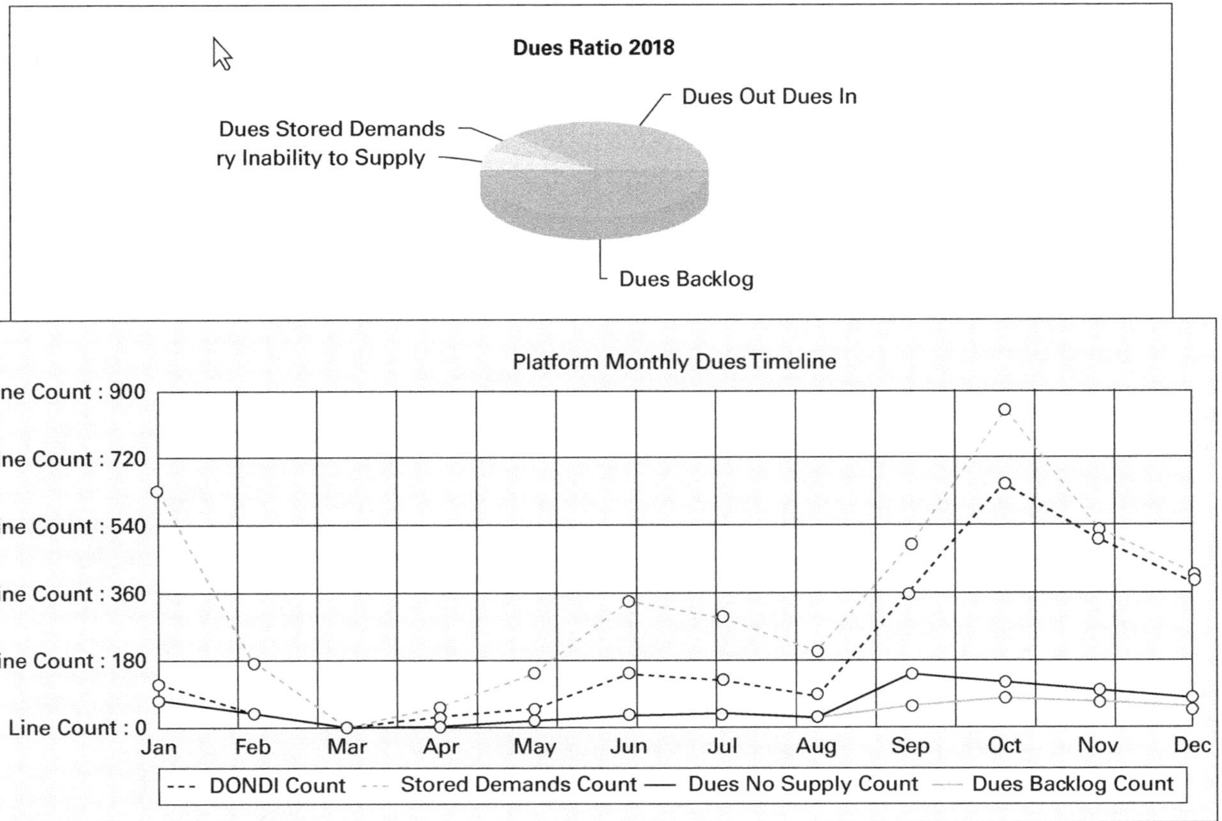

FIGURE 12.28 Page 11: High-value turnover

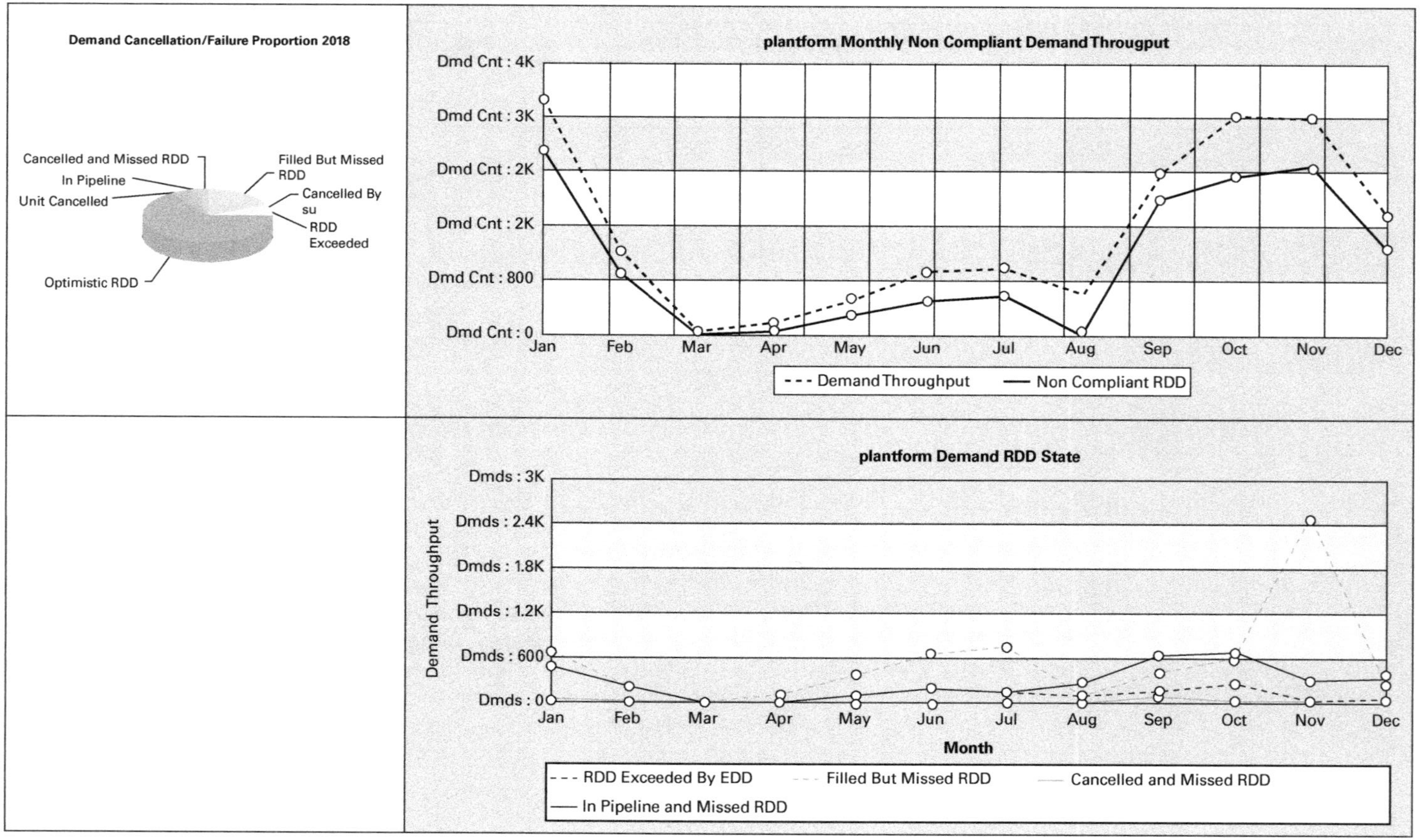

FIGURE 12.29 Page 12: Support to operations

DMC	NSN	Item Name	Owning UIN	BLB	PT Name	DMD Count	Item Count	Line Value	Current Stock	Stock Value
26AH	4133826	MAST MT RADR	D1950A	8148	Apache	58	58	£140,125,966.98	6	£16,485,407.91
26AH	5495464	MTADSTURRET	D1950A	8148	Apache	69	69	£50,436,544.00	16	£12,609,136.00
26AH	5495465	DAY SENSOR	D1950A	8148	Apache	61	61	£20,322,496.80	14	£4,741,915.95
26AH	4696708	LTU	D1950A	8148	Apache	29	29	£15,474,256.28	29	£16,026,908.26
26AH	5297446	MAIN RTR GB	D1950A	8148	Apache	31	31	£9,300,000.00	13	£3,900,000.00
26AH	6038022	PROCESSOR,SI	D1950A	8148	Apache	62	62	£9,089,741.26	26	£3,811,826.90
79D2A	3976050	ELEC COMP AS	D1950A	8148	Apache	4	4	£8,386,660.56	8	£16,773,321.09
26AH	5785352	PYLON RACK	D1950A	8148	Apache	94	221	£8,018,271.90	21	£1,870,930.11
26AH	5820432	STABILATOR	D1950A	8148	Apache	32	32	£4,779,855.08	14	£2,389,927.54
26AH	5167217	M-NSA STRUCT	D1950A	8148	Apache	7	7	£4,728,273.48	7	£5,673,928.14
36RT	8551276	ENGINE MK120	N6194Q	8157	Apache	5	5	£4,678,582.75	0	£0.00
26AH	5300694	HEAD RW	D1950A	8148	Apache	25	25	£4,292,618.00	28	£5,463,332.00
26AH	4038287	HIDAS RXP3 2	D1950A	8148	Apache	18	18	£4,128,611.58	39	£8,945,325.01
26AH	5291379	MAIN GEARBOX	D1950A	8148	Apache	18	18	£4,079,280.32	26	£6,628,830.65
26AH	4124978	BORES HARM K	D1950A	8148	Apache	9	9	£3,596,936.13	8	£3,197,276.56
005865	3234999	ALPHACMTRANS	D6461E	8436	Air Platform Systems	6	6	£3,420,000.00	40	£27,360,000.00
26AH	5183635	MPTUR RECEIV	D1950A	8148	Apache	6	6	£2,845,815.96	19	£10,814,100.61
26AH	2737610	FSP SERVOREP	D1950A	8148	Apache	21	23	£2,674,915.74	31	£4,606,799.30
79D2A	7268277	PROCESSOR	D1950A	8148	Apache	3	3	£2,167,043.46	11	£7,945,826.04

FIGURE 12.30 Page 13: International Trade in Arms Regulations (ITAR)

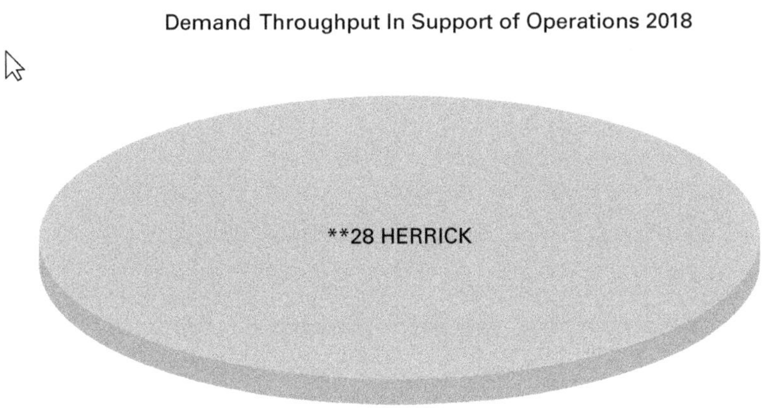

FIGURE 12.31 Page 14 – Supporting documents

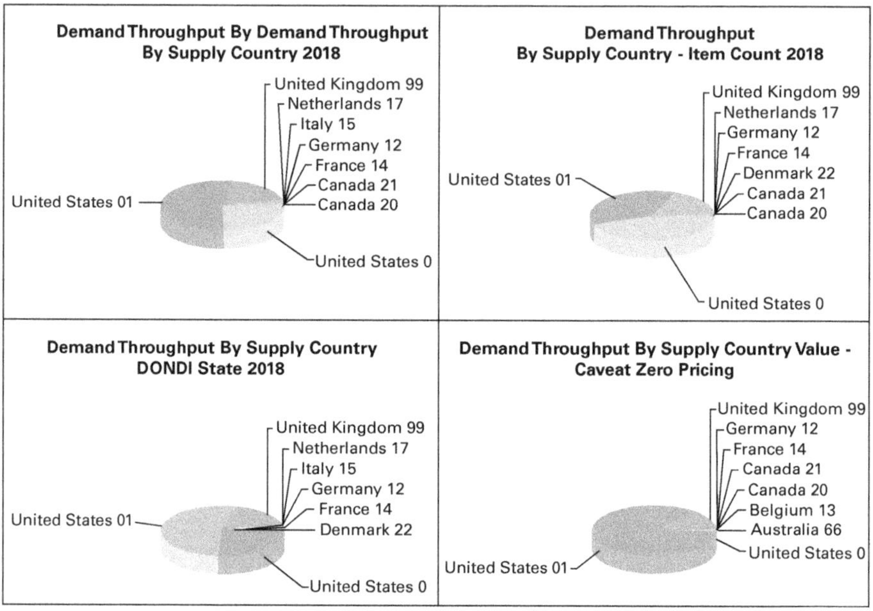

The last tab report (Page 14) provides a list of documents held in a through-life management plan (TLMP) that refer to the platform under review in their content.

As a matter of operating principle, each of the charts provided a drill-down capability into a more detailed report for each line point or pie slice as appropriate. The nature of the navigation varied from chart to chart. The time line charts drop down into a monthly report of a similar nature, with the pie charts dropping down into a slice-specific dashboard within the context of the platform under review.

Annex C – Fact Table Relational Design

As described in the body of the report, the dashboards were founded on a series of fact tables generated through a six-stage ETL process. The six stages were:

1 Extract supporting infrastructure from sources. The supporting infrastructure included database content that contained things like unit addresses, budget structures and so on. Once downloaded, they were used

to update the digital organization chart that the author had generated using his organization mapping software.

2 Extract transaction data and review programmatically the completeness and validity of the content using the supply chain process definition contained in JSP 886. Where appropriate, records that could be rendered usable were completed, those that could not were deleted. After testing and revision of the data validation and review code that had to be developed, the total volume of records deleted in any one extraction exercise was less than 1% of the total volume extracted. The end result at this stage was a single database containing, at any one time, some 2,500,000 transaction records.

3 The third stage was to use measurement criteria contained in the specified performance metrics for the resulting transaction database, for example to apply pricing data to line totals.

4 The fourth stage was to align the transaction data, in structural terms, with the supporting infrastructure data generated by stage 1. For example, transaction data contained unique identification numbers (UINs), but did not contain unit titles or other supporting attributes such as national codes. These values could, of course, be drawn from other parts of the eventual federation, but the advantage this action had was to make the transaction database easier to search on a non-relational basis.

5 The fifth stage was to apply methods of calculation to the transaction data in performance metric profiles, and then store the result in summary, or fact, tables.

6 The sixth and final stage was to reapply the primary dimensions identified during the analysis phase to the table structure of the resulting fact tables as foreign keys that could be used either as primary or composite keys.

FIGURE 12.32 Map index: mutually supportive taxonomies

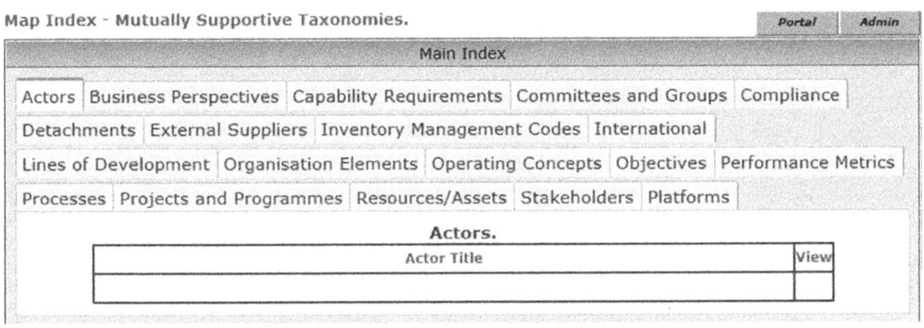

The overall advantage, while complicated in respect of ETL, meant that fact tables were a much smaller data set (on average a storage reduction of 95 per cent approximately) than the transformed transaction table, which in turn was much smaller in content that the original source data. Because the dimensioning, as a matter of design strategy, was applied to both extracted transaction data tables, it was possible, where necessary, to demonstrate a clear and definite architectural link to the source data.

The overriding advantage was speed of response to report generation requests from the end-user community.

Figure 12.33 provides a list of the fact tables (the full database structures can be made available of required), but from a case study perspective, that would be getting down into unnecessary detail.

The eventual reduction meant that the dashboards were querying against 4Gb of data as opposed to 3.5Pb, with the result that average dashboard execution was brought down to 15 seconds (as opposed to 36 hours in extremis).

FIGURE 12.33 Fact table structure

tblFactCancelledByPlatform
tblFactCancelledByUnit
tblFactDONDI
tblFactDONDIDMC
tblFactDONDIDuesIn
tblFactDONDIPlatform
tblFactDONDIStoredDemands
tblFactDONDIStoredDemandsPlatform
tblFactDONDIStoredDemandsUnit
tblFactDONDIUnit
tblFactDuesBackLog
tblFactNormalDemandMonthlyExpenditure
tblFactNormalDemandMonthlyExpenditureDMC
tblFactNormalDemandMonthlyExpenditureOperations
tblFactNormalDemandMonthlyExpenditurePlatform
tblFactNormalDemandMonthlyExpenditurePlatformNC
tblFactNormalDemandMonthlyExpenditureUnit
tblFactNormalDemandMonthlyTXN
tblFactOpCodeDMCExpenditure

Annex D - The gateway architectural concept

One of the design concepts applied by the author is that of a portal that can act as a gateway into a wider information architecture. Figure 12.34 provides an illustration of the concept. The portal consists of a series of web services (policy and governance delivery, risk register, objective and process catalogue, organization map etc) supported by a series of office automation software add-ins that provide the means to link directly from the desktop to the server side. The major end benefit is that single source of truth decision support becomes more reliable, as routes into the architecture can be better managed and controlled.

The portal provides a comprehensive navigational capability that supports cross-referencing of both applications and data on an almost infinite basis. In principle, once transaction data can be connected into the portal infrastructure by means of controlled ETL, the transaction data then become an integral part of the portal too. Nor does it require sophisticated technical or programming knowledge to operate.

The reductionist data management technique described in this case study is now an integral approach to portal implementation. The recent introduction of a document-cataloguing capability also provides the means to treat unstructured data as 'just another data source'. This in turn means that document files (and other portal components) can act as gateways into the wider data architecture too.

Annex E – The Performance Organisers' website

The portal as a gateway can be viewed as the Performance Organisers' website home page (Figure 12.35). The site itself is growing in popularity, with on average 2,000 visitors per month visiting it for one reason or another. The public site is a much enhanced and expanded capability that includes a number of components built in anticipation of the introduction into UK law of the Data Protection Bill 2018 and the EU General Data Protection Regulation. The aim is to anticipate the nature of the architectural impact of forthcoming privacy regulations, including a mix of web services and components, the aim of which is to support the effort required to meet the compliance needs of Subject Access Requests, Rights to Erasure and other related compliance liabilities.

FIGURE 12.34 Portal as gateway

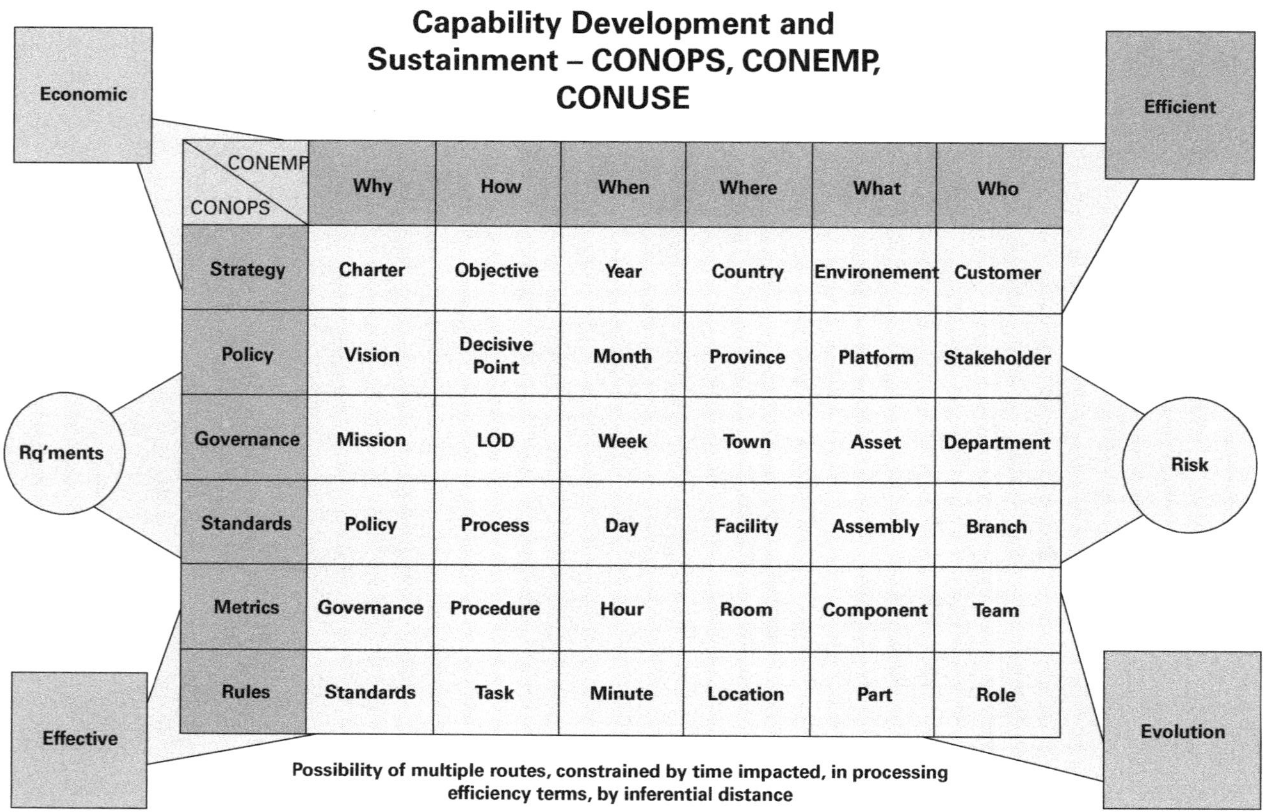

CONEMP / CONOPS	Why	How	When	Where	What	Who
Strategy	Charter	Objective	Year	Country	Environement	Customer
Policy	Vision	Decisive Point	Month	Province	Platform	Stakeholder
Governance	Mission	LOD	Week	Town	Asset	Department
Standards	Policy	Process	Day	Facility	Assembly	Branch
Metrics	Governance	Procedure	Hour	Room	Component	Team
Rules	Standards	Task	Minute	Location	Part	Role

FIGURE 12.35 The Performance Organisers' portal

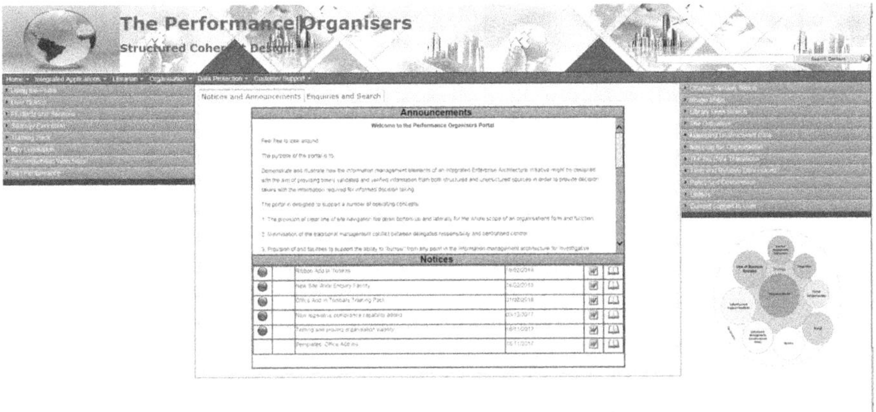

Embedded in the portal, but not active, is a partially complete digital map of the UK Armed Forces command structures as part of the possible means to track, on a geophysical basis, some code primitives that provide the means to, in effect, display supply chain routes from the manufacturers' original plants to forward deployment areas anywhere in the world.

Additionally, to further prove the validity of the methods of Cartesian cross-referencing applied in the design, the developer took a number of publicly available data sources and experimented with the possibilities offered by connecting the public data sets into the portal meta model. There have been a number of successes, which include linking up an international stock market database known as the 'GLEIF' with a subset of the NATO stock catalogue, the end effect of which is to demonstrate links from the NATO NCAGE supplier identifiers to the associated stock market company identifiers.

A second exercise involved the construction of a component that could open, read and catalogue unstructured data and maintain a link between content and document location, and then connect the resulting database using the same meta model construct with the aim of demonstrating a method of linking both structured and unstructured data. To prove the validity of the concept, a search facility was built into the portal that, from a single query, could draw data from multiple data sets, including documents, and list all associations where they could be found. The first such exercise, which the Performance Organisers refer to as the 'lithium' experiment, was successful in that a library of documents produced by the NASA battery experimental facility was linked on search to the same NATO stock catalogue subset. The net impact was that the nature of the health risk could be identified along with which items in the inventory contained the hazardous material of interest (lithium). An additional dimension gateway was also built, which provided the means to select a part item and then display where stock was held both in the base inventory and the forward supply network as indicated by MJDI.

The portal also includes the following web infrastructure capabilities:

- a process catalogue;
- an objective catalogue;
- the means to build 'fan'-type action plans based on lines of development utilizing the TEPIDOIL structure;
- a content management system;
- visitor monitoring without cookies and including the means to profile end-user browsers;
- a risk register, compliant with the aim and intent of the HM Treasury Orange and Red books;
- a RACI (responsible, accountable, consulted, informed) stakeholder assessment tool;
- an image file 'hot spot' designer with which any image file that can be displayed through a browser can be made 'active' and exploit the advantages offered by the meta construct used in the design to connect images file to just about anything.

And more. The point is to demonstrate the benefits of a structure website design underpinned by comprehensive meta modelling.

Action insights: Short cases for discussion

These short discussions and cases are insights on supply chains in action, covering issues from the past that are still applicable today. Their purpose is to provoke discussion. They are best utilized in small discussion groups. By engaging in 'reflective practice' lessons and insights from the past can be used to raise and answer questions about the future.

Innovation and competition in last-mile delivery

Action insight 1

EMEL AKTAS AND RICHARD WILDING

Increasing urbanization

The world's population is moving from rural areas to urban areas, with shifts from an agricultural economy to mass industry and services. According to the World Bank, currently 55 per cent of the world's population of 7.53 billion live in cities (https://data.worldbank.org/indicator/SP.URB.TOTL.IN.ZS). The proportion of population living in cities is 84 per cent for Oman, a country of 4.6 million people, comparable to the urbanization level of 83 per cent for the UK with a population of 66 million. Urbanization is a prominent phenomenon not only for Europe but also for the Middle East.

Cities generate jobs and income, and provide healthcare, education, financial and other services, enabling social mobility and resolution of the social and environmental problems that may exist in rural areas. With preferable working and living conditions we expect the cities to grow further, necessitating not only investment in housing, infrastructure and services but also smarter ways of meeting the increasingly diverging needs of city-dwellers.

Burgeoning e-commerce and the subsequent last-mile problem

The prevalence of the internet in consumers' lives has encouraged online shopping, with cascading effects in subsequent fulfilment of their orders. The convenience of ordering products in the comfort of one's home or office has led to a rapid increase not only in the number of people preferring online over bricks-and-mortar shops but also in the amount they spend on online shopping. Common products and services purchased online include books, fashion items, and hotel and flight bookings, as well as groceries.

For physical items such as books, clothes or groceries, the order is fulfilled by what we call last-mile delivery: the last lap in the journey of products from a business to a consumer, the destination being either the consumer's home or a collection point. Retailers have different fulfilment models for last-mile delivery: stores, dark stores, distribution centres, dedicated online fulfilment centres. The delivery distance to be covered by the retailers is analysed in two parts: 1) stem distance, which is the distance to and from a delivery zone (stem mile), and 2) drop distance, which is the distance travelled once a drop or delivery zone is reached (the last mile). The drop distance remains the same irrespective of the distance from the supplier's picking location, but the stem distance varies depending on the location of the facility where the items are picked. According to research by Business Insider, the cost of last-mile delivery accounts for the highest proportion of transportation costs at 53 per cent (http://uk.businessinsider.com/last-mile-delivery-shipping-explained).

New business models and technologies

Pressured by the economics of last-mile delivery, the industry is looking for alternative solutions. For example, in a recently completed research project, U-TURN, which was funded by EU Horizon 2020, the research team at Cranfield University investigated the idea of establishing micro-hubs with a service radius of 2km near residential areas (http://www.u-turn-project.eu). They identified distance reductions if retailers were to share this micro-hub facility and last-mile delivery were to be fulfilled from this micro-hub. The distance reductions owing to shared logistics ranged from 5 to 12 per cent, depending on the geography and the drop density. Another new business model is crowd-sourcing, where the delivery operation is fulfilled by agents acting as drivers – a concept that has emerged with the on-demand economy, accommodating the peaks in the network with flexible supply.

In terms of technologies to improve last-mile logistics, replacing current van fleets with electric vans and complementing the operation with cargo bikes, using drones, especially in remote areas, and fulfilling last-mile delivery with autonomous ground vehicles are at the top of the agenda. Electric cargo bikes are already in use in several countries (the UK, Germany, Netherlands), with advantages such as their ability to bypass traffic congestion and make more stops than a traditional van. Moreover, the total cost of ownership over their lifetime is less than half the cost of owning a van.

Drones, electric or hybrid-electric vehicles with four or more rotors, can move cargo from one point to another through the air. They can be remotely piloted or fly autonomously. A drone can carry parcels up to 15kg and are expected to break new ground in deliveries of low-weight but high-value items such as medicines. They are cost-competitive, especially in rural areas, at about 10 per cent above the cost of today's delivery model, with faster and more flexible operation.

A self-driving vehicle made for local goods transportation no longer seems too futuristic. To stop people making car trips to run errands, this new technology is expected to deliver goods to consumers sometimes even faster and cheaper than going to the store themselves. Consumers can place same-day delivery orders on the web or through a mobile app, and receive their orders at home, cancelling out at least one car trip to the store and thereby reducing congestion.

Outlook

The need for new business models to cope with increased traffic and negative environmental and social impact in urban environments could be addressed by zero-emission and connected delivery vehicles such as cargo bikes, drones and autonomous delivery robots. Several successful applications of these technologies and new business models already exist, as discussed above. What will be needed for the future is to identify which of these technologies are most compatible with the needs of specific cities, so that economic costs are not prohibitive, environmental implications are acceptable and social acceptance is achievable.

Discussion points

1. Which of these knowledge insights are applicable to you?
2. Which learnings from the past discussed in this action insight have future implications?
3. What action could be taken from utilizing this knowledge by you personally or by an organization?

The KFC crisis – a lesson in relational risk management?

Action insight 2

RICHARD WILDING

Problems like those experienced by KFC and its chicken supply in 2018 don't just happen because of a sudden mistake, accident or change in circumstances. There's usually something lurking in the history of a new supplier arrangement where the first, tiny cracks appeared.

KFC's contract with its new supply chain partners was announced in October 2017, but it's the 12-month period of procurement before that announcement that needs to be the focus when trying to understand what followed, the now-famous 'crisis'. My experience in supply chain risk has shown that disruptions of this nature don't happen magically and instantaneously; decisions made in the early stages of the transition can have a significant impact on the risk profile of the future supply chain and the severity of a potential disruption.

The transition between two models always means a very high-risk period, with some level of disruption. An organization needs to test every single assumption being made in the new model and put in place contingency plans for any assumption that includes any degree of potential wobble.

Of the key components of a supply chain strategy – processes, infrastructure, information systems – it's the people element that doesn't get the necessary attention. Organizations reviewing their supply chains and partners need to think in terms of the ISO 44001 standards for managing collaborative relationships. These take businesses through the different stages of collaborations and, critically in this context, what needs to be looked at in a separation so that both parties can 'remain whole' following the split. It's important for managing the relationship with the existing or former partner and has implications for the future partner. The instigator of the separation needs to take responsibility for ensuring there is due diligence in checking all aspects of the new model and how it works, involving all new stakeholders and partners in the process. That means detailed stakeholder mapping and analysis. Who are all those stakeholders, maybe not directly involved but still part of the supply chain network, who might be called on to provide shared services? What kinds of relationship are there and what condition are they in? What levels of goodwill and commitment will be needed from them? After all, in a world where competition is between supply chains, not individual companies, relationships are critical; a sick relationship can become a major source of risk, and supply chain management is all about the management of relationships with all stakeholders to create value for the end customer and reduce cost for the supply chain as a whole. Often proactive management of relationships is found to be lacking. Do we have metrics and processes in place to manage relationships? As larger elements of supply chain control are outsourced, the detailed knowledge of the everyday mechanics is held by the incumbent and needs to be passed on. There may be a gap between the specification and reality.

There needs to be sensible attention to value, making a real assessment of it, in order to provide a balance between cost and value. Overemphasizing either the cost or the value aspect can be dangerous in terms of increasing risks. If you overemphasize value, you can destroy shareholder value by overserving the customer. Would the average consumer notice the difference or perceived quality in 'just in time' chicken? But, at the same time, this approach does reduce inventory and therefore lowers cost. Sadly, many purchasers of supply chain services overemphasize cost, but there is little consideration of the true cost-to-serve, and service costs money.

Positives have already come from the situation, even before we have more of a KFC case study for businesses to learn from; one of them is that the spell cast over consumers about how supply chains actually work has been broken. They're less likely to be thinking in terms of a fleet of KFC trucks and KFC drivers receiving orders from KFC stores. Another positive is how KFC have demonstrated the new reality of modern business: that it's not a matter of competition between individual firms anymore but between whole supply chains. KFC, like so many other major brands, is dependent on the quality of its collaborations.

Discussion points

1. Which of these knowledge insights are applicable to you?
2. Which learnings from the past discussed in this action insight have future implications?
3. What action could be taken from utilizing this knowledge by you personally or by an organization?

Institute for supply management

Action insight 3: 'KPI alignment' feature

RICHARD WILDING

A version of this material appeared in the September 2016 issue of *Inside Supply Management®* magazine, published by Institute for Supply Management® and is copyright Institute for Supply Management®. All rights reserved. Reprinted with permission from the publisher, the Institute for Supply Management®.

In business, measurement is important: all of us know that. But equally, all of us know that the world of business is perhaps oversupplied with measures. Complex reporting systems abound, supplying metrics on almost every conceivable aspect of a business's operations. Hence the evolution of a set of metrics deemed more important than the rest: key performance indicators (KPIs), those critical measures regarded as having the greatest correlation with the overall health of the business and its operations. Undoubtedly, KPIs are a useful way of cutting through the trees and seeing the wood. KPIs are what matter.

And yet, as another well-known quote reminds us, KPIs must be chosen with care. 'What you measure is what you get. And more likely, what you measure is *all* you'll get', observed American accounting historian H Thomas Johnson. So if KPIs must be chosen with care, how should a business go about selecting them? And specifically, selecting them from a supply chain point of view?

To some people, the question isn't one that needs asking. Why not use those KPIs that are already commonplace in business: inventory turns, working capital efficiency, profitability growth, cost minimization and so on?

Look carefully, though, and you see that these are invariably focused on shareholder value. That isn't to say that they're wrong – shareholders do own the business, after all – but rather to say that they aren't operational enough to guide day-to-day decision-making.

And typically, by 'not operational enough', we mean that they aren't customer-focused enough. Because in the world of supply chain management, pretty much everything we do has the satisfaction of the end customer as its ultimate objective.

Moreover, this isn't to say that a dichotomy must exist between these financially centred KPIs and a well-chosen set of operationally based KPIs. A well-chosen set of operationally based KPIs will not only correlate well with financially centred KPIs, but also provide a firmer handle on how to influence them. Put another way, financially centred KPIs tell you how you're doing – but operationally based KPIs provide the levers to achieve your goals.

So where to start? Again, a little thought shows us that from a supply chain perspective, and with the objective of maximizing customer satisfaction, two types of metric are especially critical.

The first group of KPIs is *time centred*. At its simplest, this involves asking questions such as: How quickly did we manufacture or pick the customer's order? How quickly were we able to dispatch it? How long did it take to arrive? How variable is our performance on these measures? What are the trends? How quickly do we respond to customer queries? The golden rule: if it impacts the customer, plot it as the x-axis on a chart.

The second group of KPIs is *relationship centred*. Here, we're again looking at where we are impacting the customer, but the key focus is success based. Order fill-rate, for example: what proportion of orders is completely filled within the stated lead-time? Or first-time fix rate: how many service calls successfully deal with the customer's repair or maintenance issue on the first call? What is our customer satisfaction score? How broad is our relationship with the customer: do we collaborate with them, and is there a range of senior-level contacts?

Such questions aren't difficult to find with a little thought; you will doubtless come up with many others. Better still, the metrics to translate most of them into hard numbers will be readily available within most businesses' enterprise systems, even if present-day reporting systems don't currently report on them.

Yet one fundamental question remains. Which KPIs are the most important ones to track? For while it *is* possible to monitor 20 or so KPIs, the whole point of using a performance measure that is supposed to be *key* is in order to differentiate the important from the unimportant.

So which are these really important KPIs? The answer here is that each business must determine this for itself – there are no ready-made lists. The reason is obvious: for any given business, the critical KPIs will be those that are most appropriate for its commercial context and competitive stance, its overall business strategy and the supply chain 'subset' of that strategy.

In other words, the starting point for deciding upon a set of KPIs is the present position of the business itself, and the overall strategy and supply chain strategy that it wishes to follow. And just as a set of KPIs that aren't synchronized with these strategic requirements won't be of much help, a set of KPIs that *are* synchronized with them will be potentially of enormous help.

Are cash conservation and working capital efficiency important to the business? Clearly, a set of KPIs including metrics such as invoice accuracy, invoice cycle time, 'on time in full' rates and inventory turns will be of help.

Suppose, though, that customer satisfaction is the goal. Clearly, then, while 'on time in full' metrics will feature among the set of KPIs, so too will direct measures of customer satisfaction, complaint handling, speed of order fulfilment and so on. In each case, the trick is to identify the strategic priorities and seek out those KPIs that most directly impact on those priorities.

In short, it's not difficult. And at a time when businesses seem intent on building up ever more granular repositories of transaction and performance data – to, literally, Big Data proportions – it is also refreshingly direct.

Accumulate data stores to mine for insights and unsuspected relationships, but don't lose sight of the fact that most businesses will benefit more from scrutinizing a much smaller, albeit well-chosen, set of KPI measures that *really* matter.

Discussion points

1. Which of these knowledge insights are applicable to you?
2. Which learnings from the past discussed in this action insight have future implications?
3. What action could be taken from utilizing this knowledge by you personally or by an organization?

Harnessing social media to improve logistics and supply chain performance

Action insight 4

RICHARD WILDING AND MALCOLM WHEATLEY

R D Wilding and M Wheatley, Harnessing Social Media to Improve Logistics and Supply Chain Performance, Royal Logistics Corps Foundation, January 2017.

From marketing to electioneering, and from recruitment to publishing, the use of social media has fundamentally transformed the art of the possible. The conventional 'one-to-many' communications paradigms that have traditionally underpinned such activities have been replaced or supplemented with new socially enabled 'many-to-one' and 'many-to-many' alternatives, dramatically enhancing their effectiveness.

In the process, social media tools famously created significant shareholder value for innovators in the field – wealth surely sufficient to convince even the staunchest Luddite that whatever else social media might be, they are certainly not trivial. Eleven-year-old Facebook, for instance, has built up a market capitalization of $250 billion, with competitors such as Twitter, Instagram and Snapchat following suit.

And inevitably, proponents of social media have sought to apply them to areas of economic activity that are not directly consumer-facing. Among enterprise applications and enterprise resource planning (ERP) software companies, for instance, a range of 'me-too' initiatives has sought to apply social media techniques and tools to the world of business.

One such area of deployment is the field of supply chain management, where advocates of social media see their potential for transforming the traditional workflow and communication paradigms that underpin the working of modern supply chains.

The present appendix draws on two real-world successful applications of social media in supply chain management, and attempts to define five important lessons for managements to bear in mind as they evaluate or implement social tools within their supply chains.

This, of course, has obvious implications in the context of military supply chains, where – as with most successful innovations in supply chain management – attempts to embrace social media can eventually be expected, if indeed they are not already under way.

Why social media?

Traditional workflow paradigms within supply chain management largely follow organizational structures and relationships. From order acceptance to fulfilment and dispatch, activities are broken down into neat, logical steps, often termed 'business processes'. Broadly speaking, there is an assumption that all activities will follow the same process.

So too with communications within and across supply chains. Again, there is an assumption that communications are directed to a particular person or function, from where a response will be received. To employ the metaphor of the telephone, there must be a number to dial; or in 'snail mail' terms, an address. Making the switch to e-mail doesn't change this fundamental requirement: all it does is increase the speed of transmission, not the nature of the one-to-one communication itself.

At its simplest – and this *is* a simplification – the socially enabled supply chain dispenses with all this. Communications take place quite apart from the one-to-one diktats of the typical organization and its structure and workflows.

If there is a requirement for information, for instance, or for something to happen, a general post is made highlighting the need. Read by many, the response comes from those best placed – or most willing – to fulfil the requirement. In contrast to the telephone and the postal system, the best metaphor here is perhaps the student noticeboard.

What's more, problematic orders, or critical resources, can be 'followed', or 'liked', making sure that any subsequent relevant information is brought directly to the follower's attention. Similarly, 'tags' and other social tools can make the transition to a supply chain context.

All of which isn't to say that one-to-one communications are obsolete – far from it. But the many-to-one and many-to-many alternatives that the social supply chain enables can provide effective solutions in circumstances where the one-to-one paradigm either doesn't work or lacks effectiveness.

Perhaps the person initiating the requirement doesn't know to whom it should be addressed, for instance. Or the nature of the request is such that it is not cost-efficient or time-efficient to poll everyone in the appropriate organization, seeking a response. By using the metaphor of the noticeboard, the assumption is made that those best placed to respond, will respond.

Moreover, the use of social tools permits a richness of communication not available in a noticeboard context. Other people can comment on posts, for instance, either to add more information or add themselves to the list of those requiring the action or information being sought. It's also possible to augment messages with digital imagery, in the form of either photographs or videos. In an era where camera-equipped smartphones are ubiquitous, capturing and posting an image of a damaged pallet or misplaced consignment is the work of a moment.

In summary, if you can do it in Facebook, then someone, somewhere, is hard at work figuring out if it also makes sense to do it in supply chains as well. And – with, as we shall see, some caveats – it seems that for the most part, it does.

Social processes at work in supply chains

In recent months, the authors have been able to study the operation of the social supply chain within two distinct supply chain management environments. Together, these two examples straddle all four modes of the social supply chain: one-to-one, one-to-many, many-to-one and many-to-many.

The first environment is Travis Perkins, a 24,000-employee FTSE 100 listed builders' merchant and home improvement retailer, with brands that include Travis Perkins, Wickes and Toolstation.

For Travis Perkins, social media in the context of supply chain management means the creation of 'virtual communities' within the firm's 200+ outlet Wickes DIY estate, powered by Google+ Communities, a social media collaboration tool.

One such virtual community, Availability+, is focused on improving on-shelf availability within Wickes stores, aiming to link together geographically dispersed store-based personnel with relevant Wickes support centre personnel, drawn from functions such as inventory control, marketing, distribution and logistics, purchasing, quality and merchandising.

Availability+ augments Wickes' traditional reliance upon a call-centre-based approach to communications, where support centre staff cascade information downwards to store level, and store-level personnel in turn phone the support centre for the resolution of any problems they are experiencing.

And, phased in from May 2014, the difference in effectiveness is striking. As well as enabling store-to-store initiative-sharing – a communications process quite apart from the vertical support-centre-to-store and store-to-support-centre channels of communication – Availability+ has transformed problem resolution, slashing the time taken for problems to be resolved and queries answered.

The second socially enabled supply chain examined by the authors is that delivered by 2degrees, a specialist firm delivering supplier collaboration communities on behalf of businesses as diverse as Asda, pharmaceutical giant GSK, Kingfisher and the Irish food board Bord Bia. At its simplest, 2degrees' raison d'être is to enable businesses to leverage their supplier base to fulfil goals that would rapidly exhaust corporate bandwidth if tackled through conventional means.

Asda, for instance, funds a voluntary many-to-many community of suppliers focused around sustainability and cost efficiency, known as the Asda Sustain and Save Exchange. 2degrees' role is that of a trusted third party, facilitating communications and knowledge-sharing between suppliers, with financial gains ring-fenced from Asda's buyers.

The logic: Asda has neither the bandwidth nor the skill sets to engage directly with its entire supplier base in order to improve the sustainability and energy-efficiency of its manufacturing facilities. But collectively, in a many-to-many context, its suppliers *do* possess that bandwidth.

Underpinning such collaboration is the idea that a retailer's suppliers may have more in common with each other than with the retailer itself, thus making supplier-to-supplier collaboration a more powerful transformative tool than direct retailer-to-supplier collaboration. And while, say, two identical pork pie manufacturers might be loath to share information, owing to competition concerns, the businesses of (say) a pork pie manufacturer, a chicken processor and a sausage manufacturer are far enough apart to ease such fears.

Similarly, GSK has recognized that its own objective of reducing its carbon footprint would clearly be impacted by the fact that a third of that footprint arose from activities in its supplier base.

But no single supplier made up more than 1 per cent impact of the total, making one-to-one supplier engagement an inefficient means of engendering improvement. The answer: another 2degrees-facilitated many-to-many community, funded by GSK, and focused on sharing best practice in carbon footprint reduction.

Social limits: the impact of cultural and organizational factors

That said, case studies such as these should not be taken to mean that the use of social tools within supply chains will automatically be a success. In fact, for all the investment in applying social tools in non-consumer contexts – and make no mistake, the major enterprise applications companies are investing significant sums in doing just that – it seems that there are very few resounding success stories that can be pointed to at present. Moreover, it is not difficult to see why the uptake of social tools within supply chains need not automatically be a success.

To begin with, the undoubted success of social media in a consumer context obscures the fact that their users and proselytizers are a self-selecting group, having chosen to make use of social media tools and presumably finding that such tools fit their needs. In contrast, little is heard from those who have *not* chosen to make use of social tools, or who, having done so, find them inadequate or too cumbersome for their needs.

Clearly, in an organizational context, the social supply chain will only deliver to the fullest if adoption – and active usage – extends right across that supply chain. Put another way, the uptake and usage of social tools within a supply chain context has to find a way of drawing and engaging individuals who may be reluctant or even unwilling to engage with social tools in a personal, consumer-centric context.

Second, as will already be clear from the two case studies above, the social supply chain operates through a combination of both *flattening* the organization structure and simultaneously *weakening* the walls of its silos. The social supply chain works precisely because it enables individuals who might not necessarily communicate directly in the ordinary scheme of things to do just that, without going through 'proper channels'.

Clearly, here again, the success of social supply chain tools in an organizational context will be dependent on the extent to which a given organization is relaxed about letting that direct communication happen. Put another way, the more hierarchal and rigidly structured an organization is, the less fertile the soil on which the seeds of a social supply chain initiative must take root and prosper. This has obvious implications when considering the adoption of social supply chain tools within a military context, for instance.

Bearing in mind the above and based on our observations of social supply chains in action, we have developed five rules of which those promulgating social supply chain initiatives should be cognizant, if those initiatives are to deliver to their fullest potential.

1 *For the social supply chain to be effective, content, scale and culture are key*

At Wickes, using Availability+ is not mandatory. Likewise, line managers within those Asda suppliers who are members of the Asda Sustain and Save Exchange are similarly under no coercion to use it.

The simple fact of the matter is that in both cases, people use it because it allows them to perform their jobs better. And as a result, it is important not to be too directive about how people use such forums and virtual communities. Several things stem from this.

First, success inevitably involves ceding an element of control and empowering people with the freedom to make decisions, raise problems and provide solutions in the manner that they think best.

Second, the nature of the digital content is key: communication has to be two-way, with questions asked and answers provided. It has to 'feel' like a conversation and not like a noticeboard.

And again, this involves acknowledging that the virtual community in question will develop a direction and a culture of its own, which might be endangered if management were too prescriptive or acted like forum 'policemen'. That said, both Wickes and Asda acknowledge the need for facilitation and moderation, in order to keep communication on track, delete irrelevant postings or intervene to help resolve particular issues.

2 *Properly implemented, the social supply chain is more effective than other communication channels*

At its simplest, the social supply chain connects people who have a problem – or an information requirement – with other people who can resolve their problem or provide the required information.

Critically, they don't need to know these people already and have a relationship with them. All they need to know is this: that they can simply post a message and someone will respond. In other words, they are getting to the right person, *automatically*.

Within both Wickes' Availability+ virtual community and the Asda Sustain and Save Exchange, this has had a transformative impact. Because communication is so straightforward, and the resulting replies so rapid, individuals are much more likely to initiate communication or participate in online discussions, seeing it as a way of getting their jobs done time-efficiently.

They know that they are communicating with people whom they have never met – and most likely never will meet – but who are nevertheless precisely the right people with whom to be having a dialogue.

At Wickes, for instance, the timescale for problem resolution has been transformed. With a call-centre-based approach, a typical resolution time was three days. With Availability+, it's not unusual for problems to be resolved within an hour.

As with Facebook and Twitter, the ability to upload images quickly adds richness to the dialogue. By design, it is a straightforward affair and the work of seconds to include these images within individual posts – something that is not possible with the call centre approach.

As an example, a Wickes branch might post a message about poor packaging in goods delivered from a supplier, adding a photograph. Other branches can chime in if affected by the same issue. At which point, someone in the commercial team has all the information they need – including photographic evidence – to raise the issue with the supplier, there and then, communicating back the result within hours.

3 The social supply chain's many-to-many communication transcends the traditional vertical approach

Traditional communication approaches are vertical in direction: 'instructions' moving down from the top; 'queries' travelling upwards.

In general, a query raised at the bottom of one organizational silo must travel upwards (perhaps to the top) before it is appropriate for it to cross to another silo for actual resolution – during which time, dialogue must flow up and down this second silo until a response is formulated which can be shared with the original silo.

The social supply chain dispenses with this – and indeed, is of limited value if it *doesn't* dispense with this model.

Within Asda's Sustain and Save Exchange, for instance, the whole point is that (say) an engineering manager within one supplier can engage directly with the engineering manager of another supplier, in order to share experiences and insights into (say) low-energy lighting, heat pumps or energy-efficient compressors.

Similarly, Wickes' Availability+ virtual community has helped branches to quickly publicize individual approaches that they have found to be particularly effective in increasing sales. In one example, a branch made innovative use of a pallet, recycling it as a promotional stand for drums of external wood stain. Within three days, the uploaded photograph had been viewed over 500 times and the innovation was widely emulated at branch level.

4 The social supply chain is public, with no place to hide

As with Facebook and Twitter, the social supply chain is very public – at least within its own closed world. So, posts made by users are visible to all, although not to the wider world of internet users. Issues are raised in a corporate public forum, open for all to see, with the speed and effectiveness of any resulting resolution also open for all to see.

As in the physical one-to-one context, this encourages people to respond fully and effectively to any questions and issues raised, knowing that their peers – and their superiors – are viewing their online actions and the speed and efficacy of the responses that they make.

As might be expected, this then predisposes people to react in a 'solution' mode, not a 'discussion' mode. When problems are raised, the usual response is a solution, not a reply to the effect that there will be an offline discussion of the problem at some indeterminate point in the future.

5 Social supply chain communication is two-way, not just one-way

Traditional modes of supply chain communication are generally one-way, often constrained by workflow. A significant advantage of the social supply chain is that it unlocks a powerful medium for two-way communication, quite outside the normal protocols and circulation lists associated with conventional organizational communications paradigms and workflow.

A supply chain director, for instance, would not normally expect to be privy to reports from the front line in terms of delivery reliability, stockouts, damage and the effectiveness of promotions.

Through social media tools, such visibility is instant and ongoing. There's no onus on the supply chain director to take action to resolve individual issues (although that is always a possibility), as the job of providing that response is the work of others.

But as never before, social tools are making the workings of supply chains utterly transparent, providing – literally – a window into their detailed workings and the dialogue taking place within them.

At Wickes, for instance, Availability+ has made it possible to get near real-time feedback on how a given promotion is working, in terms of identifying the best-selling items, any errors, and any opportunities to fine-tune and improve it. And if something is clearly working exceptionally well in a particular location, it is possible to distribute it as best practice, all within a matter of hours.

Conclusion

Since its inception, the weaknesses of ERP systems have been becoming ever clearer. And the clue is in the word 'planning'. Never really intended as supply chain execution tools, they have struggled to equip businesses with the wherewithal to deal with the vagaries of supply chains in practice – and the myriad of things that don't go according to plan.

Conventional toolsets have also struggled to provide this reactive capability. For all the talk a decade ago of 'alerts' when events deviate from plan, such alerts have not proved to be the solution.

Similarly, e-mail has struggled to provide an effective reactive capability. Partly, that is for reasons of in-box overload: few indeed are the corporate middle managers who complain about an insufficiency of incoming e-mails. But perhaps more significantly, as this appendix has argued, e-mail itself is structurally flawed, being a solution to an entirely different problem.

In short, just as Facebook, Twitter, LinkedIn and their ilk have replaced e-mail in a consumer context, the omens now appear propitious for social tools to take on a bigger role within supply chains as well.

Discussion points

1. Which of these knowledge insights are applicable to you?
2. Which learnings from the past discussed in this action insight have future implications?
3. What action could be taken from utilizing this knowledge by you personally or by an organization?

The 3 Ts of highly effective supply chains

Action insight 5

RICHARD WILDING

This paper was first published in *Supply Chain Practice* Vol 5, No 3, 2003.

Introduction

In recent years the recognition that the supply chain is a source of competitive advantage has driven organizations to pursue the dual goals of achieving both value advantage and operational excellence. In many environments it has been recognized that competition in the future will not be between the individual organizations but between the supply chains they are part of.

In order to compete, effective management of the supply chain is critical. Supply chain management has been defined as 'the management of upstream and downstream relationships with suppliers, distributors and customers to achieve greater customer value-added at less total cost'. The key factors that need to be focused on are building relationships and creating value. When this is achieved, organizations become more agile and responsive; however, for many organizations this is an illusory goal.

Understanding the 3 Ts of highly effective supply chains provides a simple yet powerful framework that organizations can use to start building robust supply chain processes and structures. The 3 Ts are Time, Transparency and Trust. Each is interrelated and dependent on each other. Understanding the *time* dimension of the supply chain enables organizations to gain *transpar-ency* of what is happening within the supply chain system; when everyone knows what is going to happen and confidence is built because of transparency, *trust* develops between all the players in the supply chain. This, in turn, results in greater understanding of the time dimension, hence greater levels of transparency and then higher levels of trust. But what if one of these key dimensions is missing? The cycle is broken and transparency, trust and an understanding of time are lost. So the 3 Ts are dependent on each other, but it has been found that by using time as the starting point, organizations can create transparency and trust, resulting in significant increases in competitive advantage.

Time

Velocity within the business environment

In his book *Business @ the Speed of Thought*, Bill Gates states: 'If the 1980's were about quality and the 1990's about re-engineering, then the 2000's will be about velocity.' Velocity is distance divided by time but with direction! Many organizations have plenty of speed (ie velocity without direction, people running around very fast doing things that seem important), but velocity needs to be aligned on a goal and objective. Within the supply chain, the goal is to maximize the customer's perceived value of the product or service to be supplied. Within our velocity equation, the distance can be defined as 'the added-value journey we take a customer on', understanding that the 'added-value journey' is critical to supply chain success; the journey involves pre-transaction (what happens before the purchase is made), transaction (actually purchasing and receiving the product or service) and finally post-transaction (the customer experience after the initial purchase).

To achieve velocity within organizations, a focus on time is required. Organizations can gain advantage by taking a customer on the same 'value-adding journey' in less time or by taking customers on a longer 'value-adding journey' in the same time as the competition. In both situations velocity in increased. In order to do this, time compression is required in all processes, but in order to achieve time compression an understanding of the processes with respect to time is required.

Within supply chains, the need for improvement with respect to time-based resource management is receiving increasing recognition. Research indicates that it is not uncommon for the time spent actually 'adding value', that is, doing things that a customer is willing to pay for, to be one-tenth of 1 per cent!

It has been found that by focusing on time in the supply chain, the cost issues tend to look after themselves. Time is a common measure across all supply chain partners, whereas cost and transfer-price data are open to a variety of interpretations. In comparison to activity-based costing techniques, which are often used in the analyses of supply chains, focusing on time enables one to see 'the wood rather than the trees'. The analysis is also much faster and more effective – often using about 20 per cent of the time and resources of a traditional cost-based analysis. By focusing on time, analysis is forced down to a physical level. The time focus has proved to be easier to implement and yields rapid bottom-line results.

Time that adds value and time that does not

Value-adding time is characterized using three criteria:

- whether the process (or elements of the process) is physically changing the nature of the consumable item (ie the customer's product/service);
- whether the change to the consumable item produces something that the customer values or cares about and may be willing to pay for;
- whether the process is right first time, and will not have to be repeated in order to produce the desired result that is valued by the customer.

Discussion points

1. Which of these knowledge insights are applicable to you?
2. Which learnings from the past discussed in this action insight have future implications?
3. What action could be taken from utilizing this knowledge by you personally or by an organization?

The future of home delivery and understanding the entire parcel delivery journey

Action insight 6

RICHARD WILDING

To innovate, an organization needs to understand the complete 'value-adding journey' that a customer progresses through. Looking at the process from the customer's perspective provides insights into the future of home delivery.

The journey starts with 'pre-transaction' elements. This part of the journey may involve a consumer surfing the web, perhaps on a PC, tablet or smartphone, visiting a store, asking for recommendations on social media, reading reviews and so on: in summary, everything involved in deciding to move to the next stage of the value-adding journey, the transaction stage. The future of home delivery at the pre-transaction stage will be around choice – choice of provider and choice of delivery location.

During the transaction the item is purchased; this may be in a shop, over the internet or by telephone. The future of home delivery here requires transparency of the delivery process and a demonstration that actions are being taken and will be taken. However, this is not the end of the journey.

The value-adding journey then proceeds to post-transaction. At this point the value-adding is perceived by many organizations as the consumers' opinion of the product and their experience of using it, but this is short sighted. Post-transaction should include consideration of product delivery and collection, returns options, warranty claims and finally disposal. If these elements of the value-adding journey fail, the customer is likely never to return.

The question to ask is: what value can be created for the customer from home delivery? Critically, it needs to be easy, controlled and fun. Consumers want deliveries when they are at home, and they want reassurance about when the item is going to arrive and where it currently is. If they are not at home, they want the parcel to be left somewhere safe or delivered to a location it can easily be retrieved from.

Innovation can be defined as creating value – economic, social and/or environmental value – from ideas that are new to you. So perhaps we should no longer look for innovation within the postal delivery sector but should take ideas from other environments and apply them. Ask the question 'Which environments are best at delivering things to consumers?' and we may get the answer from, for example, fast food environments where restaurants have tried to make things as *easy*, *controlled* and *fun* as possible. *Easy* means not even having to get out of the car, *controlled* using technology and robust processes to ensure high levels of accuracy and service, and *fun* keeping people entertained as they queue.

Imagine a drive-through collection facility, a bit like your local drive-through fast food restaurant. If I miss the delivery of a parcel, I receive a text with a QR code and/or a card posted through the door. My item is taken to 'FunDriveThrough'. I drive to this facility surrounded by other well-known drive-through facilities. I hold my smartphone or card to a scanner; I am then directed to the appropriate lane for collection.

As I progress, screens play amusing cartoons to keep my children and me engaged and happy (rather like when queuing for theme park rides). My ID is automatically checked through my number plate being registered and my package is loaded into the car or passed to me through the window by happy polite staff. Are these the ravings of a mad professor or could this be an element of the future of home delivery? Easy, controlled and fun!

Discussion points

1. Which of these knowledge insights are applicable to you?
2. Which learnings from the past discussed in this action insight have future implications?
3. What action could be taken from utilizing this knowledge by you personally or by an organization?

ANSWERS TO CASE STUDIES

Case study 1

1. *In what way is the efficient integration of shipping into intermodal supply chains important for its further employment in intra-regional trade?*

Maritime services for unit loads usually do not offer door-to-door transport, but consist of the core parts of an intermodal transport chain. Their successful 'coordination' and cooperation with land-based traffic modes is essential for their further use in intra-regional trade.

2. *What is the role of efficient port operations for the enhancement of maritime supply chains?*

Successful integration of shipping into supply chains implies efficient port operations with low cargo-handling costs and short times in ports. As shown in this case, the efficient transhipment of cargo flows from trains to RoRo vessels at the port is achieved by the continuous exchange of information about the cargo flows and close cooperation between the carrier and the shipper.

3. *How do managerial and cultural parameters affect the establishment of efficient maritime supply chains?*

This case highlights the importance of cooperation and shared planning among shippers and supply chain managers for the successful integration of shipping into intermodal transport chains. The development of a management 'culture' that promotes the complementarity of inland and maritime carrier operations and relies on carrier–shipper relationships can have a significant impact on the further employment of RoRo shipping services.

4. *What are the potential benefits from the development of maritime transport chains for the supply chain actors?*

By adopting innovative logistics and management strategies for the integration of shipping into their supply chains, companies can acquire a significant competitive advantage in the market, thus reducing the per-unit transport cost of their products and enhancing the overall system efficiency and sustainability. As shown in this case, the commercial cooperation between the shipper and the carrier resulted in increased sales of shipping services for third-party units and a high utilization rate of these services, reaching about 95 per cent. Another beneficial outcome from this cooperation is the expansion of the shipper's SSS network with other partners in different regions, significantly increasing the cargo volumes of their chartered vessels.

5. *Based on this case, what can be done to facilitate the integration of shipping into intra-regional supply chains?*

The adoption of a different management approach that relies on a carrier–shipper relationship and the consideration of the transport chain as a 'whole', giving particular emphasis to the ports – the 'nodes' of the maritime supply chains, could enable the integration of shipping into intermodal transport chains, enhance the whole system's efficiency and sustainability and lead to reduced lead-times, emissions and costs for all the collaborating parties.

Case study 2

1. *Why is the healthcare supply chain complex?*

The healthcare supply chain is complex because every patient is different, and with an ageing population the healthcare needs are growing. Many patients have more than one healthcare issue and many are living with a chronic disease. Government policies for the future of healthcare recognize the need for the development of an integrated health service between the community and the acute hospitals and the development of pathways to ensure patients can transfer seamlessly through the services. It is planned to deliver more services in the community in the future and to utilize hospital care only when it is necessary, so that patients can stay at home or in the community for most of their care needs.

2. *Explain why the ED is critical to the supply chain process in a hospital.*

The ED is critical to the supply chain process in a hospital as it is often the first point of access to the acute hospital services. However, not every patient needs to attend the ED and many patients could avoid the ED if the appropriate pathways of care were in place with an access point for GPs to refer the patient. Patients that do require the ED are often very sick and the flow through the department is critical to ensure good outcomes for them. Timely access to skilled staff, access to diagnostics and access to theatre or a critical care bed from the ED are all vital steps in the supply chain process in the ED. The ED is only the front door and all the backup services are required to diagnose and treat the patient and facilitate their journey through the system. Many patients also attend the ED for minor injuries, and these patients are encouraged to use the local injury units which are part of ULHG. A large number of patients are discharged from the ED – up to 70 per cent, therefore the supply chain in the department is continuously monitored and improved.

3. *What is the function of a Bed Bureau?*

The Bed Bureau is a single point of contact for GPs to access a medical assessment in any one of the sites in ULHG. The Bed Bureau is used for patients who do not need to attend the ED. Since completion of this thesis, the Bed Bureau has been expanded to include patients requiring a surgical assessment also on the UHL site, and these patients also avoid the ED.

4. *What benefits can be drawn from the introduction of a Bed Bureau to the healthcare supply chain?*

Introducing the Bed Bureau has streamlined the process for the GPs in the region and provides them with an appropriate alternative to the ED for their patients. Previously the GPs had to ring each of the sites individually to refer their patient. This was time consuming and often resulted in the GP referring the patient to the ED unnecessarily.

5. *What suggestions can you make for improving the patient pathway in a hospital's ED?*

Admission avoidance pathways are currently being developed for patients with certain conditions in the acute hospitals setting. These pathways will be accessed through the Bed Bureau once they are developed. The particular issue arising in UHL is lack of bed capacity, and there are plans to increase the number of beds in the next few years. Isolation facilities are also a challenge and much of the current infrastructure is old and no longer fit for purpose. All new builds will be single rooms. Greater links with the community are continuously being developed under the new Government Healthcare

Policy. Many pathways will be developed across the community and the acute sectors to improve the patient journey through the system. These pathways will be accessed through the Bed Bureau.

Case study 3

1. *Critically analyse what could be the soft and hard enablers of, and barriers to, implementing LSS for this particular project and why? Critically evaluate this for SMEs and MNEs*

Soft enablers could be the manager's decision, internal willingness to change and so on.

Hard enablers could be the customers' requirement, their disappointment at the company's current performance and so on.

The barriers to implementing LSS could be lack of LSS knowledge, lack of top management commitment, lack of cultural change, lack of resources etc. These barriers are different in SMEs and MNEs. Students will have their own reasons and justifications.

2. *What could be the major strategic and operational benefits and drawbacks of implementing an LSS project in manufacturing sector and why?*

The major strategic benefits of implementing an LSS project could be lower costs, higher performance and higher customer satisfaction.

The major operational benefits could be streamlined processes, reduced waste, reduced defects and rework, good teamwork and so on.

The major drawbacks could be short term, including cultural change, receiving training, commitment of resources and so on.

3. *Calculate the defects per million opportunities (DPMO) and Sigma value of the baseline measurement and final output of this particular project and critically analyse the difference in terms of waste reduction, quality enhancement and customer satisfaction*

It is not required to calculate the precise values. The tutor will need to guide the students to understand what defects mean in this case. Here, it means failed OTD. The defect opportunities include different stages in the delivery process.

Case study 4

Describe how operational workforce planning fits into the overall business process of workforce management.

Operational workforce planning is the aspect of planning that is focused on mapping the existing skills and capabilities of labour resources against current and future operational business requirements. There are two main links into the business process of Workforce Management. Firstly, operational workforce planning provides the most accurate estimate of the direct resources required at any point in time. This supports the HR department in the ongoing management of recruitment and training plans. Secondly, it provides data used in the establishment of the labour budget and is therefore a critical part of the decision-making process for allocating labour resources across the business network.

From this case study, identify the five project workstreams and one key deliverable for each.

Project planning

Organize regular stakeholder meetings.

Work measurement

Develop labour standards for operational processes

Process improvement

Appoint Process Improvement Champions from the departmental management teams.

Productivity reporting

Validate existing data sources and re-configure reports to reflect the key performance information required to provide accurate feedback on progress.

Operational workforce planning

Scope out the requirements for the development of a planning model using best-practice methodology and use gap analysis to evaluate the effectiveness of existing planning models.

Describe the risks associated with the original operational workforce planning model in this case study and the benefits that were identified when the output from the new model was compared directly to the original model.

Risks

- Inaccurate production targets
- Inaccurate metrics used for volume drivers
- Gaps in the model where workloads were entirely based on estimates
- False interpretation of policy regarding training allowances

Benefits

- The business was able to see the true capability of its operational performance, and identified potential savings in labour costs of 15%.
- Operations managers were involved in consultations about the new modelling process and the data being applied, and were therefore more confident in the output.
- The planning team was coached in the new techniques used to ensure that the model was set up in line with best practice, and that they could maintain it going forward.
- The industrial engineer had a reliable source of information to establish priorities for process improvement activity.

Identify three ways how Industrial Engineering techniques can be used to support an organisation to improve its overall performance.

- The development of accurate labour standards to track performance at the employee level
- Establishing an effective cycle of process improvement activity across all the operations management teams
- Co-ordinating the maintenance of the planning tools used to provide financial information for forecasting, budgeting and cost benefit analysis

Case study 5

How do you start to align?

I think a corporate meeting where the major players agree that the company will buy on 'best value' is the best starting point. Then look at getting a tool to quantify value (Tim Underhill's tool mentioned above, example), and start allocating 'simple' numbers for value drivers (Downtime is $5,000, Inventory carrying costs are 20%, each KWh is 10% etc).

How should you measure your success?

Start with a few and increase supplier agreements that have an annual value improvement, and measure total TPA™ improvement per year.

What categories are the 'easiest' to start with?

Add a section on all RFPs that asks the supplier how they will create value, how they will measure it (or link to your tool that says this is how we measure value), and what happens if they do not hit it?

Case study 6

What are the challenges faced by Company X in its business?

The main challenge faced by the company is the raw material, which is timber. Although logs are renewable, studies show a deficit of around 70 million cubic metres of wood in Europe by 2020 if management of the resource continues as it is today. Therefore, if the company doesn't change the linear supply chain, the raw material cost will increase in the future.

Why does Company X want to close the supply chain loop? What are the advantages and challenges in closing the supply chain loop?

The company wants to close the supply chain loop for two reasons. The first is cost. By closing the supply chain loop, it can save both raw material costs and energy costs. The second is the company's image. By closing the supply chain loop, its environmental impact will be reduced, which will improve the company's green image.

The advantages include cost reduction and brand image improvement.

However, the challenges are also big. First, how should the company collect used furniture? Because consumers are scattered all over the country, collecting furniture from individual consumers lacks economy of scale. Second, the supply chain network needs to be redesigned to include reverse logistics. Where to locate the collection points is an important strategic decision. Third, reverse logistics management is also a challenge. How to ship used furniture and recycled materials to reduce empty running is challenging. Fourth, the decision to purchase new raw material is also challenging because of the high uncertainty of the availability of materials.

What are the key success factors in Company X's closed-loop ecosystem?

The key success factors include:

1. Top management commitment. Closing the supply chain loop is a company strategy, so top management pushed the initiative from the strategic level.
2. Phased implementation of the initiative. The company didn't rush to close the supply chain loop at full scale, but rather started small and scaled up.

Collaboration with external partners. The company partners with specialist collectors, logistics companies and customers to close the supply chain loop.

Case study 7

The questions are posed to support learning. Therefore, the answers here only points in the right direction for the reader and provides some examples. The reader should elaborate more on the answers.

Use Table 1 to discuss management principles for packaging to manage the effect of the potential delays.

To manage the effect of potential delays, the general management principles for packaging to be discussed relate to:

- Packaging postponement
- Track and trace capabilities through labelling
- Increase shelf life by securing undamaged products in containers (e.g. ventilation and avoid moisture)

- Stackability
- Unitisation

In particular, these three potential delays should discuss the following:

- *To avoid negative impacts of that the capacity in the cold storage facility is full, it is essential to have effective storage in the packhouse*: Packaging can facilitate this through unitisation, which supports co-packing. The packaging system can also be volume efficient and enable stacking for minimal need of storage space.
- *Late notification of shipping need*: Packaging should facilitate loading efficiency for rapid shipping
- *Vessel misses its time slot*: Heat protection in packaging and container together

Use Table 2 and the insights about a circular economy to discuss the impact of packaging on circularity in the case of table grapes.

A circular economy perspective on packaging means that the product and packaging values should be maintained for as long as possible, while waste is minimized and used as a resource for recycling or energy recovery. In this question, you should apply this to each step in the right column in Table 2. For instance, in the packhouse, the first challenge relates to high stacks. The load-bearing capacity of packaging affects the stackability, which, in turn, affects the amount of damaged packages. A circular economy perspective means that the load-bearing capacity should be enough to eliminate damaged packages, but still use as little packaging material as possible. The second challenge in the packhouse is to maintain the cold chain. The packaging design can help to keep the product cold, either by hindering hot air to get into packaging in a hot environment or by facilitating ventilation so that cold air reaches the product in a chilled environment. The type of temperature feature on packaging depends on the environment where the package is used. The third challenge refers to shocks. Here, packaging protection can help to avoid product damage. In the packing process in the packhouse, there is also packaging waste. To fulfil the circular economy perspective, the packaging waste should be minimized and the remaining waste should be recycled either as a new packaging material or as another type of product.

Apply first a circular economy perspective and then a sustainability perspective to the global food supply chain of packed table grapes. What are the similarities and differences in packaging system requirements?

To answer this question use the definitions of a circular economy and sustainability as well as the descriptions of similarities and differences under the heading 'Sustainable packaging'. In short:

Circular economy: A circular economy is an approach, or an instrument, for moving a business or a supply chain towards economic and environmental sustainability. In the context of packaging, the circular economy is based on the idea of an ecocycle society where product and packaging values are maintained for as long as possible, while waste is minimized and used as a resource for recycling or energy recovery.

Sustainability: From an economic perspective, this means that packaging should save more than it costs in terms of enabling supply chain efficiency and supply chain effectiveness. From an environmental perspective, sustainable packaging should minimize the packed product's environmental impact in terms of the use and reuse of resources for material, product waste, and logistics and transport operations. From a social perspective, packaging should help consumers and users to modify their behaviour in a sustainable direction.

By first applying the definitions to the case you can discuss what a circular economy focuses on and what a sustainability perspective focuses on. Then, apply the similarities and differences under the heading 'Sustainable packaging' to discuss the similarities and differences in this particular case.

Discuss food waste challenges from a packaging perspective in the case of table grapes. Based on Figure 2, what can be done to reduce the amount of damaged and wasted table grapes?

The section 'Packaging-related challenges in the supply chain' answers this question. To discuss what can be done, apply the four areas related to product waste in Figure 2 to the packaging-related challenges.

Discuss packaging material challenges in the case of table grapes. Based on Figure 2, what can be done to reduce packaging material waste?

The section 'Packaging-related challenges in the supply chain' answers this question. To discuss what can be done, apply the four areas related to packaging material waste in Figure 2 to the packaging-related challenges.

Discuss logistics and transport challenges from a packaging perspective in the case of table grapes. Based on Figure 2, what can be done to improve logistics and transport efficiency in the global supply chain of table grapes?

The section 'Packaging-related challenges in the supply chain' answers this question. To discuss what can be done, apply the four areas related to logistics and transport efficiency in Figure 2 to the packaging-related challenges.

Table 2 describes challenges regarding packed table grapes in different supply chain stages. How can the packaging system address these challenges? What potential trade-offs do you foresee?

First, analyse each challenge on packed table grapes to identify packaging features that can address the challenge. For example, such analysis on 'humidity from rapid temperature changes in container cooling' should result in that unless it is possible to slow down the cooling process there may be a need for an additional sheet, which emits sulphur to reduce water on the grapes (see description of the packaging system). A trade-off is a risk that too much sulphur can burn the grapes. Another trade-off is more packaging waste. Another example is that the primary and secondary packages needs holes for ventilation to avoid humidity and keep the grapes fresh. A trade-off is that it weakens the packages, which can affect stacking and handling. You should conduct similar analyses on each challenge on packed table grapes.

How should a farmer or producer select a packaging system for table grapes? How can different supply chain requirements be identified and included? How should costs and benefits be shared when sustainable packaging is accomplished?

The farmer or producer should identify all requirements on packaging from all processes in the supply chain from packing to consumers. Essential steps in doing so is to map the supply chain and the role of packaging in each process. Then, all requirements should be compiled and analysed in a structured way with conscious trade-offs. The answer to the first part of this question should elaborate on this. Regarding costs and benefits sharing, there is not a standardised way of sharing costs and benefits. However, it can be discussed with the different supply chain actors. Different approaches can work in different contexts. For example, if a particular packaging feature is added to only benefit one actor, this actor may be positive to pay for that feature. It can also be seen as a benefit that the farmer or producer can use in future negotiations, or a feature that is necessary to keep the business. Another example is that the price of the packed product increases when the packaging cost increases. The answer to the second part of this question should discuss these and other possibilities.

In what way can a packaging system for table grapes add competitive advantage?

The packaging system for table grapes can add competitive advantage by reducing costs and increasing the value of the packed product. Costs and the environmental impact of packaging can be reduced from logistics and transportation, product waste and packaging material usage and waste (ways to tackle each factor, see Figure 2). The value can, for instance, be increased by apportion the packaging dimensions according to consumer needs, by designing the primary packaging with features that makes it easy to open and close, prolong shelf life and present the grapes nicely, and by applying and communicating sustainable and circular packaging requirements.

Use Figure 2 to describe in what way the packaging system for table grapes can be developed to become more sustainable and support a circular economy.

Apply each way to tackle the three factors in Figure 2 to the packaging system of table grapes. Describe how the product and packaging values can be maintained for as long as possible, while waste is minimized and used as a resource for recycling in each supply chain stage.

Present ten supply chain decisions that are affected by packaging.

Shipping volume, pallet size, order frequency, track and trace decisions, warehouse equipment decisions, vehicle type, material handling decisions, packaging material purchasing, waste management and recycling decisions, etc.

Case study 8

Discovery: How would you undertake an organisational analysis as you decide which scheme would be best for your organisation?

Learners will be able to comprehend the direct and positive impact of colleagues and teams within a transport sector logistics organisation as a result of this research, which would include the roples planning, decision making, organisation, leadership and resource allocation / pooling to meet customer requirements. This exercise should allow learners to understand the current strategic objectives of the organisation to allow them to be able to assess the following through interviews and surveys across the organisation and whether this represents a short or mid-term strategy:

What aspects of planning and control are present in the organisation which drive compliance and customer satisfaction?

How are they measured?

How good are these and how good should they actually be, remember the hidden voice.

Are colleagues content, if not, why not?

What works well and what needs to be improved?

As the above represent benchmarks, how should they be recorded to make the organisation more efficient and more sustainable?

Which tools could you possibly use? Some of the learners will think that an adapted balanced scorecard would be suitable as an internal measure, to record baseline data and to use as a platform to improve the performance of the organization. Others may want to adopt a Total Quality Management approach or a Business Process Re-engineering etc.

Identification: List all of the external and internal customers that the organisation must satisfy.

This list is not hierarchical nor exhaustive but should include at a minimum the following:

Local government organisations;

National government organisation responsible for driver and vehicle standards;

Cross border organisations;

Internal departments such as HR, accounting, maintenance, warehousing, compliance managers etc.

Internal stakeholders as customers and suppliers of information;

Scheme requirements.

Choice: Which approach would you take, Scheme 1, Scheme 2 or your own independent approach. As a result of your choices, how would you rank the conventions hierarchically and what would be your reasoning behind these rankings?

Learners will be able to debate whether a short-term strategy is most important, in which case they will opt for scheme 2 which is less innovative and report driven. If the organisation has a more visible and coherent sustainability strategy then the learner will opt for scheme 1, either as a member or as a benchmark set of standards from which an organisation can undertake a primary set of operational measures to build from.

Inclusion, Quality Management and Customer Satisfaction: Quality management and customer satisfaction is a philosophy, a paradigm (set of beliefs). Scheme membership as such, drives inclusion, quality and customer oriented successful fulfilment. This is broadly derivative of Feigenbaum's concept of total control:

1. *Quality is a company-wide process*
2. *Quality is what customer says it is*
3. *Quality and costs are a sum not a difference*
4. *Quality requires both individual and team zealotry*
5. *Quality is a way of managing*
6. *Quality and innovation are mutually dependant*
7. *Quality is an ethic*
8. *Quality requires continuous improvement*
9. *Quality is most cost-effective*
10. *Quality is implemented with a total system connected with customers & suppliers.*

As a result of the learning from this chapter identify and list three ways in which a transport organisation, or if the learner is from a public sector, engineering company, operations management contractor, or consultancy etc. can develop or adapt metrics and performance indicators for each of the propositions 1–10.

Learners should be able to refer back to the chapter contents and develop a range of measures / metrics / indicators which reflects the needs for customer satisfaction and continuous improvement. It would be expected that learners can differentiate between the schemes also; the 'one size fits all approach of one scheme can be seen as casuistry in that the reasoning behind the scheme is a clever interpretation of the needs of stakeholders; albeit it with a transport sector bias, and the metrics required of different levels of membership are sophisticated without necessarily delivering proportional benefits. As such, this scheme is not only casuistry but also inculcated Here, it changes attitudinal behaviours to another set of attitudinal behaviours by consistent instruction without a 'lessons learned' phase present in the other scheme, which promotes innovation and continuous improvement rather that adherence to immutable standards. The measures developed should reflect needs to:

- Meet all needs and expectations of customers.
- Cover all parts of the organisation.
- That internal customers are equally important customers.
- Include every person in the organisation through colleague development.
- Examining all costs which are related to quality.
- Getting things right first time.
- Develop systems and procedures which support quality and improvements.
- Develop a continuous process of improvement; e.g. an innovative use of an adapted and hybridised balanced scorecard.

Case study 9

1. *Which part of a company is responsible for dealing with counterfeit products?*

In many companies, no one is responsible for counterfeit products. For companies that make high-value or regulated products, it is common to find a brand protection group that is linked to the marketing or legal departments, or both. But many companies are recognizing that brand protection needs to be linked more closely to supply chain management, because it affects internal processes and the relationship with suppliers and customers.

2. What are the financial impacts of counterfeiting on a brand owner?

Counterfeits reduce revenue because every counterfeit product that is sold is a lost sale of an authentic product. Low-quality counterfeits can erode the value of a brand and create a liability risk for the brand owner. Diverted products can undermine legitimate sales channels and harm both the brand and their distribution partners in highly profitable markets. Fighting counterfeits online, and in court, can also be expensive.

3. What happens if the brand protection strategy is incomplete, or does not align with the realities of a company's supply chain?

At best, an ineffective brand protection strategy provides the company with a false sense of security. At worst, it can actually become an asset for counterfeiters who are able to leverage the gaps to fool customers into believing that fake product is genuine, and therefore charge a higher price.

Case study 10

Priorities and strategies: The research identifies several barriers as well as opportunities. How would you prioritise these barriers and address them in the short, medium and long term?

It would be reasonable for the learner to undertake a virtual 'walk through' exercise based on their knowledge and experience, so that they could identify 'low hanging fruit' and attitudinal barriers as short term measures which then drive cycles of continuous improvement to support mid-term goals such as sustainable quality of recyclables and vertical integration of information and inventories for multiple trip packaging systems for enhanced supplier relationships. An example of this would be to mine supply data from DC to retail unit in order to predict likely returns of recyclables and packaging systems. This can aid more efficient planning of colleagues, fleets and DC operations, to support a mid-term goal of moving the point of data creation to a real time retail store level. When these benefits are multiplied and analysed, longer-term goals can be developed in relation to the three models introduced.

Choice: The three models proposed can be seen as options in relation to complex adaptive systems. As such, overall complexity results from all of the inter-relationships, inter-actions and inter-connectivities of elements within a system and between a system and its different environments. What do you think that In mapping out the systems that this case researched can you identify where more complexity of less complexity may benefit organisational efficiencies?

Learners should be able to map the current systems given the information supplied in the case and be able to comprehend where failures occur, where more complexity such as data generation at a retail unit can lead to a more balanced and holistic complex system, where innovation in a rapidly changing environment can be linked to supply chain tenets such as decoupling points, whereby the overall network benefits from the correct information reaching the network members at the correct time.

Sustainability; the research in this chapter presents a unique and novel approach to the application of JIT systems, not only showing that it is possible in operational contexts, but also that JITRL systems may offer significant benefits beyond these organisations, to distribution networks in operations within a similar environment to that of these organisations i.e. relatively high volumes of demand certainty and relatively low complexity of the materials under management. With these factors in mind, which of the proposed models would you adopt, and why? How would this choice be influenced by sustainability?

Learners will be able to develop an informed argument into their choices of option 1, 2 or 3. The interests and goals of the learners are not the same, and just because this research presents three approaches, they do not produce necessarily efficient logistics systems as a result. Learners may review these options for sustainable transportation as a policy pathway, for continuous improvement and those that see it as an endpoint. These learners may include industry professionals, policymakers and students. This research provides frameworks for an urban logistics problem, aiming to reduce the key impacts related to fulfilment of multiple retail units and the inventories they create for reverse / circular flows. The research investigates both the concept and implementation of sustainable multiple retail transport systems. However, it is of equal, if not greater importance for the learners to contextualise; if they choose not to see. the larger systems in which multiple retail transport networks are embedded, then they risk losing overall system potential impacts and efficiency gains. Sustainable transportation networks deliver more benefit as an enabling factor to drive organic improvements and efficiency gains. The learners should be able to comprehend how a system may be better served by a number of organic innovations in sustainable transport that can occur to challenge traditional systems-oriented approaches. This allows moving practices and strategies towards complex adaptive systems thinking in the creation of more sustainable logistics network outcomes.

Decision: Based on the research in this chapter and your wider experience/ organizational knowledge, which option would you choose?

Learners should be able to look at an organisation and consider its relative position in relation to vertical integration and the degree of vertical integration. From this point the learner should be able to make an informed decision about the choice that they have made and the decision process behind it, which should include a mapping exercise, a view of the current processes, the opportunities presented and a review of the assets available to them. It would be likely that a learner who has knowledge of a fully integrated and wholly owned supply and transport network would choose Option 1 as an initial choice, with a mid-term strategy of adopting option three and challenging the vehicle pool characteristics. There is no definitive correct answer here, this question has been developed with the challenging the perceptions and decision making processes of the learners based upon their ability to map and undertak process reengineering.

Case study 11

The two DF case studies outline various disruptions to supply chain operations and these can be generically categorised as breakdowns. However, given that all logistical challenges were in the absence of enemy engagement, can you identify the true source of supply chain disruption? Consider supply chain disruptions experienced in your own organisation. Perhaps poor supplier performance has impacted operations. Can you search for clues as to what may have caused these situations at a deeper level?

Quite simply, in the case of the Nordic Battle Group, the strategic documents issued by senior command, arising from a government mandate, failed to include the Logistics branch in their formulation, and this resulted in SCM manifests and resource allocations that were not fit for purpose. The Lebanon mission was significantly impacted by the seriously late communication of the Finland withdrawal to the Operations personnel of the organisation. The strategically-disruptive situation was contained only within inter-governmental and senior command actors.

Supply chain management has been described as a sub-discipline of operations management (Holweg and Helo, 2014), and the two DF case studies demonstrated that the Logistics Corps were not included in the strategic formulation process, despite the suggestion that supply chains compete, not companies (Christopher and Towill, 2002). How can we elevate supply chain management to the top management team?

My research suggests that the profession of SCM can be elevated in a number of ways:

- Create faster supply chains in order to become the 'secret sauce' of the organisation
- Use this competitive advantage as a marketing instrument at organisational-level
- Supply chain managers must become business leaders
- Increase the number of SCM doctorates
- Communication through TMT and board-level Key Performance Indictors

- SCM advocacy through major institutions such as the Chartered Institute of Logistics and Transport
- SCM media campaigns
- Education of the TMT

Until such time as supply chain management is a regular member of top management teams, how can we negotiate changes in our supply chain networks with the policy-makers? What is the threshold in your organisation for such negotiation?

My research across the full spectrum of SCM domains has shown that there are 4 broad categories for SCM negotiation with the Top Management Team:

Supply Chain Education:

- Nurture a shared understanding between the TMT and SCM
- TMT Education: Teach the basics of SCM to the TMT, broaden their operational awareness, inform the TMT of external and SCM industry self-disruptors, enable an organisational culture of change-adaption, whereby disruptions are treated as opportunities for continuous product and process efficiencies
- Reconcile TMT 'rational designs' and operational 'emergent processes' through recognition that strategies need to adjust to dynamic situations
- Cross-functional thinking, speaking a common language, co-evolution

Supply Chain Data and Metrics:

- Communication through TMT and Board level KPIs
- Deploy Logistics Control Towers
- Engage in superior data analysis and presentation thereof (ensuring the translation of SCM technical language)

Supply Chain Simulation:

- Use scenario planning tools (and thereby the removal of emotion) to gain cross-functional and customer advocacy prior to TMT negotiation
- Adopt the military decision-making process (MDMP)

Supply Chain Rhetoric and Strength:

- Ye olde ownership technique: Give the TMT ownership of the solution as well as the problem, convincing them that the solution you come up with is actually their idea
- Use of soft skills: encouraging, coaxing, cajoling, persistence

Policy-makers must acknowledge the existence of supply chain friction and factor this into the strategic renewal process so that it can be triumphed over. Can you categorise the DF logistical challenges into events that required strategic negotiation with the top management team, and those that could be autonomously and tactically responded to by the Logistics Corps? For any autonomous actions, what is the main consideration?

Negotiation Category:

- Negotiation across the top management team was needed to re-shape the troop profile for the Nordic Battle Group, such as the provision of cooks and ordnance technicians, and to secure a gross investment to the value of €820,000 for combat capability developments in Lebanon to replace the loss of assets with the withdrawal of Finland

Autonomous Category:

- A sub-tier of autonomous tactical response was found in the context of supply chain friction such as solutions to electricity provision, robust tent infrastructure, improved container utilisation, vehicle movement in Skillingaryd, provision of SUVs, the efficient use of mechanical fitters, and the provision of petrol and water

For any autonomous actions, the main consideration is that these remain within the boundaries of the core competencies of the organisation.

Case Study 12

Of all of the design factors taken into consideration which was the most significant from a business perspective?

Of no doubt the definition of the performance indicators or metrics. Performance metrics are the means for 'the business' to describe what it needs to know in order to determine viability. The original performance metric definitions were very loose in that they usually specified something high level ('how many requests for stores were delivered on time') but did not include things like methods of calculation, data sources and more besides. In the opinion of the author, performance metric definitions should be treated as key decision support requirements and should be highly detailed on a 'who, what, where, when, how, why' basis.

It would seem that there were multiples of databases/sets included in the exercise, rather than, say, the inventory systems. Why was that?

Conceptually the aim was to provide a very flexible reporting framework that could be used across the military command chain. The supply chain data base could have been used on its own. However, linking data contained in the reporting framework itself to other inventory and organisation structure databases gave a much richer investigative environment. In particular the integration provided the means to support chart navigation that would have been difficult to achieve otherwise. For example, to provide a detailed brigade level summary and from it, navigate down into individual Unit accounts.

In this document there is one scenario described. Where there any other success in respect of the provision of an ability to investigate or drill down into detail data?

One of the spin off benefits of the exercise was to expose relationships between 'things', many of which were transient in nature that would otherwise have been invisible. Quite literally, billions of potentially exploitable relationships were exposed by the combination of alignment and transition of data attempted. The issue then was determining which relationships were easier to expose for business benefit. There is no easy answer to making that kind of choice. There was only what was 'useful' depending on whether business end users asked the right questions. Nevertheless, the exposure of myriads of relationships provided the potential to explore supply chain data.

The study was quite short in duration, what kind of skills and experience were required in order to attempt it?

In order to achieve the kind of success the exercise achieved, it is the case that it requires a considerable amount of both technical and business knowledge both on operations and in barracks. The author was fortunate in that he had spent many years with front line units and in the latter years of military service, he (at his own expense) funded a series of course focusing on software development up to degree level. On discharge from the Army, he was described as the 'backbone of his Corps programming effort'. Subsequently, he worked at every level in the military command chain, up to 2* level. That is quite rare, even now. If there was a single recommendation to be made, it would be to train and groom people in data management and coding on a far more rigorous basis than is currently the case. If data is indeed the 'new oil', then it makes sense to exploit it on a more robust basis. And while that is done for military operations, there is much benefit to be gained from extending that training commitment further.

Was the aim of the study taken further?

Indeed it was. The architectural principle of using multiples of perspectives and multiples of dimensions was proven as a feasible aim. Subsequently, the MoD Joint Support chain invested in a number of special to task software tools focusing on pattern recognition (in the first instance) as a means to investigate and collate data on a much more sophisticated basis. The level of investment was significant and is ongoing but is delivering real business benefit. The key however is still reduction of the impact of 'garbage in, garbage out' (GIGO, by means of various alignments and transitions (what is often known as 'Extract, Transform and Load' – ETL) but ETL based on treating performance metric profiles as the as the key means to expressing the 'need to know' and treating them as technical specifications of requirement of an architectural nature.

CONCLUSION

This book provides a number of case studies that demonstrate supply chains in action. This book provides an insight into the decisions and approaches supply chain, logistics, operations and procurement professionals impact. It has been structured around a simple strategic framework with an emphasis on process, network and infrastructure, information system and organisation design. As editor I accept this is simplistic and more comprehensive frameworks are available but my intention was to make the structure accessible to both specialists and those just taking a glance at this critical area of business. It is recognised with the limited number of cases presented that not every topic can be addressed but it is hoped that by considering the individual cases and perhaps the book in its entirety the reader will be motivated to create action and innovate. Case studies can be reviewed individually but often it is more powerful to share with colleagues to provoke discussion, the different perspective and insights of other further enhances the impact and learning gained. It is hoped that perhaps individuals may also be motivated to tell their own story, to share by writing a case that can be included in future case study collections to enable academics and practitioners to learn and innovate.

INDEX

CPSIA information can be obtained
at www.ICGtesting.com
Printed in the USA
LVHW071730160122
708695LV00009B/600

9 780749 483708